EDUCATING ENGINEERS

EDUCATING ENGINEERS

Designing for the Future of the Field

Sheri D. Sheppard, Kelly Macatangay, Anne Colby,
William M. Sullivan

o

Foreword by
Lee S. Shulman

JOSSEY-BASS
A Wiley Imprint
www.josseybass.com

THE CARNEGIE FOUNDATION FOR THE ADVANCEMENT OF TEACHING

Published by Jossey-Bass
A Wiley Imprint
989 Market Street, San Francisco, CA 94103-1741—www.josseybass.com

Readers should be aware that Internet Web sites offered as citations and/or sources for further information may have changed or disappeared between the time this was written and when it is read.

Jossey-Bass books and products are available through most bookstores. To contact Jossey-Bass directly call our Customer Care Department within the U.S. at 800-956-7739, outside the U.S. at 317-572-3986, or fax 317-572-4002.

Jossey-Bass also publishes its books in a variety of electronic formats. Some content that appears in print may not be available in electronic books.

Library of Congress Cataloging-in-Publication Data

Educating engineers : designing for the future of the field / Sheri D. Sheppard ... [et al.].
 p. cm. – (The preparation for professions series)
 Includes bibliographical references and index.
 ISBN 978-0-7879-7743-6 (alk. paper)
 1. Engineering–Study and teaching. I. Sheppard, S. (Sheri)
 T65.E355 2008
 620.0071'1–dc22

                                                            2008039906

Printed in the United States of America
FIRST EDITION
HB Printing 10 9 8 7 6 5 4 3 2 1

CONTENTS

PART FOUR
A Way to Create

PART FIVE
Affecting the World

PART SIX
Bringing Professional Practice Forward

FOREWORD

The appliances—a coffeemaker and a cell phone—had been taken apart and the many pieces were spread out on tables at the front of the room. Photos of how they had looked when still intact were displayed. The instructor called the class of nearly 100 students to order and asked a seemingly straightforward question: "Knowing what you now know, how might these products have been designed otherwise?"

I remember the scene quite clearly. We were sitting in a lecture/demonstration hall at a highly regarded public university's school of engineering where we had spent the past two and a half days. It was a course in engineering design relatively early in the semester and the students were senior engineering majors. I had joined Sheri Sheppard and the other regular members of the engineering team for this particular site visit. Engineering was one field whose professional preparation programs were being studied by scholars from the Carnegie Foundation. I was observing the session through the lens of someone quite experienced in the pedagogies of professional preparation, especially in the training of teachers, physicians, and more recently lawyers. I knew nothing of the education of engineers. What was happening in this class, and to what extent was it representative of the central features in the formation of future engineers?

The instructor's question was intriguing in that regard. It was reminiscent of the typical query that initiates a clinical pathological conference in medicine or nursing when the staff gathers to examine a case that didn't go well and to ask how it might have been diagnosed or managed differently. Or it could be compared to a school IEP (Individual Educational Program) meeting where teachers, school psychologists, and parents gather to examine the progress of a student with special needs and to explore how the child's learning might be improved during the next semester. In each case, the event reflects a highly representative feature of the entire profession and its complexities. Medicine is all about the challenges of diagnosis, the unavoidable potholes on the road to therapy, and the inevitability of error along the way. Patients vary enormously one from the other, conditions are never entirely replicable, and the key task of medical practitioners is to learn from their experiences and avoid making the same error twice. One of the most important books on how surgeons learn is Charles L. Bosk's *Forgive and Remember: Managing Medical Failure*. Error being ubiquitous, the surgeon's job is to remember those errors and the lessons to be learned from them, not to turn away from painful memories.

Similarly, the education of young children carries an inherent uncertainty. Kids are labile and unpredictable. Teachers are merely human. An instructional protocol that worked for a child one year may simply bomb the next. So every six months to a year, educators and parents of the most challenging children deliberate together about how things have gone in the recent past and how they might go better in the future.

Which brings us back to the engineering design course. The instructor explained that the coffeemaker had been a wedding present some seven years earlier, and that, although the electric percolator remained as perky as ever, the family had moved on to an alternative technology, the drip method. He had rescued the appliance from the trash. The cell phone was almost a year old, and thus obsolete, having been replaced with a newer device with many more bells and whistles and an even more reasonable monthly cost. But these two artifacts, once paragons of design, now presented a new problem. Was there any alternative to simply adding these assemblages to the county dump? And even more important, how might they have been designed otherwise so that their disposal would not present the environmentally egregious dilemma that it currently represents?

The next hour of class was quite impressive, as students brought to bear their already extensive knowledge of engineering science, engineering practice, the art and science of design, and their understanding of the social, environmental, and economic factors that affect the ways in which such seemingly mundane devices as cell phones and coffeemakers make their mark on the lives of human beings and the condition of the world. It was a splendid design exercise, especially for seniors, because it called upon nearly everything they had been studying in their programs and challenged them to integrate those pieces into coherent plans for alternative designs. Some of the ideas were creatively goofy, some were incisively inventive, and others were solidly pragmatic and doable. They all emerged from collaborative dialogues in small groups, were immediately accompanied by hand and computer-generated drawings and models, and when each group presented its ideas, everyone else commented on each proposal with a combination of good humor and devastating critique.

An hour later I sat in a small seminar room with seven of the students who had been in the class. I commented on how impressed I was by the way the instructor framed the problem and by the intelligence of their responses. I had explained to the group the general comparative character of our studies of education in the professions and asked them how they would answer the question "What's an engineer?" if asked to characterize the place of engineering among the professions. Their response—collaboratively crafted and framed—was unforgettable: "An engineer is someone who uses math and the sciences to mess with the world—by designing and making things that people will buy and use; and once you mess with the world, you are responsible for the mess you've made."

In this way, these students had managed to construct a sentence that captured all three kinds of learning that we at Carnegie use to describe professional formation: the cognitive apprenticeship or development of habits of mind; the practical apprenticeship or development of habits of practice; and the moral apprenticeship wherein the professional develops and internalizes the values, ethical commitments, and sense of personal responsibility that is entailed in the formation of a professional.

This volume, *Educating Engineers*, is a product of several years of field-based inquiry combined with additional time devoted to data analysis, deliberations, and reviews. Under the leadership of Stanford professor of mechanical engineering Sheri Sheppard, the team has combined the deep study of engineering education with the broad comparative perspectives that develop when one studies teaching and learning across a number of parallel albeit distinctive fields. Anne Colby, a life-span developmental psychologist, and Bill Sullivan, a social philosopher, coordinated the full set of professional preparation studies over a ten-year period and bring both their disciplinary perspectives and the wisdom gained from being deeply engaged in all the professional studies. Kelly Macatangay was responsible for the coding and analysis of all the observational and survey data, bringing to bear her intimate knowledge of that data set when it came time to write this book.

There are many ways in which the education of all professionals shares a certain family resemblance. Except for the education of clergy, nearly all professional education falls short when dealing with issues of professional responsibility and ethics, in spite of the great strides in raising consciousness and awareness in recent years. Each profession has devoted great attention to the intellectual, conceptual, and cognitive aspects of learning, perhaps reflecting the impact of bringing professional education into universities a century ago. They vary enormously in how well they teach the core practices of their fields, with law and clergy attending to practice rather sparingly, while nursing and medicine emphasize supervised practice enormously. Whatever the patterns of curricular attention, however, all the professions suffer when it comes to providing sufficient attention to the challenges of integration across the intellectual, practical, and moral/professional domains.

Most of the professions we studied place the human client and his or her well-being at the center of the education process—students for teachers, patients for nurses and physicians, congregants for ministers, and clients for attorneys. For engineers, however, the artifact to be designed, constructed, or repaired takes center stage and the clients, those who will use the objects of design, have often receded into the background or remain hypothetical and imagined. In contrast, what has been so impressive about the rapidly changing countenance of engineering education is its rapid humanization. Increasingly, design is understood as a collaborative process in which different types of engineers, as well as nonengineers from a variety of backgrounds, become part of the design and implementation teams with which engineers must work collaboratively. Similarly, the process of engineering design increasingly places the human impact of design and its products at the center of the deliberations. "How might it have been designed otherwise?" is a question about the human consequences of human invention, a consideration of engineering design as a social and humanistic field as well as a technical and scientific one.

Sheppard and her colleagues have written a comprehensive account of the current state of engineering education and a compelling vision of how it might be otherwise. They constitute a team of insiders and outsiders that brings to this challenge the virtues of analytic depth and elegant comparisons. Engineering is a field that has demonstrated remarkable openness to change and reform during the past decade; the Carnegie Foundation team now urges the field to move even further.

As you contemplate the findings and proposals in *Educating Engineers*, I urge you to recognize that this volume is a critical element in a larger set of studies of preparation for professional practice. These are reports of how students can learn to profess, as lawyers and nurses, as physicians and clergy, as Ph.D. teachers and scholars, as school teachers and engineers, and even as undergraduates preparing to profess their civic and political duties in a democracy. As those engineering students expressed so eloquently, to profess is to mess with the world, and once you mess with the world, you are responsible for the mess you have made. Professor Sheppard and her colleagues have prepared a volume that helps us understand much more deeply what those words imply and how we as educators can fulfill the responsibilities of teaching more fully.

Lee S. Shulman
July 2008   Stanford, California

THE PREPARATION FOR PROFESSIONS SERIES

The Preparation for Professions Series reports the results of The Carnegie Foundation for the Advancement of Teaching's Preparation for the Professions Program, a comparative study of professional education in medicine, nursing, law, engineering, and the preparation of the clergy.

ACKNOWLEDGMENTS

Many people have contributed to this project. An external advisory committee of individuals actively engaged in engineering education, practice, or educational policies helped refine the study's core questions and research approach: Thalia Anagnos, San Jose State University; Larry Bucciarelli, Massachsetts Institute of Technology; Carol Carmichael and Carol Colbeck, Pennsylvania State University; the late Denice D. Denton, then of the University of Washington; and Susan Kemnitzer, National Science Foundation.

We appreciate additional input from the late John McMasters, then of Boeing Corporation; Charles Hodge and Frank Hughes, Boeing Corporation; Christopher Magee, Ford Motor Company and Massachusetts Institute of Technology; Karl Pister, University of California—Berkeley; George Peterson, ABET; Linda Parker, National Science Foundation; Gary Downey, Virginia Polytechnic Institute and State University; Tom Eagar, Massachusetts Institute of Technology; Richard Felder, North Carolina State University; William Wulf, University of Virginia and immediate past president of the National Academy of Engineering; James Duderstadt, University of Michigan; Gene Wiggs, General Electric Aviation; the Stanford Design Group faculty (Jim Adams, Ed Carryer, David Beach, Craig Milroy, Bernie Roth, Ken Waldron, and the late Rolf Faste); and Jim Plummer, Stanford University's dean of engineering.

We are grateful to the interdisciplinary research team who contributed to the literature review, site visits, data organization, and transcript analysis; to Cheryl Richardson and Gary Lichtenstein, who brought to the study extensive field experience in qualitative research methods; graduate student research assistants Michelle Johnson, Lawrence Neeley, and Kate Whitin; Gay Clyburn, of The Carnegie Foundation for the Advancement of Teaching, and support staff Sonia Gonzalez, Emily Crawford, and Lydia Baldwin. Lee Shulman, president of The Carnegie Foundation for the Advancement of Teaching, was also an active participant, joining in visits to engineering schools. Jim Adams and Ellen Wert provided editorial input.

Finally, we are grateful to The Carnegie Foundation for the Advancement of Teaching and the Atlantic Philanthropies, both of which provided funding for the project; to the institutions that opened their doors to us; to the instructors who opened their classrooms and labs to us; and to the many, many faculty, administrators, and students who so generously gave us their time and insights

ABOUT THE AUTHORS

Sheri D. Sheppard is the Burton J. and Deedee McMurtry University Fellow in Undergraduate Education, associate vice provost for graduate education, and professor of mechanical engineering at Stanford University. She is also a consulting senior scholar at The Carnegie Foundation for the Advancement of Teaching, having directed the Preparations for the Professions Program (PPP) engineering study. She has co-authored two textbooks on basic mechanics (*Statics: Analysis and Design of Systems in Equilibrium*, and *Dynamics: Analysis and Design of Systems in Motion*), and was guest co-editor of an issue of the *Journal of Engineering Education* entitled, *Educating Engineers: Who, What and How?* She is a fellow of the American Society of Mechanical Engineering, the American Association for the Advancement of Science. A fellow of the American Society of Engineering Education (ASEE), she was awarded the 2004 ASEE Chester F. Carlson Award in recognition of distinguished accomplishments in engineering education, and the 2005 ASEE Wickenden Best Journal of Engineering Education Paper Award. Before coming to Stanford University, she held several positions in the automotive industry, including senior research engineer at Ford Motor Company's Scientific Research Lab. She earned a Ph.D. at the University of Michigan.

Kelly Macatangay is currently a management analyst at the Clark County District Attorney's Office in Nevada and was formerly the program associate for the Carnegie Foundation's Preparation for the Professions Program. Her expertise is in textual data analysis. She has co-authored articles published in the *International Journal of Engineering Education* and *Westminster Studies in Education*. Before joining the Carnegie Foundation, she was consultant to the Board of Trustees of Ashley Educational Trust, Ltd. in Manchester, U.K., and was an education specialist at the School of Education of the University of Asia and the Pacific. She holds an MPhil in education from the University of Manchester, U.K.; an M.A. in values education from UA&P; and a B.A. in communication arts from the Ateneo de Manila University, the Philippines.

Anne Colby is a senior scholar at The Carnegie Foundation for the Advancement of Teaching, where she co-directs the Political Engagement Project, the Preparation for the Professions Program, and the Business, Entrepreneurship, and Liberal Learning project. Prior to joining the Carnegie Foundation in 1997, she was director of the Henry Murray Research Center at Harvard University. Her publications include seven co-authored and three co-edited books. Among them are *Some Do Care: Contemporary Lives of Moral Commitment* (1992), *Educating Citizens: Preparing America's Undergraduates for Lives of Moral and Civic Responsibility* (2003), *Educating Lawyers: Preparation for the Profession of Law* (2007), and *Educating for Democracy: Preparing Undergraduates for Responsible Political Engagement* (2007). A life-span developmental psychologist specializing in moral and civic development, Colby holds a B.A. from McGill University and a Ph.D. in psychology from Columbia University.

William M. Sullivan is co-director of the Carnegie Foundation's Preparation for the Professions Program, which studies the education for the professions of law, engineering, the clergy, medicine, and nursing, drawing out common themes and identifying practices distinct to various forms of professional education. The author of *Work and Integrity: The Crisis and Promise of Professionalism in America* (2005) and a co-author of *Habits of the Heart: Individualism and Commitment in American Life* (1996), Sullivan also works on the link between formal training and practical reflection in effective education. He has co-authored *Educating Lawyers: Preparation for the Profession of Law* (2007), and most recently, with Matthew S. Rosin, *A New Agenda for Higher Education: Shaping a Life of the Mind for Practice* (2008). Prior to coming to Carnegie, Sullivan was a philosophy professor at La Salle University. He earned a Ph.D. in philosophy at Fordham University.

INTRODUCTION

Engineering has never mattered more. The explosion of new information technologies, robotics, biotechnology, the increased blending of invention with scientific discovery: these are powerfully affecting every area of life, often in unexpected ways. Information technologies are not only speeding communication, but also creating upheavals in how work is carried out and how business is organized worldwide. Environmental and societal issues require local and global solutions. Engineers, at work at the center of all these developments, are also essential to efforts to grapple with the ramifying consequences of such rapid innovation. What engineers know and can do are critical resources for American society and the world.

This is also a moment of transformation in engineering practice. The engineering profession that helped bring about our ever more technological future is also being changed by it: engineering practice has become exponentially more complicated just when new communication technologies make it possible—and business pressures make it imperative—to work rapidly and effectively, and the conditions of engineering work are rapidly changing.

The intensified, global chase after greater economic value has placed a premium on technological innovation, in turn spawning a dramatic rearrangement of the design, production, marketing, and distribution of all manner of goods and services. The increasingly large gains go, more than ever, to the swift, nimble, and well organized. Whereas stable, national corporations once set the terms of employment and directed the work of engineers—who were mostly expected to solve rather than to formulate their problems—now global and weblike corporations organize chains of design, supply, and marketing, shifting the sites and forms of engineering practice.

Today's engineers, situated in distributed, often global chains of supply and distribution, formulate complex problems as well as solve them. Increasingly, they work with other technicians and managers who bring different viewpoints and sometimes different languages, cultures, and outlooks. These developments have dispersed engineering work, as in the many forms of outsourcing to other contractors and other countries' engineers. Some even ask whether these developments are replacing loyalty to firm and profession with personal self-marketing and image management as the key values of engineering practice.

However, what most distinguishes contemporary engineering work is that it demands a sophisticated command and understanding of the interplay between the natural and artificial. The world is so heavily shaped by collective technological interventions into nature that the dividing line between nature and human-influenced environments is becoming blurred, and new fields such as bioengineering and nanotechnology may erase the line altogether. Indeed, an emerging problem for the public at large is how modern society is to manage and actively adapt itself to new habitats enabled by these "blurred" technologies.

By necessity, engineers will be crucial players in resolving this problem, for, increasingly, engineering prowess is seen as a key to the progress of civilization. There is clearly some truth to this faith in the power of problem solving: consider what advances such as sanitation systems, power, flood control, and communications have made possible in terms of liberation from toil and deprivation. Yet as engineering prowess, particularly at the regional and national levels, is ever more tightly connected to economic vitality through technological innovation, a potential hazard is that technological innovation may "more and more be understood without reference to its human ends, but rather as an end in itself or a means to economic ends" (Williams, 2002, p. 30), a "technological momentum and drift" in which serious deliberation about purposes is displaced by the purely technical solution (Hughes, 2004).

What is the relation of engineering education to today's whirl of innovation? To the profound changes in engineering practice and professional responsibilities? With such a vortex of change in the world of engineering, it is not surprising that leaders in government and industry—the primary employers of engineers—have undertaken serious efforts to understand what is happening to engineering practice and the knowledge on which it draws. They have even tried to scan the future in search of the optimal direction in which to steer engineering education.

The public has a serious stake in the preparation of engineers to design and manage our technological world. Our motivation for this report on engineering education in the United States is to provide a better understanding of how engineering schools prepare future professionals, particularly in light of the new challenges now confronting engineering worldwide. In this effort, we explored three central questions: Do the academy's conceptualizations of what engineers must know and be able to do align with the new realities of professional practice? Is the engineering curriculum organized and delivered in ways that align with what engineers must know and be able to do, now and in the future? And if not, how might it be?

The Study Behind This Book

Our book is the result of a study in which, over the course of several years, teams of researchers from The Carnegie Foundation for the Advancement of Teaching visited a variety of programs to examine current educational practice in U.S. engineering schools. During these visits, we focused on the practices of teaching and learning that shape future engineers, considering both strengths and weaknesses of current curricular goals and teaching practices, especially in light of the major changes in professional practice in this new, global era. Although we made an extensive review of the literature on contemporary engineering education, our primary goal was to understand, through field research, how the educational practices of the schools form future engineers.

Toward that goal, after piloting our methodology at Santa Clara University, we visited eleven mechanical and electrical engineering programs at six engineering schools:

- College of Engineering, California Polytechnic State University (Cal Poly)
- Carnegie Institute of Technology, Carnegie Mellon University (CMU)
- Colorado School of Mines (Mines)
- College of Engineering, Georgia Institute of Technology (Georgia Tech)
- College of Engineering, Architecture and Computer Sciences, Howard University (Howard)
- College of Engineering at the University of Michigan, Ann Arbor (Michigan)

We focused on mechanical and electrical engineering because, of the twenty-five different engineering fields currently named by ABET, the accrediting body for engineering education (ABET, 2007), these two concentrations together produce over half of the engineering graduates in the United States each year. They have also long been, and remain, central to engineering innovation. Thus these fields provide useful vantage points to observe both continuities and changes in the core of engineering education.

In selecting schools where we would spend time on campus, talk to faculty and students, and observe classes, we looked for evidence that faculty were experimenting with educational practices and that their undergraduate programs had well-articulated mission statements that appeared to be consistent with program elements. In addition to these criteria, we sought differences: it was important that the schools be distinct from one another in terms of size, public or private status, geographic location, and institutional mission so that collectively they would represent a spectrum of educational settings and environments. (For details about the study, see the Appendix.)

This study is a first step in exploring the composition and effectiveness of today's engineering education in light of the challenges described, most recently, by the National Academy of Engineering in *The Engineer of 2020* (National Academy of Engineering, 2004) and *Engineering for a Changing World* (Duderstadt, 2008). We believe that our descriptions from the classroom serve as a complement to those studies. We can well imagine additional exploration of similar questions at the graduate level, as well as international comparisons, for our approach lends itself to wider application than the limitations of time, personnel, and resources permitted us.

Preparation for the Profession

This study of engineering education is also part of a larger research project of The Carnegie Foundation for the Advancement of Teaching. The Preparation for the Professions Program—a multiyear, comparative initiative—examines the education of professionals in five fields: law, the clergy (Jewish and Christian), nursing, medicine, and engineering. These studies build on each other as well as on the Carnegie Foundation's long tradition of studying professional education that stretches back to the Flexner Report on medical education of 1910 and *Engineering Education*, the study authored by Charles R. Mann in 1918.

However, although this report draws on the findings from the Preparation for the Professions Program's growing body of experience with professional preparation in other fields, the study's perspective was primarily influenced by the profound changes in engineering practice itself. Therefore, we seek to describe the education of engineering students today—and to offer a vision for future generations of students.

We also note the movement in the United States, over the last thirty years, to increase K–12 students' interest in engineering, part of a larger effort to promote the science, technology, engineering, and mathematics (STEM) fields. Along with foundations and industries, federal, state, and local agencies have promoted and supported this movement, with a particular interest in expanding and diversifying student participation in STEM fields—and, thus, the workforce, for historically these fields have been populated by white males. In addition, as more nations around the globe begin to build technological capacity among their own citizens, concerns have been raised about the possibility that the United States might begin to lag behind. Those concerns have developed into calls for the education of engineering leaders in the United States, not just expert technicians.

Findings

We found that in the midst of a profound, worldwide transformation in the engineering profession, undergraduate engineering education in the United States is holding on to an approach to problem solving and knowledge acquisition that is consistent with practice that the profession has left behind. There are, however, pockets of innovation, and these, along with the example of medical education and new findings from the learning sciences, suggest to us that engineering educators can transform their programs so that students' learning experience more effectively prepares them to meet the new demands of professional practice.

Specifically, we found that undergraduate engineering education in the United States emphasizes primarily the acquisition of technical knowledge, distantly followed by preparation for professional practice. Laboratory and design experiences are understood as applications or adjuncts that follow the learning of theory in engineering science and technology courses. Concerns with ethics and professionalism, which have new urgency in today's world, have long had difficulty finding meaningful places within this historical model, for not only are programs packed solid with the technical courses, but also there are limited conceptual openings for issues of professionalism. Yet these four years are a crucial moment for professional formation: unlike law and medicine, in engineering the first professional degree is the undergraduate degree.

Further, we found that the dominant curricular model, which might be best described as *building blocks* or *linear components*, with its attendant deductive teaching strategies, structured problems, demonstrations, and assessments of student learning does not reflect what the significant and compelling body of research on learning suggests about how students learn and develop and how experts are formed:

o In the engineering science and technology courses, the tradition of putting theory before practice and the effort to cover technical knowledge comprehensively, allow little opportunity for students to have the kind of deep learning experiences that mirror professional practice and problem solving.

o The lab is a missed opportunity: it can be more effectively used in the curriculum to support integration and synthesis of knowledge, development of persistence, skills in formulating and solving problems, and skills of collaboration.

o Design projects offer opportunities to approximate professional practice, with its concerns for social implications; integrate and synthesize knowledge; and develop skills of persistence, creativity, and teamwork. However, these opportunities are typically provided late in the undergraduate program.

o Students have few opportunities to explore the implications of being a professional in society. Moreover, the work of providing such opportunities is often outsourced to other academic units.

We are not the first to suggest that engineering education could be improved through new strategies for the curriculum, teaching, and assessment. Although there is value in many of the long-standing approaches to engineering education, we are not persuaded that incremental improvements to the current model will result in engineering education that is aligned with the work of and demands on the new-century engineer.

In our visits to engineering schools, and in our reading of the literature and meetings with leaders of the field, we were struck by the emerging possibilities of a focus on professional practice—a nascent response to the profound changes in engineering practice, informed and supported by new findings in the learning sciences. If students are to be prepared to enter new-century engineering, the center of engineering education should be professional practice, integrating technical knowledge and skills of practice through a consistent focus on developing the identity and commitment of the professional engineer.

What would this mean in the curriculum, in the classroom? Rather than offering courses that touch on professional understanding and commitment merely as a curricular afterthought; rather than hoping that students gain, through an experience in a course from another discipline, a deep sense of the complex ethical issues they will face as professionals, engineering programs would begin from the habits, commitment to competence, public responsibility, and accountability that are core to professional practice and would build students' capacity to learn, over a lifetime, in service to the profession. Such an approach would fully recognize that the technical knowledge that enables engineering problem solving is forever expanding and that tomorrow's creative solutions will come from engineers who revel in deep complexities.

The current linear components structure will not support such a focus, for it is not a matter of making room for more attention to lab, design, or ethics or even using more effective teaching and assessment strategies for these components. A focus on professional practice will require *remaking* undergraduate engineering education, networking the components in ways that strengthen and connect them into a cohesive whole. This could be accomplished through a set of design principles that represent the best of current understanding of the learning sciences and medical education, and by using teaching strategies that support the integration of knowledge and skills and engaged learning.

We fully recognize that making such a profound shift in focus will take an enormous amount of work on the part of faculty and administrators. However, we are persuaded that shifting the focus to a broader conception of professional practice is the direction that engineering education needs to take. Throughout the book, we offer concrete examples of innovative and effective ways faculty are making engineering education more responsive to present and future needs of the profession.

The Plan of the Book

The book is organized into six parts. In Part One, we look at engineering practice, and, in particular, the changing demands on engineers, and then take a broad look at U.S. undergraduate engineering education, including its historical context, and consider what engineering education for professional practice might look like. In Parts Two, Three, Four, and Five, we describe what we learned, particularly from our classroom observations and our conversations with faculty, students, and administrators. In doing so we follow the familiar "blocks" of the current curriculum: engineering science courses, lab, design, and professionalism, and we ask the reader to consider the current alignment of learning goals and pedagogy. As we look at each in turn, we suggest what the learning sciences could contribute to new thinking about engineering education. In light of the descriptive analysis in Parts Two through Five, we consider, in Part Six, how education might be refocused on professional practice, and we invite the field to consider how the entry-level degree for professionals might better align with current and future needs.

A Tool for Change

We offer this book to engineering faculty and administrators, national leaders in the engineering profession, and higher education leaders as a catalyst for reflection and assessment of engineering education. We hope that it causes the reader to explore a core question: *What are today's educational practices and how well do they support the development of tomorrow's engineer?*

This questioning may happen at the individual level. For example, faculty members creating and teaching analysis or design courses may be drawn to the particular sections of the report that describe their areas of the undergraduate engineering program. We hope that individual faculty members will consider their courses in the context of the entire program. We imagine that this question might also drive department- or program-wide affinity or working groups as they review programs, discuss pedagogy and assessment, or consider curriculum changes. Similarly, we imagine that professional societies, as well as accreditation and funding agencies, might undertake a similar process using this book as the basis for study and recommendations.

Ultimately, however, our goal is more ambitious than prompting reflection or incremental improvement. Our goal is action, for we believe that incremental improvement will lead only to a more optimized linear model of education that will, if not at the moment of its redesign, quickly thereafter become once again "overstuffed." To accomplish this task, we need to undertake what Vincenti (1990) termed "radical" design and develop a new approach to undergraduate engineering education, the core of which is professional engineering practice, not historical tradition. Both the learning sciences and our sister profession, medicine, offer much to draw from. This redesign, as one of its requirements, should have continuous revitalization and rejuvenation.

Thus, through this book, we extend a challenge to the engineering community: Reflect, assess, debate, design, and prototype a truly networked engineering education, one that engages both student and teacher in learning in context. Engage as colleagues and make the redesign of engineering education a national undertaking for the next five years. Redesign engineering education to prepare the new-century engineers that today's problems demand.

PART ONE

PREPARING THE NEW-CENTURY ENGINEER

PROFESSIONALS, EXPLAINS LEE SHULMAN, provide a worthwhile service in the pursuit of important human and social ends; possess fundamental knowledge and skill; develop the capacity to engage in complex forms of professional practice; make judgments under conditions of uncertainty; learn from experience; and create and participate in responsible and effective professional communities (Shulman, 1998).

Engineers, as do other professionals such as physicians, nurses, lawyers, and clergy, work within ever-increasing complexity and changing conditions. As the external environments for engineering practice have changed, so too has the substance of the work—the problems engineers address and the knowledge they draw on to do so. At the same time, their relations to work and the workplace as well as to their colleagues are also changing dramatically.

Although engineering schools aim to prepare students for the profession, they are heavily influenced by academic traditions that do not always support the profession's needs. From the time that the formal training of engineers in the United States was first patterned after the French model—a curriculum of basic sciences, technical subjects, and humanities, with theory taught before application—through the middle of the twentieth century, engineering education struggled to establish its place in the academy and earn the recognition of practitioners, both responding to and being shaped by the values of the academy. The solution has always been to add more rather than to consider the overall design. Thus a jam-packed curriculum focused on technical knowledge is the means for preparing students for a profession that demands a complex mix of formal, contextual, social, tacit, and explicit knowledge.

The case of engineering education, however, is not unique. The Carnegie Foundation's studies of the education of lawyers, clergy, physicians, and nurses have also found that professional education has been dealing with the challenge of integrating knowledge and practice in a way that more fully prepares students to enter the profession.

The foundation's reports recommend that professional schools, because they are responsible for the preparation of practitioners, should aim for an increasingly integrated approach to the formation of students' analytical reasoning, practical skills, and professional judgment. Although some engineering schools have introduced programs, teaching methods, or curricular structures that attempt to integrate these professional goals, none offers a comprehensively networked approach.

In this first part, we look first at the profound changes in the profession of engineering. Then, to begin our consideration of how U.S. engineering education aligns to current and future needs, we describe the current linear components model that we found so prevalent and the nascent networked components approach that integrates knowledge and practice.

I

THE NEW-CENTURY ENGINEER

ENGINEERING PRACTICE IS, in its essence, problem solving. There are, of course, many ways to describe this work. The U.S. Department of Labor describes engineering as the application of "the theory and principles of science and mathematics to research and develop economical solutions to technical problems ... the link between perceived social needs and commercial applications" (U.S. Department of Labor, and Bureau of Labor Statistics, 2007). The outcome is often fabrication specifications, the creation and production of a physical artifact, changed personal or public knowledge, new technologies, or a changed state of the human condition.

ABET describes engineering practice as "a decision-making process (often iterative), in which the basic sciences and mathematics and engineering sciences are applied to convert resources optimally to meet a stated objective" (ABET, 2007, p. 2). The problems that engineers respond to are typically ill-defined and underdefined; that is (1) there are usually many acceptable solutions to a design problem, and (2) solutions for design problems cannot normally be found by routinely applying a mathematical formula in a structured way (Dym and others, 2005; Dym and Little, 2008). A former official of the National Science Foundation observed, "In essence, engineering is the process of integrating knowledge to some purpose. It is a societal activity focused on connecting pieces of knowledge and technology to synthesize new products, systems, and services of high quality with respect for [for example] environmental fragility" (Bordogna, 1992, p. 1).

However, as the enormous changes in technology that engineering has brought about are precipitating profound changes in society and daily life, they are precipitating similarly profound changes in engineering practice. The most central of these is a change from a *linear conception* of

3

problem analysis and problem solving that presupposed a more stable organizational and physical environment to a *network, web, or systems understanding* of engineering work. The new environment for engineering is forcing the formulation of problems and interactive design of solutions to the center of professional activity. This represents a significant change in focus, away from problems in which "the number of variables was severely constrained, and problems could be reduced to quantitative dimensions" and solved by the use of knowledge and techniques common to all involved, and toward "complex systems" that are "so heterogeneous that interdisciplinary interactive groups sharing perspectives and information are needed to create and control them" (Hughes, 2004, p. 78).

New-Century Engineering: A New World of Problems and Problem Solving

Historically, the engineer's assumed perspective was outside the situation or problem—that of a disengaged problem solver who could confidently model the problem in objective, mathematical terms and then project a solution, framed largely in terms of efficiency and technical ingenuity, affecting a system uncontaminated by the frictions of human relationships or conflicting purposes. This concept of the professional as neutral problem solver, long central to engineering practice and education, is now outmoded, due in part to its own unintended consequences. For example, developing automobile technology and national policies with little regard for the social or ecological effects has proved to be a narrow-minded policy in the United States but one with potentially catastrophic ecological effects if continued in China.

Because engineers' work directly affects the world, engineers must be able and willing to think about their ethical responsibility for the consequences of their interventions in an increasingly interlinked world environment. Working with others, in this country and around the world, to understand and formulate problems, engineers are immersed in the environment and human relationships from which perception of a problem arises in the first place. Writing about this newer engineering sensibility, Rosalind Williams has described it as the viewpoint attendant upon living within a "hybrid world in which there is no clear boundary between autonomous, non-human nature and human-generated processes" (Williams, 2002, p. 31). The effects of engineering problem-solutions—their interventions into affairs—are being "fed back" to the engineers working, often in groups with other specialists or lay people, to define and solve problems within a common set of purposes.

The shift from an outside to an inside perspective can be understood as a shift from engineering for "them" to engineering for "us." Although this new point of view may be disarming, at the same time it holds the potential to inspire new thinking, for a shift from an outside to an inside perspective highlights the complex social, physical, and informational interconnections that enable modern technologies to function. As the globalizing economic system illustrates, division of labor produces great efficiencies by enabling each component of a complex interacting system to focus on maximizing the achievement of just one goal. However, the system as a whole is also likely to produce consequences not intended by the designers. These may "feed back" on both the system and its environment, sometimes in ways that threaten the continued efficiency of the system and the sustainability of its environment. Today's growing list of ecological problems, to say nothing of economic and social problems, have brought home in alarming ways the unintended consequences of many of our greatest technological triumphs.

Changing Knowledge

Professional practice depends on a specialized body of "engineering knowledge." As Vincenti offers, "Engineers spend their time dealing mostly with practical problems, and engineering knowledge both serves and grows out of this occupation" (Vincenti, 1990, p. 200). A distinctive feature of this specialized knowledge is that it includes what philosopher Gilbert Ryle called "knowing that" (Ryle, [1949] 2000). Shavelson and Huang add to Ryle's "knowing that" (that is, declarative knowledge), "knowing how" (that is, procedural knowledge), by suggesting that disciplines also rely on schematic knowledge, or "knowing why," and strategic knowledge, "knowing when certain knowledge applies, where it applies, and how it applies" (Shavelson and Huang, 2003, p. 14). The knowledge that engineers must bring to bear in their work includes knowing how to perform tasks, knowing facts, and knowing when and how to bring appropriate skills and facts to bear on a particular problem.

Another distinguishing feature of engineering knowledge is that it is not simply and totally a derivative of science. It is "an autonomous body of knowledge, identifiably different from scientific knowledge." (Vincenti, 1990, pp. 3–4). The idea of "technology as knowledge" (Layton, 1974) credits technology and, by extension, engineering, with its own significant components of thought: "This form of thought, though different in its specifics, resembles scientific thought in being creative and constructive; it is not simply routine and deductive as assumed in the applied-science model. In this newer view, technology, though it may *apply* science, is not the same as or entirely *applied* science" (Vincenti, 1990, p. 4).

Moreover, the knowledge engineers draw on is increasingly dynamic and complex. To successfully integrate process and knowledge, engineers must not only stay informed about new and emerging technologies but also be aware of knowledge and skills from other domains. As Table 1.1 suggests, engineers call on wide ranging knowledge, from theoretical tools to contextual knowledge. Taken to a high degree of detail, such a list could even include such things as marketing, finance, and sociology that are critical for particular engineering enterprises.

A Changing Process

Engineers are continuously balancing and negotiating tensions. For example, engineers must strike a balance between moving a project toward completion with incomplete knowledge or imposing delays to allow more complete knowledge to be gathered and employed. In *Designing Engineers*, based on ethnographic studies of three design projects, Bucciarelli makes the case that engineering is not an instrumental process: it is full of uncertainty and ambiguity. There is neither a routine solution nor a defined script for doing the work. For the software engineers in Perlow's 1997 ethnographic study *Finding Time*, this manifested itself in the engineers' feeling that they were perpetually in crisis mode as they dealt with competing demands, frequent interruptions, and shifting deadlines.

Collaboration

Increasingly, engineering work is a highly collaborative process (Bucciarelli, 1996). There is just simply too much to know and to do. The scope, timeframes, and complexity of most projects require the effort of teams of engineers—experts in some aspects of engineering practice working in coordination with other experts.

Teamwork has inherent tensions. As Rubenstein observes, "the same problem, two different value systems; therefore two different criteria, different decisions, and different solutions. This is the problem of problems, the subjective element of problem solving and decision making ... Two people, using the same rational tools of problem solving, may arrive at different solutions because they operate from different frames of values and, therefore, their behavior is different" (Rubinstein, 1975, pp. 1–2).

Table 1.1. Types of Knowledge Used by Engineers

Knowledge Type	Description
Theoretical tools: math-based and conceptual	Mathematical methods and structured knowledge; scientific, engineering, and phenomenological theories; intellectual concepts. "Engineering science" consists of specific combinations of math and science around particular engineering domains.
Fundamental design concepts: operational principles and normal configurations	"Operational principle" describes "how [a device or technology's] characteristic parts fulfill their special function in combination with an overall operation which achieves the purpose"—in essence, how the device or technology works. "Normal configurations" describes what is typically taken for the shape and arrangements for a particular class of devices (technologies).
Criteria and specifications	Technical criteria appropriate to a class of devices or technologies, including numerical performance criteria, such as impact performance criteria in the automotive sector or pressure vessel standards in the chemical industry.
Quantitative data	Physical properties and quantities required in formulas and required to demonstrate device performance. Understanding of procedures and processes for generating such properties and quantities.
Practical considerations	Tacit knowledge, typically learned on the job, generally not codified. In addition, rules of thumb and heuristics ("design considerations," Vincenti, 1990).
Process-facilitating strategies	Knowledge of tools and strategies for project management, leadership, teamwork, communications, and management.
Contextual and normative knowledge	Knowledge of values (personal, professional, cultural), norms (what is acceptable, expected behavior), contexts, and contextual factors that constitute the artifact's ambience.

Sources: *Vincenti (1990), Koen (2003), and Kroes (1996).*

As the size of the engineering team expands and the members of the team become more diverse, these tensions become more complex. The members of the teams are, indeed, changing. From its nineteenth-century beginnings, American engineering has taken a course of upward mobility, providing a route for generations of ambitious, technically oriented young people to rise into the middle class, often going on to careers in industrial management. Engineering's status as an undergraduate professional degree continues to give the field an advantage in attracting upwardly mobile students—in contrast with medicine and law, both of which, in the United States, require costly graduate study—and since the 1960s, non-whites and women have entered the field. Although engineering lags behind other professional fields, including law and medicine, in its percentage of minority and women students and practitioners, it has seen an increased representation of these populations. For example, prior to 1970, women made up less than 1 percent of the students graduating annually with a bachelor's in engineering; they now make up over 20 percent of the graduating class. Similarly underrepresented groups now make up 12 percent of each graduating class. Still, these numbers fall short of their representation in the general population.

Collaboration is also a process that crosses time and cultures. Increasingly, engineering endeavors involve teams scattered across continents, working toward a common purpose. Corporations are moving aggressively, tapping into technical talent wherever they can find it, recognizing that synergized, distributed expertise can bring both needed engineering and cultural knowledge to a project, which holds the potential to build new markets.

The New-Century Engineer

What professional goals and values might guide the engineer in this new, networked context? As we suggest in Part Five, the codes of engineering ethics in the particular engineering specialties, when taken together, point to a set of overarching values and goals of the profession. All of the codes acknowledge the overall mission of the profession as contributing to human welfare. In line with this mission, they describe the overriding importance of public safety, health, and welfare, and protection of the environment in all that engineers do (Little, Hink, and Barney, 2008; National Academy of Engineering, 2004). They also stress the responsibility to be competent in one's work, to be careful not to misrepresent one's competencies, and to continue building one's competence through ongoing professional development.

Globalization of engineering work has added urgency and complexity to each of these goals. To enact them, the "new-century engineer," needs attributes that connect "engineering's past, present, and future" (National Academy of Engineering, 2004, p. 54; see also Downey and others, 2006; Shuman, Besterfield-Sacre, and McGourty, 2005; and Oberst and Jones, 2006). In *The Engineer of 2020*, the National Academy of Engineering (NAE) describes nine attributes that build on strengths inherited from the past while incorporating the qualities that are becoming critical in the changing world of engineering practice, with its more public and inter-active aspects of designing and working with today's complex new technologies, for more complicated problems.

The first two attributes, "strong analytical skills" complemented by "practical ingenuity," are long-familiar goals of engineering education. Engineers must be able to employ "science, mathematics, and domains of discovery and design to a particular challenge and for a practical purpose" (NAE, 2004, p. 54). However, although engineers must be able to use science and mathematics in their thinking, this thinking is not oriented toward theory but to "discovery and design" for particular purposes in response to specific challenges. In other words, an engineer's analytical thinking is framed by and used in the service of practical ends. With "skill in planning, combining, and adapting," the engineer uses both science and "practical ingenuity" (p. 54).

The engineer also needs "creativity," described as the ability to respond to challenges by combining in new ways "a broader range of interdisciplinary knowledge and a greater focus on systemic constructs and outcomes" (p. 55). Engineering practice increasingly demands an approach to problems that resembles engineering design work. Attendant to creativity is a fourth attribute, which NAE calls "communication," a way to address the need for engineers to become more "accountable": because they will increasingly work as part of interdisciplinary teams, engineers must be able to explain their thinking to diverse audiences and partners as well as think with others in order to arrive at solutions to problems (p. 55).

A fifth attribute, "mastery of the principles of business and manage-ment," stresses the need for engineers to understand—and act in light of—"the interdependence between technology and the social and eco-nomic foundations of modern society" (p. 55). If they can do these things, then engineers will be able to exhibit "leadership" that acknowledges "the significance and importance of public service ... well beyond the accepted roles of the past" (p. 56). Complementing leadership is a greater sense of "professionalism" and "high ethical standards." These attributes are connected to a quality that "cannot be described in a single word" but encompasses "dynamism, agility, resilience, and flexibility" (p. 56), character traits that need leadership, high ethical standards, and professionalism to give them balance and point. None of these attributes can be developed quickly. Hence the need for the final attribute: engineers must be "life-long learners" (p. 56).

We believe that Shulman's description of a professional encompasses the professional values described in the engineering codes and NAE's nine attributes: the new-century engineer provides a worthwhile service in the pursuit of important human and social ends, possesses fundamental knowledge and skill, develops the capacity to engage in complex forms of professional practice, makes judgments under conditions of uncertainty, learns from experience, and creates and participates in a responsible and effective professional community.

Preparing the New-Century Engineer

We are convinced of the direction and scope that the profession is now taking and thus the necessity of cultivating in aspiring engineers the knowledge, skills of practice, and understanding and commitment to enact these values and attributes in daily professional life. The task, then, is not only to identify the specific engineering knowledge, skills, and values that students need as they enter the profession but also to determine what kind of educational experience and what approximations of professional practice will best position students to continue to develop them. Because engineering schools initiate but do not complete the formation of their students as engineers, starting the process in such a way that the students' progress toward greater engineering competence can continue and be sustained is no small task.

2

TECHNICAL KNOWLEDGE AND LINEAR COMPONENTS

ALTHOUGH THE 1,740 UNDERGRADUATE engineering programs in the United States vary in their emphases and serve diverse student populations, they are remarkably consistent in their goal: U.S. engineering education is primarily focused on the acquisition of technical knowledge. Indeed, over its two-hundred-year history, the formal education of engineers has consistently emphasized the study of concepts and ideas grounded in mathematics and the physical sciences; offered practice of skills, strategies, procedures, and techniques seen as central to engineering practice; and called for development of understanding of professional and cultural ethics and standards.

U.S. undergraduate engineering programs also share a remarkably homogeneous curriculum and pedagogy. Our reading of ABET self-study reports; interviews with faculty, administrators, and students; classroom observations; and reading of the history of engineering and engineering education all pointed directly to four building blocks—or, as we call them, linear components—that make up engineering education. Each block has its own cluster of courses that have distinct, although not necessarily explicit, learning goals and a particular approach to pedagogy and assessment.

The Four Linear Components

The largest block of the engineering curriculum is made up of the mathematics, science, and a body of knowledge called "engineering science," often referred to as the "fundamentals" or, as faculty told us, the major part of the knowledge that every engineer ought to master. These courses make up the greatest number of credits or units in the program, and the course sequences, some of which are layered four and five courses deep, suggest to students not only that theory precedes practice, but that one needs to move from theory to practice in a particular sequence.

Students begin with mathematics and physics, chemistry, or increasingly, biology courses, taught theoretically and by faculty outside the engineering program. In their sophomore year, students continue math and science courses while beginning the engineering science sequence; they also identify a concentration. The engineering science courses may reintroduce concepts and skills the students encountered in science and mathematics courses, this time with a focus on their uses in engineering. Emphasizing deductive reasoning, faculty present students with methods for solving problems, along with paradigmatic examples of problems and solutions, making extensive use of blackboard or Microsoft PowerPoint. Students learn as individuals, largely by applying formulas and rules to the solution of structured, "right-answer" problems, whether in class, as homework, or on exams.

By their junior year, the students will have completed the mathematics and science requirements, and they start taking the technical, or "analysis," courses particular to their field of engineering. These technical courses introduce new concepts and skills derived from and aligned with those the students encountered in the engineering science courses. Using these second-generation principles, students evaluate such engineering elements as gears, bearings, circuits, transistors, and other key technologies of their particular fields.

The upper-level courses also employ lecture and right-answer problems for homework and exams, and the labs connected to the courses are used largely for demonstrating the concepts, although students may be asked to develop systems. At their very best, technical courses ask students to solve open-ended analysis problems and tackle design exercises. The engineering faculty responsible for teaching the engineering science and technical courses often do not have much freedom in defining content, as most of these courses are prerequisites or requirements, and course material has been established by the curriculum committee and the field.

Seniors continue taking technical courses, some of which broaden the range of engineering elements they are exposed to or deepen their experience with those elements they already know. The senior year generally concludes with a design experience, in which the instructor, who might be an adjunct faculty member from the field, acts as a coach or guide, and students are challenged to develop entirely new skills.

From Theory to Practice

Lab courses are usually either appendages to theory courses or extend the teaching of formal concepts begun in theory courses. In the lab, students see theory in action, learn to prototype, and try to debug ideas. Here, however, the setting and teaching are quite different from those in theory courses. Faculty or graduate assistants explain procedures and then coach students, who generally work with lab partners.

Thus students generally experience problem solving as a linear, two-step process that involves first acquiring a body of technical knowledge and then generating models and analyzing engineering systems. The tradition of putting theory before practice reflects the notion that "engineers needed grounding in these 'fundamentals' to have command of basic principles that could be applied to a variety of technical problems" (Williams, 2002, p. 40).

Practicing Design

Design is a relatively recent addition to engineering education, and the central focus is teaching students to define needs, generate many possible solutions, and move toward an optimum solution. Although some programs offer first-year design experiences, design is generally reserved for the senior year. The design projects of the final year are often unstructured problems that demand imagination and teamwork. The projects may either simulate engineering practice or present graduated experiences of it, and assessment often focuses on communication and teamwork. It may appear to students as both a welcome introduction to the "real world" but also an anomaly in their experience of a deductive model of science applied.

From Student to Professional

ABET accreditation requirements now specify that students can take up to 36 percent of their total 120 to 130 undergraduate credit requirements outside of technical studies, in the humanities, business, and social sciences. Explicit inclusion of the humanities and what we now call the social sciences in the undergraduate engineering program dates to the early nineteenth century. The purpose behind the long-standing expectation is lofty: "The fields of humanities and social sciences from which some courses must be selected include history, economics, and government, wherein knowledge is essential to competence as a citizen; and literature, sociology, philosophy, psychology, and the fine arts, which afford means for broadening the engineer's intellectual outlook" (Grinter, [1955] 1994, p. 82; see also Mann, 1918; Society for the Promotion of Engineering Education, 1930; Bucciarelli and Kuhn, 1997). The assumption is that exposure to the humanities and social sciences will contribute to the students' "development of both a personal philosophy which will insure satisfaction in the pursuit of a productive life and a sense of moral and ethical values consistent with the career of a professional engineer" (Grinter, [1955] 1994, p. 76).

Although they are required, the humanities and social science courses, including ethics, are not treated as integral to the business of becoming an engineer. With the exception of the ethics modules in some capstone design courses, liberal arts requirements remain appendages rather than central elements of what is required to learn to be an engineer. Students generally choose courses rather haphazardly from a list of those that meet distribution requirements, and the learning in those courses is seldom integrated with their development as engineers. Too often, these courses are seen simply as hurdles to be cleared, standing in the way of rather than informing the process of learning to be an engineer. The courses and their content remain largely disconnected from the technical education program, and it is largely up to the student to bring them together, if they are brought together at all.

We might then more accurately say that engineering students have curricular experiences that may or may not expose them to the societal implications of engineering work. The ethical standards, social roles, and responsibilities of the profession, often framed around avoiding wrong-doing, are treated as ancillary elements of engineering work. Students are rarely afforded multiple opportunities to actively struggle through ethics problems in classroom discussions and assignments that would help them connect the ideas, principles, processes, and habits of mind of engineering.

As it stands now, the liberal arts component of most engineering programs does not realize its potential to inform practice in these rich and compelling ways. This means it is unlikely that the goal, expressed as important by both faculty and employers (Lattuca, Terenzini, and Volkwein, 2006), of students learning to consider the implications of engineering in global and social context can be adequately achieved.

Four Unbalanced Blocks

Figure 2.1 presents a visual rendering of engineering education, depicting what we have observed about of the historical "linear components":

Figure 2.1. Linear Components Model

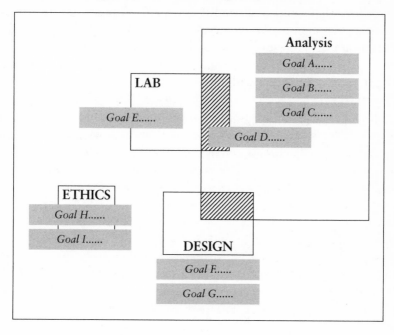

how undersized design and laboratory are, relative to the multiple roles they play a student's development, including being the best proxy for a clinical experience, and how distant and small are considerations of professionalism—ethics, social responsibility, integrity, lifelong learning. Moreover, where the boxes connect, the relationship is unidirectional—hence "linear" components.

The linear components represent a result rather than a plan. Over the history of engineering education, the remarkable expansion of scientific knowledge and the increasing professional prestige associated with it encouraged engineering educators to respond by adding science-based courses to the already extended and overloaded curriculum, thus further reducing the provision for laboratory, social science, and the humanities. Today's curriculum is as "congested beyond endurance" as Mann found it in 1918 (p. 25), if not more so.

The packed curriculum results in practical problems. The conceptual difficulties and pace at which the material is presented, in addition to the manner of its presentation, contribute to attrition (Seymour and Hewitt, 1997). Critics have noted that the workload of science and math courses can be so overwhelming that students end up losing interest in the profession for which they are being prepared. Furthermore, the curriculum is such that it is almost essential that students be committed to engineering from the day they matriculate: "discovering engineering" at some point during—or after—undergraduate studies and being able to shift into the field is very uncommon.

Engineering has the highest persistence rate of any undergraduate major: 57 percent of students who matriculate in engineering remain there. The next highest is business at 55 percent, followed by sciences and mathematics at 44 percent and computer science at 38 percent (Ohland and others, 2008). However, engineering has the lowest percentage of students migrating into the field: only 7 percent of students who major in engineering did not matriculate in engineering, whereas for all other fields the comparable number ranges from 35 to 59 percent (Ohland and others, 2008). Though women and underrepresented minority students generally persist in engineering at the same rates as majority students, their overall absence from the engineering student body, relative to their presence in the general population, remains striking.

However, we believe that the reasons for trying to effect change in engineering education go beyond the need to address even such important problems as these. The historical model of engineering education treats learning as a deductive sequence, in linear fashion, suggesting a form of mechanical causation in which each component propels the next in line. Proficiency in "engineering science" counts most, and the proper progression is always from scientific theory to engineering practice. The implied theory of knowledge is that engineering is in the main deductive.

Our field observations of engineering programs, described in detail in Parts Two through Five of this volume, suggest that this impression is strongly reinforced by the deductive strategy used in teaching the core subjects of engineering science. Formal knowledge overshadows practical experience, even experiments under laboratory conditions, and suggests that the engineering student, if not the engineer, is an individual competing with other similar but mutually disinterested individuals for achievement. The strength of the pedagogy is such that it competes with the goals of team-based learning, including capstone design experiences.

It is, of course, possible to maximize the potential for learning in the linear curriculum. We saw, and describe here, many innovative approaches to teaching in the traditional curriculum. However, the pieces remain blocks, and though we might rearrange them or change their size, they remain blocks, with all the attendant limitations on the structures that can be built with them.

Aligning Preparation to Professional Practice

The innovations we observed suggest that it is possible to network the components in such a way that engineering education would be better aligned to the profession. Less concentrated on engineering science and analysis courses, a networked approach would integrate theory, laboratory, and design experiences at each phase of the program in a spiral configuration of developing professional competence.

For example, in some programs that we observed, the starting point for students is an overview of the profession as well as some experience of design activity, even when students have hardly any real scientific knowledge to guide and complement that activity. The idea behind this approach is that efforts at design and questions about the nature and scope of engineering are valuable, even or especially at this stage of learning. In experiencing a simplified approximation to engineering practice, the novice nonetheless gets a sense of the breadth of engineering's dimensions.

These first encounters with the field as a whole can be important motivators to learning. They enable the student to grasp firsthand the value of acquiring difficult knowledge and skills that engineering work entails. The students' experiences with design and other dimensions of professional practice are often continued in different contexts through the subsequent years of the program.

Students entering a networked curriculum would encounter engineering from the first as a clearly professional and inventive field. Developing and maintaining competence in professional practice would be understood as a spiral process that builds and draws on various kinds of knowledge and skill, importantly including deduction and scientific analysis, but understanding and commitment as well. With professional practice as a center, students would encounter engineering as a field that requires working closely and effectively with others not only to solve problems but to formulate them as well.

We believe that the widening difference between the new demands on the profession and the inherited model of engineering education has created the conditions for a transformation. A shift from the linear components of the historical curriculum to a networked approach would align with both professional practice and new understanding about learning, teaching, and the development of professionals.

3

A HISTORICAL CURRICULUM
IN A NEW ERA

MUCH OF UNDERGRADUATE ENGINEERING EDUCATION has remained the same since Jefferson's 1802 legislation establishing West Point although the emphasis given to the various components of the curriculum has shifted over time, to keep pace with burgeoning scientific and technological knowledge and to increase the status of the discipline. As the history of engineering education indicates, today's model represents the accumulation of a number of design decisions, though memory of these has tended to fade over time, making the present form of engineering education seem, misleadingly, far more inevitable than it actually was.

A Technical Orientation

Early engineering schools prepared students for work that was understood to encompass a wide range of "industrial, commercial and public activity" (Society for the Promotion of Engineering Education, 1930, p. 129). Courses like "Topographical and Hydrographical Surveying," "Machine and Freehand Drawing," and "Masonry and Carpentry" addressed the demand for agriculture and mechanics. As industry expanded, the professional or practical courses quickly shifted their focus to manufacturing concerns. In shop courses, students learned to operate machine tools; in graphics courses, they learned to communicate product geometries as drawings.

Hence, in the early years, scientific knowledge and industrial practice were the focus of these technical schools, whose aim was to train men who could use the rapidly growing scientific knowledge to address the needs of a growing economy and to improve production. However, because of its practical orientation, engineering education was seen as a threat to traditions of higher learning that valued Greek, Latin, history, philosophy, and theology (Mann, 1918; Society for the Promotion of Engineering Education, 1930; Grayson, 1993). This perceived threat led to pressures from both the academy and industry. Engineering struggled to earn academic credibility and professional recognition. In an effort to "professionalize" engineering, educators began putting stronger emphasis on science and math and promoting a scientific approach to the practice (Coxe, 1894; Mann, 1918), such that science and math, with "humanistic" studies, became significant components of the curriculum and helped engineering schools achieve academic respectability.

Theory Versus Practice

From the mid-1800s to the end of World War I, engineering curricula swung back and forth between heavy practical training on the one hand and pure science on the other. What started as a curriculum focused on design and fieldwork, which became the pattern of civil engineering and later mechanical engineering, eventually began focusing on scientific method and experiment (Grayson, 1993).

At the same time, engineering education struggled with the growing tension between advocates of broader education and those who promoted practical training for immediate employment. However, in the early 1900s, as the nation experienced a surge in economic growth and inventions, engineering education began focusing on the sciences to meet productivity demands. With the growth of electrical engineering, laboratory instruction began increasing in popularity, thus overshadowing the once-dominant shop work.

Joining the Academy

By the turn of the twentieth century, as a new university-based way of training engineers gained ascendancy, engineering became an academic field along with other professions that were entering the university in search of legitimacy through association with scientific research. This new emphasis developed at the height of the second industrial revolution, as new technologies based on advances in internal combustion, chemistry, and electricity spawned huge new industries and set mechanical and electrical engineering on an upward swing in numbers and influence.

Thus the bachelor's degree became the sought-after credential for entry into engineering practice. Civil, mechanical, and electrical engineers typically began their training firmly within the larger structure of American higher education. By this time, the undergraduate curriculum combined a strong core of mathematical and scientific courses with a substantial requirement of courses in the humanities and other liberal arts. "The basic process of engineering education should be an undergraduate curriculum of coherent and integral structure, directed to the grounding of the student in the principles and methods of engineering and to those elements of liberal culture which serve to fit the engineer for a worthy place in human society and to enrich his personal life" (Society for the Promotion of Engineering Education, 1930, p. 84). Significantly, it also emphasized practical experience in laboratories and shops, including design experience.

The undergraduate curriculum developed through close working relationships among the engineering schools, professional associations, and American industry. Indeed, for the past hundred years, corporations and corporate philanthropy have sought to spur and support development and coordination in engineering schools and the preparation and training of engineering faculty.

Into an Era of Engineering Science

Since the cold war's intense military competition with the Soviet Union and rivalry in space exploration, U.S. undergraduate engineering education has emphasized engineering science and research. The massive national effort to intensify studies in science and technology brought the education of engineers, like the training of physicians, to the forefront as a major concern of the national government. Just as medical education has been importantly stimulated and shaped by the National Institutes of Health and the National Institute of Medicine, so the National Science Foundation (NSF) and the NAE, drawing on distinguished engineering talent, have given impetus to better preparation of engineers. For engineering education, the result has been a displacement of practical experience and design to the margins of a more scientific, less "practical" engineering curriculum. As we describe in greater detail in Part Six, the result for medical education has been an overhauled approach, with greater integration, that focuses on the entirety of professional practice.

When the NSF was established in 1950 as an independent government agency, as part of the national strategy to address the nation's defense and welfare needs through scientific and technological research, engineering schools began recruiting academic researchers rather than practicing engineers. The NSF awarded funds through competitive grants, and the schools needed faculty members with strong mathematical and scientific research capabilities if the programs were to compete successfully for these important grants.

Thus, in the decade between 1950 and 1960, engineering education experienced a true paradigm shift, from an applied, practical focus to a mathematical, engineering science focus (Grayson, 1993; Pister, 1993). The growing research culture continued to thrive with the creation in 1964 of the NAE—a private, nonprofit organization—to advise the government and conduct its own studies on matters concerning the economic and social implications of engineering and technology.

At the same time, productivity and efficiency became the central forces of industrial growth, and by the late 1970s pressure for innovation forced the engineering curricula to give special attention to design and methods used to teach engineering design that go beyond "the routine." Throughout the 1980s and into the 1990s, university-industry interaction intensified through corporate research and development projects, industrial contracts, and entrepreneurial initiatives. The increasing collaboration with industrial partners and the changing demands of engineering work emphasized the need for educating engineers not only in engineering science, mathematics, and other discipline-specific tools but also in nontechnical skills such as teamwork, communication, negotiation, and integration necessary to operate in a complex and ambiguous environment (Bucciarelli and Kuhn, 1997; Prados, Peterson, and Lattuca, 2005). In these decades, increased pressure to include more technology in the curriculum, particularly computer-related technology, squeezed the already packed curricula to the point that the freshman design courses were eliminated or scaled back significantly at most schools (Evans, McNeill, and Beakley, 1990).

Now, as the U.S. economy has become more enmeshed with the rest of the world, voices expressing worries about the competitiveness of American technological workers—and engineers in particular—are becoming louder and more insistent. In this context, questions about the value added by U.S.-trained engineers have come to the fore, as government, industry, and the academy seek to define an American comparative advantage in relation to the engineering workforces of rising industrial powers such as China and India. Behind all this lie the new technologies of the microprocessor and integrated circuitry—the sources of today's information, or what could be called the third industrial revolution. These events have outpaced the educational processes built around the post-war engineering science model.

Chronic Issues

Since the Mann report of 1918, engineering education has received criticism about the curriculum and pedagogy, to the point where these have become a set of chronic challenges or issues. Again and again, engineering education has been faulted for trying to teach too much, believing that a comprehensive background in mathematics and sciences is a prerequisite to the learning of practice.

For example, just as the Mann report noted the overcrowded curriculum and inadequate assessment as well as a need for integration of theory and practice and better retention, so Duderstadt refers to the curriculum as an "obstacle course" (Duderstadt, 2008, p. 34), commenting that "the science-dominated engineering curriculum has also led to an overdependence on the pedagogical methods used in science courses—large lecture courses, rigidly defined problem assignments, highly structured laboratory courses—all of questionable utility for teaching the most important technical skills of engineering: the integration of knowledge, synthesis, design, and innovation" (Duderstadt, 2008, p. 33).

Similarly, Duderstadt's observation that "As the knowledge base in most engineering fields continues to increase exponentially, the engineering curriculum has become bloated with technical material, much of it obsolete by the time our students graduate" echoes the so-called Wickenden report: "Our primary concern should not be with content, but with mastery of the methods of learning and we believe a cumulative effort to be of greater worth than ever widening spread" (Society for the Promotion of Engineering Education, 1930, p. 147). In 1955, the "Grinter report" called for more integration of laboratory and design, as well as the humanities, observing, "Engineering Education must contribute to the development of men who can face new and difficult engineering situations with imagination and competence. Meeting such situations invariably involves both professional and social responsibilities" (Grinter, [1955] 1994, p. 74).

In the early 1990s, Karl Pister commented, "We have taken a great deal for granted in designing curricula and we badly need to revisit both the input and output ends of the process" (Pister, 1993, p. 66) and suggested in the 1995 report that he chaired, that as "there is no simple, universal prescription for dealing with complexity and constant change ... To meet the challenges that the nation faces, each engineering college or school should enter a period of experimentation, monitored by self-assessment and feedback from industry" (National Research Council's Board on Engineering Education, 1995, p. 2). More so now than ever, we believe that the time has come for engineering education to make profound changes so that education for the profession is just that—aligned for new demands on the profession. Although doing so may not eliminate all of the challenges inherent in preparing engineers, we believe that a new approach can reduce or eliminate many of the chronic issues.

Beyond the Blocks

Research on how people learn offers a way to rethink engineering education that addresses engineering's chronic issues and offers a way of thinking consistent with new-century professional practice. The fundamental discovery made in the recent research into learning, which has explored how experts in any domain actually think and act, is that all forms of competence, in both thinking and skillful performance, develop through a process of guided experience that in some ways resembles the traditional entry into professional life via apprenticeship. Some theorists have even called the process of guiding novices toward expertise a *cognitive apprenticeship*, describing the specific processes of thinking that enable beginners to make progress in learning. Careful descriptions of the development of experts—ranging from athletes to scientists to chess players and musicians—reveal that high-performing individuals share a set of features that seem common to expertise.

What Experts Know

The first of the features of expertise is the ability to know a great deal and, most crucially, to have that knowledge readily available in ways relevant to the activities of their practice. In their particular domains of activity, experts have mastered well-rehearsed procedures for handling knowledge based on experience. This observation holds whether the field is chess or musical performance or the practice of medicine. Experts' superior ability to relate their knowledge to problems stands out when compared with that of novices in a field.

Confronted with complex problems, experts can assess the complexity in ways that enable them to bring their knowledge and experience to bear quickly and efficiently. Novices, by contrast, although able to solve problems that have been carefully structured in advance—such as the problem sets provided by mathematics and science textbooks—are often at sea when confronted by open-ended or poorly structured situations.

Experts can also read situations. They quickly size up what is salient, asking which facets of a complex situation are important for solving a challenge. They often do this without stopping to think, judging situations holistically. This is what makes expertise appear so mysterious, even magical, to the beginner. Beginners develop expertise gradually by employing feedback from competent coaches to improve their performance. However, as practitioners become more competent, moving into greater degrees of expertise, their knowledge and skill become tacit, second nature. They have less need to painstakingly think through problems and can instead use their growing experience to approach solutions efficiently and confidently (Bransford, Brown, and Cocking, 2000).

From Novice to Competent Practitioner

What might the learning sciences contribute to engineering education? First, it is important to grasp that students are on a trajectory from novice to competent performance as practitioners. That is, students must learn to move from solving highly structured problems involving formal concepts, as in their theoretical courses, toward building ability to both formulate and solve less structured, more uncertain kinds of problems. In one sense, this describes a linear progression.

The surprising insight from learning theory, however, is that the most efficient way to facilitate this transition is not a simple one-way movement, starting from structured "theory" courses and ending with unstructured design. In a professional practice like engineering, competence is manifest in the ability to read complex and ambiguous contexts and to carve out from them the important and productive problems that can then be addressed with precision through structured problem-solving techniques. Developing this capacity requires not a once-and-for-all movement from theory to application, but a continuing back-and-forth between general theoretical principles and the particularities of the problem situation as the student builds more sophisticated skills through experience.

UNDERSTANDING COGNITIVE DEVELOPMENT Engineering education differs from most other professional education in an important way: the students are primarily eighteen to twenty-two years old. Engineering students are thus still in a formative phase of cognitive development. The learning and developmental sciences can help engineering educators understand cognitive development and thus better approach teaching for the goals of knowledge in the discipline, skills of practice, and understanding and commitment.

In their extensive work on college students' cognitive development, Patricia King and Karen Kitchener have described the development of what they call *reflective judgment*: the judgments individuals make about ill-structured problems for which there are multiple possible solutions (see, for example, King and Kitchener, 1994). As individuals develop mature reflective judgment, their epistemological assumptions and their ability to evaluate knowledge claims and evidence and to justify their claims and beliefs change. This progression, which King and Kitchener categorize into seven stages, clusters into three levels: *prereflective thinking, quasi-reflective thinking,* and *reflective thinking.*

o At the lowest level, prereflective thinking, individuals imagine knowledge to be certain and absolute, though they are aware that not everyone has knowledge in any given area and sometimes the truth about an issue is not yet known even to authorities. At this level, they acquire knowledge from authorities or from direct personal experience.

o At the next level, quasi-reflective thinking, individuals recognize that some problems are ill structured and inevitably include elements of uncertainty. Pascarella and Terenzini explain: "Knowledge claims come to be seen as requiring justification and evidence ... Reasoning and evidence are offered in support of beliefs, [and] the individual begins to realize that others' views may be more strongly reasoned and supported" than one's own so if one is to convince another, one has to provide a stronger justification. "[K]nowledge [about unstructured problems] is considered subjective, context specific, shaped by the individual's perceptions and interpretations of the evidence and criteria for judging ... In accepting knowledge as contextual, the individual recognizes the legitimacy of other views and conclusions" (Pascarella and Terenzini, 2005, p. 37).

o At the highest level, reflective thinking, individuals "recognize that knowledge is never a given but rather the outcome of inquiry, synthesis of evidence and opinion, evaluation of evidence and arguments, and recognition that some judgments are more solidly grounded and defensible than others. Beliefs are judged with respect to their reasonableness, consistency with the evidence, plausibility of the argument, and probability in light of the assembled information. The individual also recognizes that judgments may be reviewed and altered on the basis of new information, perspectives, or tools for inquiry" (Pascarella and Terenzini, 2005, p. 38). This is the kind of thinking that engineers draw on in high-level analytic problem solving.

The undergraduate years are an opportunity for a critical transition in cognitive development. Most students arrive at college at the last stage of the prereflective level, believing that knowledge is gained through personal experience or by finding out the right answers from authorities. Although they may lack the skills to deal with ill-structured problems, their growing "recognition that knowledge is sometimes uncertain" indicates that they are ready to move "toward more complex stages of thinking" and can start differentiating "categories of thought" (Pascarella and Terenzini, 2005, p. 37). Undergraduate education can advance students' reflective judgment so that they enter the stage of quasi-reflective thinking: able to use reason and evidence in forming, evaluating, and justifying judgments—to engage, in other words, in analytic problem solving.

What are the implications for engineering education? First, the curriculum and teaching and assessment strategies must be designed and enacted to help students realize their potential for cognitive growth. Second, because the undergraduate program yields the professional degree, the program must be designed to position students to continue to develop toward the reflective thinking—the high-level analytic problem solving—of experts.

FROM UNDERSTANDING TO ACTION These are significant professional responsibilities for engineering educators, ones that require thoughtful and creative attention to every aspect of the students' experience. In our campus visits, we saw many opportunities for faculty to put into action a new understanding of the process of learning and cognitive development. For example, faculty in engineering science courses can provide "scaffolding" within which students can learn to attend to the context of design problems with more disciplined awareness. Gradually, as the beginner masters the basic rules of the activity and acquires the fundamental knowledge underlying those rules, the teacher introduces more of the complexity of situations characteristic of the profession itself. As students acquire more facility, the instructor can increase the complexity of the problems presented, opening up to the full complexity of actual practice situations. This process should happen both in individual courses and over a program.

In moving from structured situations to more ambiguous ones, the role of the teacher is primarily to show the novice what to look for and then how to characterize unclear situations. Using feedback and coaching, the instructor's goal for student learning is the central engineering practice of formulating problems and solving problems. This is rarely a simple task. It requires careful movement from an initial approach to testing the approach by evidence. The instructor feeds back corrections to the initial approach. In this iterative process, the novice begins to learn from experience. The formal knowledge acquired earlier begins to serve largely as a disciplined basis for thinking and trying out solutions rather than a source of ready answers. Through design experiences of increasing levels of complexity and decreasing scaffolding, students are able to develop a repertoire of abilities to size up situations and approach the solution of problems with skill and confidence (Dreyfus, Dreyfus, and Athanasiou, 1986). In time, the student learns to approximate what experts do and develops skills for future learning on the job.

A Framework for Evaluating Engineering Education

Engineering, the profession that builds society, has profoundly affected the world through technological innovations. In turn, these innovations have affected the practice of engineering, facilitating not only new ways of thinking but also new global partnerships and alliances. Are today's approaches to teaching engineering learning appropriate to educating the engineers who will help to shape this new world? Is U.S. engineering education capable of fostering a new generation of engineers who will embark on solving problems with competency, responsibility, and accountability—in other words, as engineering professionals?

As we describe and discuss, over the next four parts of the book, the goals, curricular structures, pedagogies, and assessments employed in U.S. engineering programs, we ask the reader to consider three questions:

1. Where in their educational experience do students acquire and develop each dimension of professional expertise: engineering knowledge, skills of practice, and the understanding and commitment expected of today's professional engineer? How, if at all, do the traditional components of the engineering curriculum—engineering science, laboratory, and design courses—map onto these aspects of professional expertise?

2. How is this learning accomplished, and who among faculty and staff is responsible for each of these dimensions? Who, if anyone, is charged with ensuring that the continuity necessary for the students' developmental trajectory is maintained?

3. What counts as evidence that students are in fact moving toward competence in engineering knowledge, skills of practice, and understanding and commitment? What are the important markers of this progress, and how is such progress assessed?

PART TWO

A FOUNDATION TO BUILD ON

THE PRINCIPLES AND THEORIES that inform an engineer's assessment of an engineering problem in order to predict, estimate, calculate, or optimize the function of an existing or imagined system or device, given its particular attributes: these are generally considered by the academy as the body of knowledge that every engineer ought to learn, even if they are not always used in practice. Students are expected to acquire this knowledge principally through courses in physics, chemistry, biology, and mathematics; engineering science courses, such as "Electromagnetics," "Fluid Mechanics," and "Statics"; and technical knowledge and analysis courses, such as "Analysis and Design of Analog Circuits," "Stress Analysis," and "Kinematic Synthesis." The goal of this coursework is to provide a technical knowledge base—to equip the student for the practice of engineering by providing them with the math-based theoretical tools, operational principles, and normal configurations described in Table 1.1.

This core of engineering science and technical courses is expected to provide the basis for the rest of the curriculum and serve as the bedrock of conceptual knowledge for professional practice. The principles and theories are the ones that faculty believe students should know by heart and be able to retrieve easily when working on an engineering problem, for they are considered central to the systematic study of the design, operation, and production of engineering systems grounded in basic mathematical and scientific principles. A professor at Cal Poly describes this set of tools as the "table of multiplication that everybody needs to know" because it "has a strong connection to everything [students] are going to do later."

Developing specialized knowledge should be central to engineering education. However, as we observed in sophomore engineering science courses through upper-division technical courses, the focus of the effort is largely on transmitting a body of knowledge, training students to apply this knowledge in solving well-posed problems. Yet in professional practice, problems are rarely well posed. They require approximation and judgment—thinking at the highest level of reflection.

To acquire robust analytic problem-solving skills, students need repeated, staged experiences in doing analytic problem solving, experiences in which they get a lot of feedback on the process. Even before they have a great deal of technical knowledge, they can begin doing analysis. In the main, however, we found that these courses generally fail to fully engage students in analysis in a systematic way, despite the fact that there are no other places where students might build the strong analytic problem-solving skills that are so important to their profession.

We are not the first to observe that this overriding emphasis on teaching technical knowledge focuses on learning the knowledge *per se* and not enough on learning the knowledge so that it will be usable toward effective professional practice. We are also not the first to note that teaching an enormous amount of content does not guarantee that students will necessarily even learn or remember it, let alone be able to use it in engineering situations. We are concerned that the pedagogy and assessment that are common to the core courses are not designed to help students move farther along the continuum of cognitive development, toward reflective thinking.

As the specialized knowledge that an engineer must draw on increases exponentially, engineering educators face two significant professional challenges. They must make tough choices, selecting knowledge and skills that will position students to enter professional practice. They must also learn new ways to approach teaching that will help their students move toward the levels of thinking and judgment needed for professional practice.

In this section, we describe what is taught in these courses and the teaching and assessment strategies used toward these goals. As we do so, we ask the reader to consider (1) to what extent these courses should have the dual goals of teaching technical knowledge and teaching how, when, and where to apply it as part of engineering work; and (2) how well these courses are achieving either of these goals.

4

"KNOWING THAT" AND "KNOWING HOW"

IN ITS REPORT on the goals of engineering education, the American Society for Engineering Education (ASEE) defined the science taught in the engineering sciences courses as "the study of physical phenomena utilized in artificial or man-made devices and systems as distinguished from basic science which is concerned with the phenomena of nature" (American Society for Engineering Education, 1968, p. 437). In the words of a faculty member, these courses have a "fundamental role in the curriculum. If [students] don't learn that, they're in real trouble. The particular course material integrates into most of what they take later on in ... design." Without it, said another faculty member, "You wouldn't have an engineering program. This is where the tools come from."

What are these tools? Typically, technical courses are aimed at "knowing that" or knowing specific engineering principles, concepts, and theories that govern engineering systems as well as the mathematical tools that offer an accurate representation of these concepts.

We observed that the faculty and students feel enormous pressure to cover everything, for this body of knowledge—the concepts, theories, and principles considered the foundation on which to do engineering work— is also the foundation of the linearly organized engineering curriculum. A faculty member described the content of these courses as "something you need to learn ... before you get to the next series of courses."

Thus, opportunities for the kind of deep learning and understanding that allows students to become, over time, sophisticated, independent learners are lost in the effort to teach everything. Although faculty told us that it is important for students to "know how"—and know when, where, and why those principles are applied to analyze engineering problems and

Figure 4.1. Components of "Knowing That" and "Knowing How"

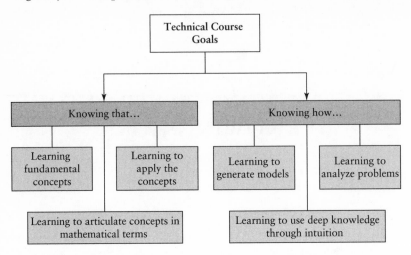

situations—we found that students have few opportunities to develop this dimension of their knowledge.

Through our interviews with faculty, we identified the components of "knowing that" and "knowing how" depicted in Figure 4.1. The challenge facing engineering educators, we believe, is not so much coverage but teaching for students' deep knowledge. Faculty members must be supported in drawing deeply and creatively on their professional expertise, their "pedagogical content knowledge"—knowing both the subject matter and how to convey it effectively (Shulman, 1986; Cochran, 1997).

"Knowing That": Principles, Theories, and Concepts

One of the primary learning goals of the engineering science courses that students typically take, starting in their sophomore year, is "knowing that"—knowing the fundamental principles, theories, and concepts of engineering. The factual and conceptual knowledge, or "declarative knowledge" (Shavelson and Huang, 2003) presented in these courses is drawn principally from the natural science and mathematics that students are expected to have learned about in their first year, now applied to engineering problems in a specific and concrete way.

Learning the Fundamental Concepts

The concepts introduced in the first engineering sciences courses are highly abstract and not easily comprehensible. This is a primary reason why engineering is often regarded as a difficult subject to teach and learn. Faculty members generally agree that the difficulty is intrinsic to the subject matter, often described as "too mathematical or too abstract."

In electrical engineering, for example, students learn concepts like circuits, mutual inductance, and frequency response, as well as Ohm's laws and Kirchhoff's laws, as they are applied to electric circuit systems. Represented in terms of mathematical formulas and equations, the concepts are difficult to grasp unless teachers develop useful ways of facilitating a deeper understanding and extended retention (Farah and Samaan, 2001).

Learning to Articulate the Concepts in Mathematical Terms

Mathematics is the language of engineering. For example, when an engineering principle is applied to a case, it is often translated into a mathematical formula, which in turn is restated in an equation that is ultimately solved, thus revealing a particular engineering system's behavior or condition in a quantitative sense. Students must learn this "second language." Thus, learning the concept that the principle embodies is just one aspect of the work in the engineering science courses; students must develop the fluency to describe the concept in quantifiable terms.

Indeed, the biggest challenge for faculty teaching engineering science courses is helping students interpret the physical world in mathematical terms. Students generally find it difficult to relate math to real objects around them or to engineering practice. They struggle to make the connection between mathematical representation and the real-world manifestation of the concept. As one faculty member noted, "making that jump is the piece that they seem to find the hardest." Another faculty member explained, "[T]hey have to wrestle with situations where you give them a problem in plain English, and they have to translate it into a mathematics problem. And one thing that is being stressed in these courses is that if somebody comes to you as an engineer and asks you to solve a problem, the problem will be stated in plain English ... How do you get this problem that is stated in plain English translated into an abstract problem and use your way of thinking to solve it?"

Learning to Apply the Concepts

By the end of their engineering science courses, students are expected to be able to use fundamental principles to solve specific and well-defined problems. Even though these so-called applications problems may be framed around realistic systems, geometries are usually simplified and unnecessary details have been removed, for it is assumed that students must achieve a certain level of understanding of a concept before they can actually learn how to apply it. Further, it is assumed that the more they practice applying a concept, the deeper their understanding of the concept becomes. Yet unless students move beyond matching patterns as their strategy for solutions, they are unlikely to fully appreciate how the concept itself serves as the primary guide in navigating the problem.

"Knowing How": Analytic Problem Solving

In addition to "knowing that"—having a firm grasp of the theories and principles—students need to "know how"—how, when, where, and why to use the theories and principles in analyzing engineering problems or situations. Without knowing "how," they are not prepared for high-level analytic thinking, for this knowledge and this skill are essential to their cognitive development. Thus technical courses should also aim at preparing students to apply these concepts, using mathematical derivations or modeling to analyze an existing or imagined engineering system or device in order to provide a basis for its improvement, enhancement, or development.

Procedural, schematic, and strategic knowledge (Shavelson and Huang, 2003) all involve modeling and analysis, two distinct though interconnected intellectual skills critical to analytic problem solving. Although students can learn these skills within or across the different technical courses of an undergraduate program, it is typical for most courses to focus first on learning the theory. Only after a certain level of exposure, with the expectation that they will understand, are students introduced to application—how these concepts might be used to formulate and solve engineering problems through modeling and analysis.

Modeling is the process of creating a representation of an engineering system or device in a way that illustrates and explains the relationship among the parts that make up the system. (Engineering uses both physical and mathematical models; in this chapter we are focusing on mathematical models; physical modeling takes place in the lab.) Whether students work with a mathematical model or a conceptual model that captures, justifies, or clarifies the operational principle of the engineering system it represents, modeling part or all of the system is a component part of analysis, for, in a more general sense, *modeling* can describe building a prototype to simulate how the system or its parts behave.

Thus analysis takes the student a step further in the process to evaluate an existing or imagined engineering system or device to determine when, where, and how to apply the appropriate principles in order to understand or predict its behavior. The process of analysis therefore requires breaking down a complex engineering problem that represents the system in parts, applying the basic principles to address each of the parts, and determining the appropriate connections among those parts in a way that best addresses the problem.

Teaching students how to generate models and analyze engineering systems principally contributes to their practice of analytic problem solving while at the same time enhancing their understanding of the fundamental principles and theories they use. As students become proficient in modeling and analysis, they develop knowledge about the concepts in such a way that they can use them intentionally.

Learning to Generate Models

Knowing a theory is one thing, but using it to make, change, or improve engineering systems is quite another. Solving engineering problems entails identifying the theories and principles essential to the problem and defining their optimal relationship. Without a good grasp of the principles in physical terms, however, students will find it difficult to think in a relational way.

As a model is a representation that embodies the operational principles of a device or system and defines the criteria for the system's design and production, it provides the framework for evaluation of the design, operation, and production of a system that satisfies a set of predefined attributes and constraints. Models are used to represent the physical world. They constitute an attempt to articulate a possible solution based on an idealized representation of the physical world. As one professor put it, "We don't make [physical] prototype after prototype without first trying to predict performance and how it will work; we have tools [analysis] that help make the best guess."

A model, however, is only a conceptual view of the result. It is an abstraction of the essential elements based on the system of the device's operational principles. Hence, it is only as good as the person's grasp of the concepts that the system embodies. In cases in which the problem demands a particular solution that meets certain specifications or constraints, mathematical modeling is inevitable. In generating mathematical models, students must know the parameters and implications of a theory and its relation to other theories, be able to translate them into mathematical terms, and be able to move fluidly between concepts and mathematical representations. As one faculty member observed, difficulty in doing so often implies that students lack an understanding of the principles or the mathematical language: "Well, if you're talking about doing an integration of a function, $f(x)$, they can do that. All you have to do is change f to be something physical and give x a different name, and then they can no longer do it. They cannot do that transformation of taking a physical thing and model it mathematically and then do that a little more mathematical manipulation on it. And that's a question about a missing comprehension or understanding of what's going on."

Learning to Analyze Problems

In professional practice, analysis requires a deep understanding of the principles and how, when, where, and why they should be applied to engineering problems. Analysis involves a number of skills that rely heavily on good judgment and practical reasoning. Analysis also involves the synthesis of ideas, negotiation, and reconciliation between competing and perhaps incomplete ideas, as well as a strategic approach that involves resource evaluation, validation of choices, consideration of ethical implications of candidate solutions, and optimization of decisions made.

We found, however, that because engineering technical courses in general and introductory engineering science courses in particular tend to focus more on teaching the principles, students have few opportunities to actually "do" analysis. As we discuss in the final chapter of this part, presenting the principles in context captures some aspects of the analytic problem solving such that students can be made aware of the need to be discriminating in identifying the relevant information of a given problem.

"Knowing Why": Engineering Intuition

In professional practice, although application, modeling, and analysis are central to problem solving, engineers draw on the tacit knowledge of expertise. Some faculty members teaching technical courses talked about "engineering intuition" as a critical aspect of analytic problem solving, and we would add this to the goals of teaching technical knowledge. Engineering intuition, they explained, involves judgment and, to some extent, back-of-the-envelope calculation, which requires knowledge of the fundamental engineering principles combined with common sense. Engineering intuition—that quick and immediate perception or judgment of an engineering problem or situation and its possible solution—comes from experience, developed through constant exposure to engineering principles and their application in the context of engineering systems and devices. It is what some term "deep knowledge."

One manifestation of engineering intuition is an automatic response, the ability to analyze a problem without engaging in any serious calculations. Sufficient for less complex solutions, it may also be the first step of a more complex analysis. Students can learn to make a quick assessment of the problem at hand and identify what needs to be resolved. As a faculty member remarked, "[Y]ou typically solve first in a coarse manner ... I don't think that we [teach] this deliberately; but by the time they finish they have gotten the idea. Maybe we should have a 'back-of-the-envelope calculation' course."

Intuition, faculty told us, can serve as a guide and help students keep their approach to a solution focused on the key issues as they develop a sound and suitable model of analysis. Having a good sense of the dynamics of a problem can help students craft a reasonable solution approach to a problem prior to doing any rigorous conceptual or mathematical analysis. Moreover, faculty observed, the accuracy of their conclusions increases and errors are minimized: "There is a difference between analysis and math; analysis involves learning the art of what matters and what does not. It is interesting to watch them mature in this thinking. In engineering analysis you often have to decide what to keep and what to remove. This is where that intuition comes into play. You keep your eye on what you want to solve. A good model depends on what you want to accomplish; you cannot answer this in a vacuum. This is one of the differences between a mathematician and an engineer." (See, for example, Redish and Smith's 2008 exploration of the distinction between mathematicians' and engineers' use of mathematics.)

Developing Knowledge for Professional Practice

That faculty may not be realizing the full complement of student learning goals they identify as necessary suggests the need to rethink the strategy for developing technical knowledge. We do not suggest that engineering educators should abandon teaching the fundamental concepts and principles, but we are persuaded that engineering educators can approach the goals in new ways, through the context of professional practice.

Doing so will mean making very difficult choices about course content and curricular design. It will also involve new approaches to teaching and assessment of student learning so that students are prepared to engage in analytic problem solving that demands a high level of cognition: the generation of models of possible solutions, the evaluation of model solutions against the problem statement and the desired solution at each stage of the process, the negotiation of constraints and attributes, and the consideration of the ethical implications of the candidate solutions. As we describe in Chapter Six, engineering science and technical courses can encourage such reflective thinking and analysis. Yet, as we discuss in the next chapter, the pedagogical strategies and assessments we observed in many technical courses are at cross-purposes with these goals.

This faculty member's comment aptly sums up the need for change:

> [A]n important aspect is to teach the students to be able to distinguish the important parts from the nonimportant parts. Because we live in the world of information overload . . . there's no end to the amount of information you can gather about any particular thing. But it is very important that you know what the important pieces are and which the unimportant pieces are. And so in that sense, the students should learn how to start out by having an overall view of things and then decide what aspects they are looking at, and what analysis therefore is important to perform for this. And if they cannot do that, they just become formula chasers or handbook chasers or whatever. And then they don't know where to go.

5

LISTENING, SEEING, DOING

IN A SOLID MECHANICS CLASS that we observed, the teacher lectured on calculating shear stress. He used the overhead projector to guide his lecture but relied mainly on the blackboard, drawing diagrams on one section and scribbling formulas on the other. For the bulk of the class period he talked about the formulas with variables. Toward the end of the session, he plugged actual numeric values into the equations for two different examples that illustrated the calculation of stress on differently configured beams.

This approach is typical of engineering science courses. The teacher introduces a rule or a principle, explains the concept using diagrams and formulas, substitutes the variables in the formula with actual values to illustrate a concrete case, and finally performs the calculation, hoping that students will see how the solution relates to the fundamental principle and to the physical artifact to which it is applied.

Whether in classrooms or theater-style auditoriums, the teachers take full control of the transmission of knowledge. It is a method that regards the teacher as the expert who transfers knowledge to a group of novices. Faculty repeatedly demonstrate the principle being applied to particular cases. As one professor explained, "Students have to keep seeing it over and over before really understanding it"; another pointed out that students "have to keep seeing it" before they can "do it."

As illustrated in Figure 5.1, the dominant pedagogy for the dominant component of the engineering program is *deductive*.

Based on our observations and interviews with faculty members, it seems that Mann's description of the teaching practices at MIT when it opened in 1865 holds to this very day: "[I]nstruction was given mainly by lectures, in which the professor presented to the class a logically well-organized explanation of the general principles and theories of the subject

Figure 5.1.   Deductive Method of Teaching an Engineering Principle

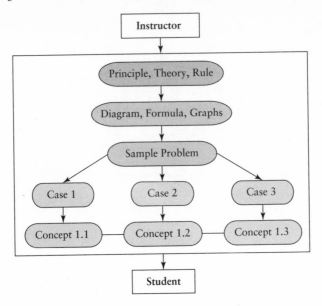

in hand. Lectures were illustrated by experiments and accompanied by blackboard demonstrations. The students took notes, recited on them at regular quiz hours, and worked problems that illustrated the principles and theories presented" (Mann, 1918, p. 37). With increasing enrollments in the twentieth century, "interrogations and blackboard demonstrations" became the popular forms of pedagogy in engineering schools and have remained so as generations of faculty, facing large classes and increasingly pressed to cover the material, draw on their own experience as students.

The process of learning, thinking, and doing sends a powerful, unspoken message that students receive as information about how an engineer works. Having no other experience, they take the classroom to represent the profession. The deductive method of teaching, which faculty may reach for because it is convenient, thus forms students' understanding of engineering work. Likewise, through assessments of what they know and can do, students develop an understanding, whether accurate or not, of what the profession counts as important knowledge and skills.

What Counts?

Consider homework and exams. The frequency of homework assignments in engineering science and technical courses is sound pedagogy, for students are afforded multiple opportunities to practice and get feedback on their work—at relatively low stakes, for the homework typically counts toward the overall course grade: about 10 to 15 percent, just enough to ensure that students do it. However, the numerous textbook problems the students are asked to solve each week of the term, although they range from structured to open-ended, generally fall in the structured end of the range and do not sufficiently challenge students to move to a deeper level of understanding and skill of analysis that helps move students toward reflective thinking.

Exams, generally mid-term and final, account for 85 percent of the student's final grade and are intended to assess students' skill in using engineering tools. Like the homework problems, most exam questions are single answer and process oriented, and require a demonstration of the steps used to arrive at the answer. Students are expected to show their technical skill in applying the mathematical formula to a given problem by substituting the given data and running a series of equations to calculate the correct answer.

Thus, although learning to use concepts to analyze real-world problems is an important goal for technical courses, we observed that students generally have very little opportunity to develop these skills. In the push to cover the fundamental concepts, students' main activities are (1) applying the concepts to textbook problems that often are not representative of the current engineering practice and (2) generating simple models focused on specific principles. Students cannot use principles as tools for developing solutions unless they have a good grasp of the concepts in the first place. To develop that good grasp, they need opportunities to process the information.

Tasks such as story problems, for example, provide such opportunities. However, as faculty members told us, open-ended or story problems, though ideal for supporting the goals of the engineering science and technical courses, seldom appear on exams:

> We don't tend to ask very many story problems on exams because [students] don't have enough time to properly sit down and evaluate it and also it's very difficult for us to evaluate it, because if they take the wrong tack on it, then they're in trouble. And the real problem with that is of course that they can argue pretty convincingly that their tack on it may well be within the way of looking at the problem. Unfortunately, when you have exams and you have an exam grading, it tends to be focused too much on how well you use the tool rather than how well you choose which tool to use.

In other words, what counts, the faculty told us, is not whether the student learns to think like an engineer, to use the tools of engineering creatively and responsibly, but that the student can identify the tools in the toolbox. Thus the predominantly single-answer-problem exams are consistent with the deductive pedagogy. The exams, focused on the mathematical tools and their specific uses, fail to provide opportunities for students to synthesize these tools to form their engineering judgment on problems that are more complex.

Consequently, what counts for the students is "getting through." Students told us that they try to gain enough exposure to the different types of problems and their solutions, if only to acquire a good sense of how the former matches the latter. They believe that going through the exercise of solving a wide range of sample problems will help them choose the right solution for every problem—and do so quickly: "I always just do the homework again as fast as I possibly could to ... prime myself for the test." They look for the key components of a problem, identify the problem type, and apply the correct formula in order to solve for the answer. As the students noted, the objective is to solve as many problems as possible in the shortest time: "The tests are usually long, so it is best that you try to do practice problems fast."

Moreover, the focus of the typical assessment does not allow students to make an important cognitive leap. Although the problems on the exams are fundamentally similar to those in the homework, faculty and students alike told us that if a problem on an exam is presented differently from the way the students found it in the textbook, students have difficulty solving it. As one student commented, "One of the reasons I think that a lot of people do not do well in that class is because the exams are so different from the homework. It is the same exact material. It's just presented in a different way and each of the problems requires you to sort of think slightly differently. So the problems are the kind of problems that would not show up on the homework, and that is where a lot of people got very low."

Without a deep understanding of the concepts, students rely on patterns of solutions that they assume to be easily transferable to problems with a similar framework. When they meet a case that does not match the pattern they have constructed, they do not recognize the principle. They are not prepared to jump across the cognitive gap. Nor are they well positioned to translate from the English version of the situation to the math-based representation and thus a set of decisions about how sound the situation is. As a faculty member commented, "There would be certain problems that some students just cannot seem to figure out unless they kind of map it to some other problem that they've done that they kind of see worked out ... If you give an exam or you give them a problem that doesn't look like any of their homework problems, you'll see that some of them will do very well because they'll take all the basic principles and they'll re-apply it, and some of them would get really stuck."

Making the Cognitive Leap

To help students make the leap from solving straightforward applications of the concepts to the using the concept as a tool in understanding a system, some faculty members, we observed, put greater emphasis on the students' understanding of the principles or concepts. One faculty member explained: "On exams, I tell them that 90 percent of the grade is in the approach and their understanding; not whether they wind up with numerically correct answer. If they explain to me in words but don't have time to do it, they can still make an A. If they can explain all the concepts and how to do it, they don't have to do the work."

As one faculty member noted, "They tend to . . . try to load into the brain as much information as possible the night before [an exam] and they dump it . . . I'm trying to break them of that because the brain has got a limited capacity. What you've got to do is to know where to go for things and how to derive things from those principles and . . . what is the relationship between this, that, and the other stuff."

According to a faculty member at Michigan, the focus of assessment must be on how one thinks about a problem, not just the correct answer. To do this, he deliberately challenges students to respond to open-ended questions to determine how well they understand and synthesize the concepts they have learned. His method of assessing students is reflective of his teaching: he puts a lot of emphasis on acquiring a solid understanding of the concepts and strongly discourages memorization of facts. In his view, getting students to think in this way is not easy. It demands reaching out to individual students and helping them adopt this attitude toward learning.

It is through understanding the relationships that students learn how to use the concepts for their particular value and how to use them as a basis for further learning, as this faculty member explained:

> You can't really grade it . . . because they may get the answers by luck, though you never know whether they've just memorized the whole string of stuff . . . I want to know that they really got what those concepts are . . . I allow them to take in . . . a sort of formula sheet . . . and then I tell them that basically they shouldn't try to remember anything that is more than they can get on that sheet of paper. It's a hard job . . . it's part of the culture . . . the difficulty is to get them to realize that

it's the relationships between things that are important rather than the actual facts.

Aligning Assessment with the Learning Goals

Some faculty members pose questions that challenge students to think of the concepts from a systems perspective and to learn to synthesize those concepts as they figure out an answer to a problem. A faculty member at Michigan, for example, focuses the students on learning to use the engineering tools on a systems level, where different concepts are interconnected, and to make decisions as they approach specific problems:

> I ask questions like "If you have a such and such structure loaded in such and such a way, where is it going to fail first? Which point in the structure is going to fail first?" So, I'm looking for whether they can take all of the things that they learned in the whole course and prioritize things … I'm generally looking on that level rather than on the detail level. But I do also examine their ability, of course, to do certain basic types of calculation. But wherever possible, I try to throw in stuff that is into these more general questions.

Using Formative Assessment

Assessment treated as constructive feedback in an ongoing learning experience is often called *formative*, as opposed to mid-term or end-of-the-course *summative* assessment, when a grade is at stake.

Some faculty told us that they develop (and assess) students' analytic problem-solving skills by using open-ended problems, focusing the students on the approach to the problem rather than on their final answer. What counts is how well the student considers the principles that are relevant to the situation. Because the homework is such a small part of the grade, the assessment is formative. It provides a low-stakes opportunity for the student to learn how to analyze complex problems and understand that analysis is not a simple application of the principles but a process of idealizing a complex problem and figuring out a strategy that best solves the problem, while taking into account the constraints and attributes of the desired solution.

As faculty in the study observed, demonstration of the student's ability to work through an analytic problem-solving process is a fundamental aspect of formative assessment: "I assign three to four problems a week, which are graded on a scale of one to five by a course grader. They get a one if they show the method, a pattern. They get more points if they draw the free body diagram, equilibrium, force definitions. I'll take off a point if they get the wrong answer. I'm more concerned that they understand and can do the methodology than ... getting the right answer."

Meeting the Challenge of Grading the Process

Although a focus on problem solving is an effective learning strategy, grading it in summative situations is a challenge, as there can be many parts to a solution. The teacher must evaluate the student's solution and process. We noted some creative approaches. Faculty members at CMU, for example, give credit to the process as well as the final answer by using a point system that reflects a practitioner's ability to take on an engineering work. Students earn points for every correct segment, component, or phase in their problem solution. The more points the student earns, the greater her chances are of being hired to do a particular job. As a faculty member explained, this helps students not only to devote the necessary care and attention to details, but also to appreciate the demands of the practice in relation to their performance: "Sometimes I take the approach that we're talking points, engineering points. They either make it, or they don't. It's really as simple as that. And it kind of gives them a different feel for not the ten points but that this is their livelihood. It works out pretty well. That is the difference between zero and ten. You either get the contract or you don't. That's exactly it, and they need to appreciate that."

CMU students get the message: being able to think and argue about a solution to a problem is more important than recalling and applying mathematical formulas to solve for the right answer: "[I]f you can explain how to approach solving the problem, it is as valuable as the equations. It is more valuable in terms of real life. I will be able to look at a cantilever beam and know how it will bend, I will not have a naive approach using mathematics; it is more of an intuitive sense." Students genuinely appreciate being challenged to be critical about a problem and understand that the challenge enhances their learning. They told us that the assessment impels them to value critical thinking rather than remembering formulas or solving mathematical equations without understanding how this relates to the problem statement. Said one student, "On the last stress analysis test, I did not get to solving one of the problems. I wrote an essay on what was going on, and got 19/25 points. On another problem, I did all of the equations and cranked through the math and got the wrong answer; it got 12/25. He focuses on how well we understand, and not on cranking through the numbers."

6

LEARNING FOR PROBLEM SOLVING

FACULTY SEEM TO FEEL COMPELLED to teach as much of theory and principles as possible, in the belief that this will equip students to perform engineering tasks. However, simply transmitting knowledge through lecture does not guarantee students' comprehension or their ability to apply it or do analysis based on it. Students cannot convert principles into solutions unless they have a good grasp of the concepts in the first place. Students need opportunities for processing the information, to make it usable knowledge.

Although the historic formula of lecture, demonstration, follow-up homework, and exams is perceived as efficient for today's large class sizes, typical of the core courses, we wonder whether deeper convictions or disciplinary habits inform the choice. Do faculty believe that students must first hear about a principle before they can examine particular applications of it? Do they believe that they must focus on delivering the principles efficiently and thoroughly in order to equip students with the basic tools of their profession? Do they assume that a student's understanding of a principle is aided by the repeated demonstration of its application to specific cases?

Although the deductive approach to teaching in engineering science and advanced technical courses might seem a clean and organized way of introducing new material, it does not encourage students to be actively involved in their own learning. Moreover, repeatedly demonstrating the application of a principle does not necessarily help students learn or understand the material; in fact, it precludes the opportunity to learn how, when, where, and why the principle is applied, to develop the understanding of the phenomenon necessary for high-level analysis—opportunities to develop the cognitive skills of reflective thinking.

Findings from current research on learning suggest that engineering educators, individually and collectively, could significantly improve student learning, particularly in the foundation courses. With information and insight that our teachers never had about learning, and with a world of technical and scientific knowledge that continues to expand at rates unimaginable to previous generations of educators, it is time to rethink our teaching strategies. Engineering educators now have the tools to consider how students learn, what impedes their learning, and why students consider some knowledge and skills easier to process than others, even though they might seem equally complex. We now know the importance of articulating to the learner *what* it is we are trying to teach and *why* we teach. We now know that teaching in the context of the profession that students are aspiring to be a part of motivates and improves learning.

The content of the engineering science and technical courses should be considered in relation to the whole of the program that prepares students for professional practice, with the goal of guiding students in developing a robust set of problem-solving strategies and the ability to continually expand their knowledge of the technical world. The technical knowledge is one aspect of the professional—the new-century engineer—who provides a worthwhile service in the pursuit of important human and social ends, possesses fundamental knowledge and skill, develops the capacity to engage in complex forms of professional practice, makes judgments under conditions of uncertainty, learns from experience, and creates and participates in responsible and effective professional community.

Solving Problems and Problem Solving

It is assumed that in-class problems and homework give students the opportunity to immediately apply what they have learned, to think through the process of problem solving without the time constraints typically encountered in exams, to develop their problem-solving skills, and consequently to enhance their understanding of the material. However, as we note in the previous chapter, because most engineering science courses rely mainly on textbook problems with answers at the back of the book, many students tend to focus on the answers as they work through the problems. As a result, they work toward getting the exact solution that the book presents, often ignoring the thought process that justifies their solution.

Likewise with single-answer problems: if students are asked to determine the current i_2 and the V_5 in the given circuit, they do not have to think about how the principle relates to the elements—such as current and voltage—of the problem based on the desired state or condition of the engineering system, such as the circuit. Single-answer problems focus students on one or two principles, showing application in a concrete way. (Structured laboratory experiments, which we discuss in Part Three, also do this.)

Solving right-answer problems is not necessarily problem solving: the problems that students are typically asked to solve do not build the kind of problem-solving skills they will need later in their program or in practice. They do not lead to the habits of mind that, whether the students become engineers or not, are such valuable contributors to work and citizenship.

Developing a Conceptual Framework

Problem solving demands understanding. To be problem solvers, students need to gain both a deep understanding of some basic principles and the ability to organize and restructure them for later use. One of the key findings from research comparing experts and novices reveals that the "ability to plan a task, to notice patterns, to generate reasonable arguments and explanations, and to draw analogies to other problems are all more closely intertwined with factual knowledge than was once believed" (Bransford, Brown, and Cocking, 2000).

Students learn with understanding when they have the opportunity to develop a conceptual framework for the facts so that they are not trying to store them as disconnected pieces of information. With a conceptual framework, they can transfer or apply what they have learned to other situations, thus gaining the ability to develop competence in problem solving.

Although introductory engineering science courses are particularly aimed at helping students learn the fundamental principles and the mathematical tools that represent them, teachers can contribute to the ultimate learning goal of analytic problem solving by encouraging students to internalize and construct a framework for conceptual understanding. Whether the instructor uses visual representations of the principles, cases or story problems, or laboratory experiments, helping students, early on, to think analytically about what they are learning will help them synthesize and generalize their knowledge and use it in their future learning.

Rehearsing Analysis

Sophomores at Colorado School of Mines (Mines) told us that analysis is critical to problem solving: "We are learning to deal with any sort of problem, not just equations. As I am studying, I look beyond the equations. I ask myself if I will be able to look at a problem."

Making a distinction between the simple application of equations based on memory and the thoughtful process of strategizing an approach to solve a problem, the students recognize that there can be a number of ways to arrive at a solution and that they must make a decision based on their understanding and careful evaluation of the problem. Said one: "There are an infinite number of ways to solve a problem—it is just about finding the most efficient way. I tend to write down everything I know, and then look for a strategy, as opposed to just applying equations. At first I was focused on memorizing equations, now I am focused on the thought process. Even if I see a new problem, I have a thought process."

In solving complex problems, for example, the Mines students are asked to simplify or break a problem into parts and figure out which of the parts are crucial and likely to have the greatest impact on the solution. They take a complex problem to a manageable state with the use of their knowledge of the fundamental principles, identifying the tasks involved in carrying out the solution while considering and optimizing the available resources. As the students told us, practicing skills of decision making builds their problem-solving capabilities: "You need to know how to prioritize the tasks. You need to be able to identify what is important and what is not, since there is not enough time. [You need] to be able to define what has to be done. Given that we have more work than is possible, you need to learn how to have a strategy."

Teaching Inductively

As the learning sciences suggest, an inductive method of teaching is one way to help students learn to use the fundamental concepts for robust problem solving. As illustrated by Figure 6.1, the teacher focuses on cases that the students could work on to help them develop an understanding of the phenomenon that these cases represent before a principle is introduced.

For example, a teacher might begin the class with a problem, such as how to hold a two-hundred-pound weight using a piece of paper and paper clips, and ask the students to figure out the fundamental elements that are critical to the problem. Based on their existing knowledge and experience, students attempt to explore possible cases given the attributes and constraints of the problem. As they work through this process, they develop a sense of awareness of the key elements that seem to be relevant in all the cases, such as load, stress, or strength. Subsequently, they begin

Figure 6.1. Inductive Method of Teaching an Engineering Principle

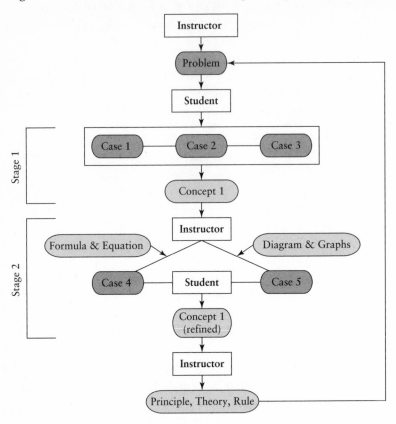

their concept-formation of each of the elements based on the phenomenon observed.

Building on the learning experience, the instructor introduces new cases and, along with the students, identifies their fundamental elements. Although formulas, equations, graphs, or diagrams may be applied, the instructor uses them as tools in helping students refine their concept-formation. As students acquire a more refined understanding of a concept, the instructor introduces the principle and reconnects it to the problem.

The two major differences between this approach and the deductive method described in Chapter Five are (1) the teacher's early introduction of context, thus encouraging students to think in real terms; and (2) the potential for students to be more reflective about their own learning as the learning experience becomes more iterative and less linear. Although the inductive method can be messy and challenging, its impact on student learning can be enormous.

Examples from the Faculty. In our site visits, we observed the inductive approach in action. A Michigan faculty member, for example, begins with specific problem cases (for example, how to break a piece of wood in two) to help students visualize and conceptualize the principle of stress before it is introduced. In his view, students must first experience or observe the concept that the principle embodies at various stages and forms. We listened to him tell his students how he plans to guide them in creating an experiential basis for understanding a principle:

> You'll learn the theoretical material by trying particular cases and say, "Oh, in this situation this happens and in some slightly different situation this happens. Can we generalize this into a more general theory?" rather than "Let's start from a whole series of axioms and work our way down." I can tell you what something is, but until it's been part of your life for a period of time, you don't really have a very rich concept of it. You just have a definition ... So, every time you use the concept of stress in a new example, your concept gets a little bit richer regarding coloring you get out of it ... And then I want to say, "Okay, now we've got as far as this, we've built up some concepts. Let's go back and revisit some of our original ideas. Maybe now we can generalize them a little bit because we've got more experience of what the concepts mean."

A faculty member at Mines often shifts between the inductive and deductive modes. Using familiar cases and objects, she presents the phenomenon that best describes the concept of stress before actually working through a series of equations to explain it mathematically. As her description of her lesson suggests, presenting examples that students can relate to helps them grasp the concept and retain it in their memory: "When we talk about vessels, which are boilers or pipes, then I give an example like a basketball or a Coke can. I was sitting in a kitchen and heard an explosion. It was Coke that had frozen and it popped. It was a classic pressure vessel. They fail lengthwise ... And my final example is a hot dog: when you grill it, it splits. They laugh, but I think they remember the big stresses that pull it apart ... everybody has seen that and they go, 'Oh yeah.'"

Learning in Context

The theories and principles at the center of engineering science and analysis courses can be learned in the context of an engineering problem, system, or situation that in some ways represents the practice. Learning

in context suggests that the learners are given the opportunity to interact with the body of knowledge in a way that connects with the practice
for which they are being prepared. This approach helps students relate
what they are learning to how it might be used. It presents the subject
as a body of organized and meaningful concepts and not "a mere list of
disconnected facts" (Bransford, Brown, and Cocking, 2000, p. 24).

Learning in context often results in a deeper understanding of the subject. This means that teachers should think of ways to introduce principles
and theories in context to help students establish the relationships between
concepts, thus supporting their understanding and enabling them to both
internalize it and transfer knowledge to other contexts. In this way, students are encouraged to see the bigger picture of what they are learning
and to have a better appreciation of the subject matter. Moreover, making an immediate connection to something real or familiar often motivates
students to be engaged in their own learning, because they are able to relate
well with the object that embodies the phenomenon they are attempting
to learn. In technical courses, for example, students are more likely to
be able to make the cognitive leap, moving from straightforward application of concepts to using concepts as tools in analysis. Students see
and experience the messiness of real problems and use the tools to work
through it.

For example, through an inductive approach, demonstrating and
explaining the process of using a principle or theory to solve real-world
problems can help students appreciate the explanation for the appropri-
ateness of the principle and use that to form their understanding of the
concept. By doing this, "learners are given access not only to what they
see, but to what the [teacher] is seeing and sensing, plus the [teacher]
can give further explanations about what she is doing" (Merriam and
Caffarella, 1999, p. 245). This is done not once, but several times,
each time using different examples or cases to help students develop a
conceptual framework for understanding the principles.

As we suggest in the previous chapter, as a strategy for contextualiz-
ing the concept, if a single-answer problem can be presented in a word or
story form, it can provide a rich context for understanding the application
of the principle while presenting the elements relevant to the problem as
they appear in the story. The goal is to help students learn how to apply
a principle to a particular problem by using a formula that defines the
principle and restating the formula as an equation using the given data.
Establishing an early connection between the engineering principles and
problem exercises or laboratory experiments or a classroom or simulation demonstration enables students to see the relevance of what they

are learning and increases the likelihood that they will acquire a better understanding. Teaching application in context, however, is not an easy task if the course structure does not support it. For example, laboratory assignments require particular facilities, and creating appropriate story problems requires a certain level of imagination and background in engineering practice.

The opportunity to work with hardware while learning to apply a principle or theory is a good way of putting the subject matter in context. An engineering science course that has a laboratory component attached to it offers real-time application of concepts, as it provides immediate connection to and feedback from the physical world. As we discuss in Part Three of this volume, laboratories are great opportunities for providing students with hands-on experience in applying fundamental concepts to physical artifacts in a way that resembles practice. This teaching strategy has the potential for bridging theory and practice because of the immediate representation of the theory in a physical form and the opportunity to understand the concept from a different perspective.

If a program faculty coordinate with their colleagues in mathematics, physics, chemistry, and biology, they can provide examples or cases derived from industrial and professional situations. Examples that suggest the larger context in which the knowledge that students are learning is applied may lead to deeper learning of the basic knowledge and be motivational for some students. The key is including appropriately framed technical and nontechnical aspects of the situation, at a developmentally appropriate level, and getting students actively involved. (Such engineering cases are available at www.civeng.carleton .ca/ECL/; dissection cases are available through EngineeringPathways: www.engineeringpathway.com/ep/; ethics cases are available at www .onlineeethics.org/eng/cases.html; and simulation games are available at http://bridgecontest.usma.edu/.) The roles students play in these exercises can vary from hearing or reading the case and writing up an analysis, to role-playing one of the characters in the situation, to authoring new exercises based on observing industrial practice. A student's role, which specific aspects of the case are emphasized, how the student's work is assessed—all should be thoughtfully designed based on learning goals.

Homework assignments that put subject matter in context. In nonlaboratory settings, one practical approach to learning how to analyze is through homework assignments that involve actual industry problems as opposed to fictional exercises that are simply passed on every year. For example, a faculty member at CMU takes advantage of his interactions with industry in putting together problem materials that students could work on for their engineering science course. Unlike structured problem examples with clear parameters, industry-based problems come with several unknowns. They are rarely neat packages. Current engineering problems give students the experience to work on real-world issues without the simplistic or unthinking application of familiar solutions.

Bringing Professional Practice into the Classroom

Unlike most universities, Carnegie Mellon University (CMU) offers not only a capstone design course but also a capstone analysis course that provides opportunities for students to experience solving actual engineering problems through modeling and analysis, making a stronger connection between engineering science and practice. It is what a faculty member considers "a transition to actual engineering practice." Industry often provides CMU students with real engineering problems requiring heavy analysis in support of engineering design. As a faculty member explains, students act as engineers by defining and clarifying problems, developing models, making assumptions about their proposed solutions, and conducting rigorous analysis:

> Often, industry folks come in and bring in problems either that they have worked on, or they're working on, or they would like somebody to work on. And they pose the problem, usually orally, and students act as engineers. They are engineers. We treat them as engineers. What I tell the students is that it is not design, but it is the kind of problems that you might do in support of design ... And what we want to do with this course is bring all of these together and say, "Look, there's an engineering problem" ... All engineering problems are complex and require probably everything that you can bring to the table. And that's what we want to do. We want our students to be able to at least get a good taste of it before they go out and face their first such problem.

The capstone analysis course is an attempt to bring professional practice into the classroom through analytic problem solving. The problems are difficult and require a multitude of knowledge and skills, thus helping students get a sense of what real engineering work might entail. Aimed at helping students realize the importance of knowing what information is needed to solve complex engineering problems and how to find and synthesize that knowledge, the course encourages students to learn on their own and to think beyond what is already known.

As the faculty member teaching the course explained, students are challenged to decide which concepts to use and whether or not to seek additional knowledge. The industry problem encourages them to integrate what they have learned and to develop a way of thinking that recognizes the need for continuous learning:

> (1) to be able to synthesize the knowledge that they have gained in other courses, and (2) the recognition that they need other information to be able to solve engineering problems and that they need to figure out what it is that they need and how to go out and get it. Not everything will be given to them ... So, once again, how do they put it together and recognize the complexity of the problem; how do they put together what they have learned and recognize what else it is that they need to find out that they may not have learned?

Of course, the capstone analysis course, for all its strengths, is not sufficient to help students "put it together" unless it is truly a capstone to a program of staged development of analytic problem-solving skills, in which each technical course gives students opportunities to learn, in parallel, technical knowledge and skills of using the knowledge as a tool of analysis—in the larger context of professional practice.

PART THREE

A PLACE TO EXPLORE

AS ENGINEERS EVALUATE CANDIDATE SOLUTIONS to problems, they use a variety of tools to predict performance: analytic and physical models based on heuristics, science, mathematics, and rules of thumb. The engineer works with information or evidence describing the current state while at the same time trying to establish, through testing, the model's attributes in the desired state. This thorough investigation and experimentation of possible solutions is possible only in a laboratory.

In the undergraduate engineering curriculum, the laboratory prepares students to measure, test, observe, and experiment. It gives students the opportunity to work with hardware, measure properties, test theories, and observe and predict product behavior using a scientific and systematic approach. The lab also offers material context for understanding and learning the fundamental concepts and theories of mathematics and science. In the laboratory, students learn to work with data to explore possibilities for generating solutions to problems. They develop problem-solving skills as they work in a practice-like setting where theories may or may not work and instrumentation fails intermittently.

Although laboratory work may begin as early as the freshman year, most of it occurs in the sophomore and junior levels. One might assume that this advanced-level experience includes open-ended experiments that encourage students to learn how to deal with the uncertainties and problems associated with experimentation, for, as most engineers would agree, "real laboratory situation is not neat, not shiney [sic], gives the right answer only 5% of the time, and breaks down several times a week. A realistic laboratory project is thus one that incorporates these unpleasant yet challenging features ... in addition to standard laboratory exercises, the student should fail to achieve success, get frustrated and get dirty" (Scott, 1983, p. 67).

In other words, the undergraduate laboratory should be the place for students to explore: to generate solutions to real-world human problems, develop a sense of the possibilities of resources, and integrate the appropriate analytical tools in a low-risk setting where the only consequence of failure is learning (Dean, 1983; Grossman and others, 2009).

What we found in our study was something less than this ideal, however. Although laboratories provide an important practical dimension to student learning, they serve chiefly as a supplement to lectures, a place to validate the theories taught in the classroom. Driven by the foundational courses to which they are linked, either structurally within a single course or thematically as a stand-alone course, they are expected to reinforce, illustrate, verify, or test the engineering principles introduced in the theory classes while developing students' practice-related skills. Depending on the course objectives, laboratory work comes in different forms, ranging from "cookbook" or structured exercises to open-ended projects, with varying degrees of teacher control and student autonomy.

We found many examples of innovative practice in the lab and in the *use* of labs. However, we saw that it is rare for engineering programs to have a program-wide lab plan that scaffolds and supports learning as students work with real systems. We also found that despite the individual efforts of lab instructors, engineering programs in general undervalue lab relative to its impact and potential to help students move toward professional practice.

Although the laboratories provide important opportunities for integrating theory and practice, they are plagued by resource and staffing issues. Wankat and Oreovicz's 1993 observation that apparatus are often outdated or inoperative and courses are assigned to new professors or graduate teaching assistants was confirmed during our visits more than a decade later. Labs were a problem in most institutions we visited. A number of faculty members talked about the money required to "populate the lab with equipment and support it and keep it running" as well as the need for a well-established maintenance program.

The situation is not new. Although the laboratory has long been considered a part of the preparation of engineers, the attention it has received relative to the rest of the engineering curriculum components is minimal. Because of costs, it has long been difficult for engineering schools to keep laboratory instrumentation and facilities up to date and supportive of the new technologies. Moreover, because the laboratory has generally been considered an extension of or "appendage" to the more "important" courses in the engineering science sequence, it has long been neglected (Kopplin, 1965). In fact, during the mid-1900s, laboratories suffered a great deal: laboratory equipment and facilities were limited or in poor condition, and laboratory courses were radically reduced and often assigned to new teachers and teaching assistants. In our study, we found that between the continued heavy emphasis given to the theoretical component of engineering curricula (Bucciarelli and Kuhn, 1997) and the resources necessary to maintain, develop, or improve teaching laboratories, the laboratory's potential remains untapped.

The undergraduate laboratory has enormous potential for helping students connect theory and practice. The laboratory offers a place for activities that connect to robust analysis and problem solving. Laboratory experience can both reinforce students' understanding of theory and cultivate their creativity and critical thinking. The lab can increase students' appreciation for the significant work, beyond mathematical analysis, that provides the basis for building and testing technology to solve human problems.

The laboratory is also an excellent means of bridging engineering analysis and design through activities such as testing, experimental modeling, and simulation. It offers students something analogous to the clinical experience that medical practitioners consider critical to their training. Hence, a good laboratory is one that helps students gain insight into real engineering work—where failure is the norm, not the exception (Scott, 1983).

In the chapters that follow, we look inside the engineering laboratory, offering as examples some of the particularly effective approaches we observed. After we describe the learning goals we discovered there, the curricular arrangements we found, and the prevalent pedagogy and assessments, we offer a discussion of innovative practice that makes the lab truly a place to explore.

7

THEORY AND SKILLS

"PEOPLE LEARN DIFFERENTLY ... Some get it from the equations and understand it. Some need to see it on an oscilloscope to make it integrate properly ..." This faculty comment is representative of the primary use of the engineering laboratory—helping students understand the core concepts.

Another faculty comment, however, points to the promise that the laboratory holds: "A large majority of students will tell you that it is the hands-on, tangible experiences that they have in their program that are the most meaningful ... I just had a conversation with a graduate student yesterday, and he said that if he could have it his way, he would get rid of all [lectures] and just do the lab. Particularly for engineers, the idea that they have the opportunity to experience the system and its behavior and respond to various situations is a very important part of their education."

Although the faculty we spoke to agreed that the experience in the laboratory is an essential component of the engineering curriculum, they were not explicit about learning goals beyond its function of reinforcing fundamental concepts and developing practice-related skills such as measurement and testing. Indeed, the engineering faculty—and more broadly, engineering education—are not explicit about the goals for student learning through work in the laboratory. That we had to infer them through our interviews, classroom observations, and review of ABET documents and other literature is telling of the role that the lab plays in the engineering curriculum.

We observed six major learning goals in operation in the laboratory: (1) learning fundamental concepts; (2) learning to use the concepts to solve practical problems; (3) learning to work with complex engineering systems; (4) learning how to communicate; (5) learning to work in teams; and (6) learning to acquire attitudes of persistence, healthy skepticism,

Figure 7.1. Learning Goals for the Engineering Laboratory

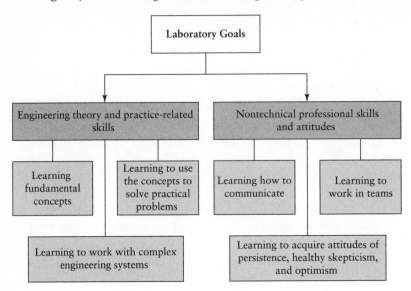

and optimism. As Figure 7.1 illustrates, we consider the first three to be goals for learning engineering theory and practice-related skills and the other three as goals for learning nontechnical professional skills and attitudes.

Because the lecture hall is generally considered the primary place for presenting the theory, and the laboratory the place where it is applied, the central goals of the lab are aimed at mastery of engineering science and the development of problem-solving skills through the dynamic interaction of engineering principles, physical evidence, and hardware. We observed that these learning goals are typically addressed sequentially, through experiments with increasing levels of complexity. Although a few faculty members we observed or interviewed offer creative ways of achieving some of the learning goals, the general trend is to begin with the goal of learning a concept, using basic experimental methods to conduct laboratory exercises. In time, students learn how to solve complex problems using a variety of tools and data that may present competing ideas.

Engineering Theory and Practice-Related Skills

Most lower-level teaching laboratories aim to help students develop awareness and acquire basic understanding of the fundamental engineering concepts introduced in engineering science courses. Learning a fundamental concept, like Hooke's Law or conservation of energy, means recognizing the concept's strengths and limitations, its distinct character- istics, and its unique behavior or functionality.

Learning the Fundamental Concepts

Using hardware and physical evidence or data, students typically observe the phenomenon that the concept embodies. Instructors use a device or a model to demonstrate the concept or supervise the students while they conduct highly structured, tightly scripted experiments that generate fairly consistent results even when done repeatedly. Following step-by-step or "cookbook" instruction, students focus on one concept or a few closely related ones.

Such controlled experiments give students the opportunity to observe certain conditions associated with the concept or its representative abstract model and to relate them to the phenomenon that the concept or model embodies. The experiments serve to validate or confirm what students already know in theory about the concept and enhance their understanding of it (Hazel and Baillie, 1998). Thus the experience in the laboratory gives the concept some depth, dimension, and perspective for the learner. It helps students see what the concept means in practice because of the physical context it provides.

The concept of elasticity, for example, can be better appreciated if actual experiments for observation, measurement, and testing using different materials are performed. The idea of moving from a theoretical to a prac- tical approach to learning helps students acquire a deeper understanding of the relevant features of the concept. Students told us that the lab experi- ence helps them understand and visualize the principle that they are trying to learn: "[T]he homework ... there is nothing physical there ever. How can you understand something without actually doing it?"; "[A] resistor, it's just a squiggly line; and for capacitors, just these two parallel lines. But you know, without lab, how do you know what they actually look like? How are you going to put them together if you do not do it in the lab?"

Learning to Use the Concepts to Solve Practical Problems

Some experiments focus students on applying an engineering theory to solve a practical problem. We observed that students engaged in these types of experiments often think in terms of a well-defined problem to which a theory or set of theories are applied in order to arrive at an appropriate or a best possible solution. On the other hand, we did observe faculty who focus students on how and why a particular theory should be used to solve a problem, taking them well beyond the mere familiarity with the concept gained by observing how it relates to a given set of data and hardware.

In these last-mentioned cases, we observed what Wankat and Oreovicz (1993) described: in a well-designed lab experience, building on the fundamental concepts, students actually learn how a particular theory is used to solve a problem. Along with learning experimental skills—like how to plan an experiment, conduct measurements, operate modern equipment, and record or interpret data—students can begin to understand the connection between their application of a theory and hardware and the desired outcome, given a practical problem.

The students are not just observing a phenomenon that is consistent with their understanding of a theory, nor are they just following a recipe to validate their expectations; rather, they are given the opportunity to choose the steps that would best lead them to the anticipated result based on their initial understanding the theory. Hence they learn to decide what to do, given what they have and based on what they think should happen. As one student explained, "In the electronics theory class you saw today, we learn the theory behind a certain device. We learn how it functions at a fundamental level. In this lab, we apply that practically."

Learning to Work with Complex Engineering Systems

As we discuss in Chapter Eleven, we observed that some faculty organize the laboratory environment in a way that more closely approximates engineering practice. In these settings, instructors require their students to work on projects or conduct investigations involving a number of fundamental principles or theories. Students are asked to solve a problem with no clear indication as to which fundamental principles to use. The instructor may offer some indication about the desired outcome, but the experimental approach and the choice of which theories to use to solve the problem are left to the students.

In most cases, students must first conduct an evaluation of the problem and negotiate the various components that may affect the problem-solving process. They try to figure out the elements of the experiment, select the relevant data sets, identify the concepts that might be useful to test or manipulate the data, and decide which experimental method would be most appropriate to solve the problem or achieve their goal, given the circumstances surrounding the investigation. These unstructured laboratories have an element of design that requires students to use their ingenuity, thus requiring greater autonomy and offering practice in both formulating and solving problems.

Working on open-ended experiments is an excellent means of preparing for professional practice. Unlike theory classes or cookbook laboratory exercises, open-ended or project-based laboratories do not offer a clean and clear-cut process of problem solving. Often students must first make a diagnosis of the problem before deciding on their experimental approach. However, a sound diagnosis of the case does not necessarily guarantee a successful experiment. Students need to be reminded that failure in the experiment may be caused by several factors, including damaged equipment or deficient models due to unknown theories affecting their analysis. One faculty member at CMU emphasizes the need for students to realize that understanding the physical world can be a painstaking task: "You tie them to physical reality in a lab. If you are talking and drawing, they can be off in magical thinking; they are not tied to reality. Lab is about physical reality, where you must sweat the details and make yourself one with that. The subtleties and bugs are important; you cannot just plug two things together and assume that they will work and that the measurement apparatus will not affect things. The lab is opaque; labs obey all of nature's laws, not just the ones you know. It forces them to get their heads into this game."

Learning to work with unstructured, open-ended problems about complex engineering systems helps students not only learn how to use engineering concepts in an imperfect environment but also acquire proficiency in negotiating the uncertainties as they struggle to understand the world around them. A faculty member explains: "The main thing is requiring them to generate numbers from imperfect laboratory data ... When you see, let's say, the typical stress strain diagram drawn out from a metal, there's no error. You go to the lab and there are all kinds of interesting ways to make errors. There's mismeasurements, there's miscalibrations, there's misalignments, and all these things can come back to haunt them now."

Students working on open-ended laboratory experiments can expect significant challenges that test their knowledge and understanding of engineering principles, due to the range of possible outcomes. Indeed, it is important for students to learn how the interaction of the theories, hardware, and physical evidence may affect the process and outcome of their investigation: they learn that results are not always consistent with their computer simulation or modeling and that they must be creative in their approach to engineering problem solving.

Nontechnical Professional Skills and Attitudes

Consistently, we saw that faculty use the lab to develop nontechnical skills that contribute to good practice. In particular, we noted, they attempt to initiate students in the social aspects of the practice and prepare them for more complex forms of interaction and communication required in design and project-based learning.

Learning How to Communicate

The ability to translate and transmit findings into a readable and professional report is a skill that industry expects from engineering graduates. It is considered an important aspect of engineering work. As part of their laboratory work, students may be required to keep a lab notebook in which they can write all their data and keep a record of their laboratory procedures and processes. They are then required to produce a written document that communicates their findings to a wide audience.

In keeping this notebook, the faculty suggest, students can be reminded to assume that their audience is not aware of the process of their investigation and therefore must be brought into the development of their thinking: "One of the things that we put a lot of effort on in all lab courses is technical communications. While assessing an answer from a technical point of view is one thing, presenting it to someone who has not gone to all the derivations is another issue ... while they might be very good in coming up with an answer, it's difficult for many of them to present it so that people can understand and follow what they have done."

Another faculty member explained:

> I have them each write a discussion individually. So you have all these data now, taken as a group and then tell me what it means ... Not just, "well we're a little bit off here." I want to know, how much is [a] little? Be very specific. So it would be like a report to your boss in industry. "You had me do this. This is what I found." And it's something I insist on in just about all of the labs I teach. They just have to sit down and translate the numbers into words, and it just takes doing it and doing it. And this is something over the years of teaching, I've probably had more people come back and say "Thank you" and "Gee! I had to do this and it was just like you're doing a lab report."

Learning to Work in Teams

Today's complex engineering systems require the collaborative effort of experts, both engineers and nonengineers, across multiple fields. Thus, functioning as part of a team is a significant component of professional practice. Moreover, the intricacies associated with a global economy demand flexibility and social interactions that can bring about greater "synergy and harmony" among engineers from diverse cultural backgrounds (National Academy of Engineering, 2004).

Although students often work in teams in the lab, and faculty acknowledge that the laboratory can be an excellent venue for introducing students to collaboration, we rarely saw an explicit focus on learning about and learning the skills of teamwork. As we discuss in the following chapters on pedagogy and assessment in the lab, the challenges of leading, coordinating, and grading group work create challenges and even disincentives to this important experience.

Learning to Acquire Attitudes of Persistence, Healthy Skepticism, and Optimism

Beyond specific skills and knowledge, we saw that the lab can be a place to develop a set of attitudes or personal qualities that are widely understood by faculty to be important to success in engineering, in particular optimism and persistence tempered by healthy skepticism.

Students at Cal Poly, for example, told us that they are trained to think that every problem, no matter how difficult, has a solution. When a solution does not seem right, they are urged to keep an open mind and think of other possible solutions while recognizing that certain theories should guide their problem solving. For example, if an engineering system does not work, it is highly unlikely that the whole system has failed. They have to reevaluate components of the system or review the assumptions that may have influenced their investigation towards the wrong direction. One student told us, "[I]f something comes out wrong, I must have made a mistake somewhere." The student chuckled, then went on, "If you go through some solution and the solution does not make sense or does not physically work out, then it kind of goes back to the engineering thinking that you have been trained to do and you go about it in a different way, possibly take a different path to the solution."

A professor at CMU explained that, in his view, students should not expect the laboratory work always to match their expectations. They must approach their engineering work with a healthy skepticism—knowing, for example, that there can be errors in measurements; thus he urged them to be persistent and optimistic in their problem solving. As Hoover and Fish noted in *The Engineering Profession* (1950), "all values resulting from measurement have one quality in common: they are all inexact, they are all approximations to the actual magnitudes of the things measured ...

[a measured value] is subject to inescapable error" (p. 247). It is how students deal with or handle these errors to solve an engineering problem that make these teaching laboratories an important preparation for practice.

Failures in testing are almost always inevitable and should be considered as part of the experimental process. Hence one needs to have a positive disposition toward failures and be persistent in finding out how to solve a problem. As one faculty member told us, "I like to see students realize things don't always work the way they expect. Overcoming that is important. Not only do you learn the technical things to overcome the problems, but the attitude and the experience of how to solve the problem and move on ... The basic robotics they will probably forget. That's fine. It's these higher-order principles that will last them forever." The faculty member's remark suggests that it would be better for the students to forget a few basic engineering concepts than to disregard this positive attitude of optimism that has far greater consequences in their professional lives.

8

LAB IN THE CURRICULUM

THE ENGINEERING LABORATORY generally takes two forms: laboratory-enhanced engineering science courses and stand-alone laboratory courses. In the former, lab is an integral part of the course. A stand-alone laboratory course, on the other hand, is not linked to any particular course but may require one or more pre- or corequisite engineering science courses. Both may be part of a series of laboratories spread across the curriculum in a logical and deliberate progression. Hence, the students may experience a collection of laboratory-enhanced engineering science or stand-alone laboratory courses.

That the engineering laboratory is considered by many to be a follow-up or supplemental activity for learning fundamental engineering concepts is evident in both the curricular arrangements and, to a lesser extent, as we discuss in the next chapter, the teaching and assessments we observed.

Laboratory-Enhanced Engineering Science Course

The conventional way of connecting theory and practice is through a combined lecture and laboratory course. Each week, faculty introduce a new theory and application of a particular engineering phenomenon. The lecture addresses the theory and modeling; then, in the lab, the students explore, measure, test, or evaluate the theory.

Although a laboratory-enhanced engineering science course provides opportunities for students to connect theory and practice, its lecture and laboratory components require thoughtful coordination and planning to support the course's learning objectives (Wankat and Oreovicz, 1993). If the laboratory component is aimed at helping students learn and reinforce a fundamental concept, then the laboratory is likely to be straightforward, as students will have been given a preview of the relevant theory in question. If the objective is to stimulate or encourage critical thinking prior to the introduction of a theory, then the laboratory might provide opportunities for students to explore the experimental process on their own, which means offering less-structured experiments, with guidance and supervision to make the students' learning experience worthwhile.

An exceptionally well-coordinated laboratory-enhanced engineering science course is "Fundamentals of Electrical Engineering" at CMU. Offered at the sophomore level, and the last course required of all engineering students, it is primarily focused on fundamental topics related to engineering devices and systems. It is typical of CMU courses in that it comprises two lecture sessions of one and a half hours each, an hour of recitation, and three hours of lab work per week. The course demands a high level of integration and coordination between the lecture and the lab components. As one faculty member said, "That's easier said than done; to create a set of weekly labs that run along perfectly in parallel with the lecture is a real challenge ..."

It is worth the effort: a well-coordinated laboratory-enhanced engineering science course has great potential for supporting student learning. Students told us that the immediate and direct application of theory to practice in a laboratory setting often motivates them to learn the difficult material that engineering science courses introduces. The *act of doing* helps them appreciate the usefulness of what it is they are learning.

Similarly, a Michigan graduate student instructor explained how the laboratory can help students make sense of and appreciate the value of the principles they learn in the theory classes it supports. For example, in a lecture on signal analysis, students initially learn the theory and the mathematical formulas associated with the representation of periodic signals. In the laboratory, students learn to apply the tools or principles to explore the representations of the signals. Using signals generated by two musical instruments playing two different notes at the same time, with each note representing a signal, students learn how the principles can be used to determine the spectrum of the combined signals and to separate the signals to eliminate one of the notes. This laboratory exercise is then directly linked to a practical problem in which one seeks to remove an unwanted signal that interferes with the overall sound.

As the instructor explains, "We've got laboratories where we actually *use* the material that we're presenting in lecture ... So we're trying to shift focus from purely theoretical to something that's more applied ... it motivates the material that they'll be learning so that we can say, 'Well, why do we need to learn this?' 'Because you can do *this* with it.'"

Stand-Alone Laboratory Course

In some institutions, laboratory is a stand-alone course linked to one or several pre- or corequisite courses, and the material may or may not be limited to a single course. Although requiring students to take theory courses concurrently with stand-alone laboratory courses may help bring theory and application closer together, it takes deft coordination to time the presentation of the theories and the lab experience in a way that facilitates the students' connection between the theoretical and the practical.

At Cal Poly, for example, students take "Electric Circuits Analysis Laboratory II" alongside "Electric Circuit Analysis II"; the laboratory experience can easily refer to the theory course. Students who are taking "Fluid Mechanics Laboratory" must have taken the two theory courses on fluid mechanics. At Georgia Tech, students taking "Digital Design Laboratory" are required to have taken two to three other courses, with the option of taking one of them concurrently.

We noted that if the lab has more than one pre- or corequisite, it provides an opportunity to introduce experiments incorporating several closely related theories that students should have learned through the different courses. Complex experiments promote higher levels of thinking while encouraging students to wrestle with potentially divergent concepts. However, because the application of new knowledge does not happen immediately, students in a stand-alone laboratory may find the shift from theory to practical application more challenging than they might in a laboratory-enhanced analysis course. Notwithstanding their prior exposure to the concepts in their theory courses, students often still need a refresher on the theories before they can actually perform the application in the laboratory. Instructors of stand-alone laboratory courses that are dependent on prerequisite engineering science courses typically begin with a mini-lecture on the relevant principles before engaging students in the experiment.

Despite the challenges, stand-alone laboratory courses closely linked to two or more pre- or corequisite courses can make use of engineering systems-oriented experiments involving several theories to promote integrative learning and critical thinking, both of which are skills of high-level analytic problem solving. Students can work with experiments that demand synthesis and a systems-wide approach and, in the process, learn how to navigate sometimes conflicting ideas.

A Series of Teaching Laboratories

Some engineering programs use a series of laboratory-enhanced engineering science or stand-alone laboratory courses, a deliberately arranged succession of individual teaching laboratories in which the experiments focused on specific theories are closely linked and gradually build from basic skills needed for highly structured experiments to complex, open-ended experiments requiring sophisticated problem-solving skills.

Programs that use a series of teaching laboratories do so on the assumption that students acquire and develop engineering skills and attitudes over time through repeated, increasingly independent performance. Although they require the highest level of coordination and monitoring, they offer a lot of potential for connecting theory and practice.

For example, Michigan's electrical engineering program offers a series of laboratory-enhanced engineering science courses across the sophomore and junior levels. Five basic courses correspond to the five major areas of electrical engineering: systems, circuits, solid state, optics/electromagnetic, and computers. They are supported and enhanced by follow-on core courses that provide depth to each of the major areas. A laboratory component is embedded in most of these basic and core engineering science courses. The students take three of the five courses as a series, each course a prerequisite of another. The theories introduced in the basic courses are further explored in the core courses and are ultimately brought together in a major design experience in the student's final year.

Replicating Professional Practice

The three-year Multidisciplinary Engineering Laboratory (MEL) sequence of stand-alone laboratory courses at Mines is designed to replicate industrial practice by creating laboratory work that gradually introduces traditional engineering fundamentals from various disciplines such as electrical circuits, fluid flow, and material stress into integrated systems (King and others, 1999). This sequence of courses—MEL I, II, and III—begins in the sophomore year. In MEL I, the teaching laboratory is focused on physics and introductory electrical circuits courses, moving slowly from basic science to engineering science through controlled engineering science laboratory work. In MEL II, through less-structured experiments, students enter the domain of engineering design. In MEL III, students work on industrial projects involving sophisticated systems. Throughout the sequence, students are challenged to connect the fundamental concepts from other courses as they work on engineering systems with increasing complexity. This approach to laboratory experience is an attempt to present the field of engineering from a multidisciplinary perspective to help students develop problem-solving skills.

In fact, the MEL sequence has become an alternative approach to the circuits, fluids, and strength of materials courses that traditionally have been offered separately. In some ways, this educational innovation is also a product of an institutional effort that stirred interest among Mines faculty to rethink ways of improving engineering education. The MEL structure is a systems experience approach aimed to support the students' organization of knowledge and their understanding of the relationship of concepts from various courses. As students are required to build and analyze laboratory-scale systems, their thinking skills are enhanced and their expertise in discipline-specific components is developed.

Although MEL is an innovative approach to laboratory instruction and offers students greater opportunity for working on engineering systems problems because of its multidisciplinary nature, its demand for coordination and faculty engagement are beyond what most institutions might be willing to invest in. As one professor from another institution explained, "We've done a little bit of cross-fertilization ... But to bring in some students from mechanical engineering, some students from bio, some students from nuclear, and do a project together, we haven't reached that level of coordination, which to my mind is an extremely high level of coordination ..."

Coordination and Credit

The faculty member's remark about coordination raises one of several challenges to making the laboratory truly a place for students to explore. Coordination of laboratories is one chronic issue; the disproportionately low number of credits the courses carry is another.

A laboratory experiment entails many steps that may be repeated several times, and the time and effort involved naturally increases with the complexity of the experiment and the conditions under which it is conducted. Typically, students support their lab work with a detailed report that discusses the process and results. Writing the reports—and writing them well, of course—requires additional time. Yet for all the effort, and despite recognition of what the experience can offer, lab generally carries fewer credits than do "classroom" courses.

Laboratory instructors and students alike struggle with the discrepancy between the amount of time they devote to lab work and the number of credits given for it:

Student 1: My 241 lab, I thought that it was too much ... It required too much work for the amount of units it was actually worth ... It made it challenging 'cause there were some lab reports in our case that would take us about eight to nine hours to actually try to get it done. And that is not just coming from me; that is coming from a lot of students.

Student 2: [O]ne thing that bothers me is that the labs actually do take a lot of time. I think they should be worth more units or credits than what we are getting right now because ... I think actually that is a little more important than lecture. I mean, lecture helps you understand everything, but lab is where you are applying everything and understanding everything. And I think it is a pretty important part that needs more credit.

Although faculty realize the value of the laboratory to students' professional preparation, they cannot ignore the students' frustration about the few credits they earn for the effort they invest. Maintaining students' enthusiasm for the lab despite the lack of recognition for it is difficult for all parties. We noted that educational goals are often compromised: some faculty members simply limit the amount of time students can spend on the experiences, requiring students to get their work done within the laboratory period. This of course only adds to the challenge, as teachers try to develop laboratory assignments that can be completed within the allotted period:

There's a different instructor who does the same thing in another class we're in ... He expects the lab to be done at the end of the lab period. But it takes you the whole lab to do it, so they had to turn it [in] the next day. And every time they have a lab ... we have a midterm the very next day. So we know a few people who spend all night, thirty-two-page lab write-up, and he had a midterm the next day and he's failing both classes. It's not easy trying to be good in lab and be good in class. You can't do both.

Some institutions, however, have recognized the need to restructure. At Michigan the one-credit-hour laboratory supplements to the lecture classes have been combined to cover major engineering topics, forming two laboratory courses with four credit hours each. The thermal and fluid sciences lab became a single course, and the material and mechanics course combined with the dynamics course became another laboratory class (Tryggvason and others, 2001). The change was a hard-won effort.

9

LEARNING IN THE LAB

HANDS-ON WORK IN THE LAB allows students to develop a refined understanding of the nuances of a concept—what the concept is and is not, or what it can and cannot do. It clarifies the boundaries of the concept and provides a practical approach to understanding it. Hence a good laboratory experience is likely to support students' ability to retain knowledge. Some students learn best if they see the concept translated into something tangible or physical. Just like the hues of a painting, laboratory gives the concept some depth, dimension, and perspective for the learner. It helps students see what the concept means in practice by providing a physical context.

In this chapter, we map out the pedagogies that we observed in the engineering labs and our insights into the relationship between teacher and student and between the student and the knowledge or skill that these teaching strategies rely on.

Learning the Fundamental Concepts

In the labs attached to lower-level engineering science courses, the instructor attempts to show the dynamic interaction between the physical evidence and theory to help refine the concept and give it context. The physical evidence—the data, for example—provides information about the potential response or behavior of the theory and the possible use of hardware to explore or achieve a desired response. In the same way, the theory guides the use of hardware in examining the evidence to generate the ideal results.

The teacher's role is to guide students in their attempts to follow instructions carefully and precisely to arrive at a predicted outcome. As depicted in Figure 9.1, the teacher asks the students to follow a set of

Figure 9.1. Demonstrations and Controlled Experiments

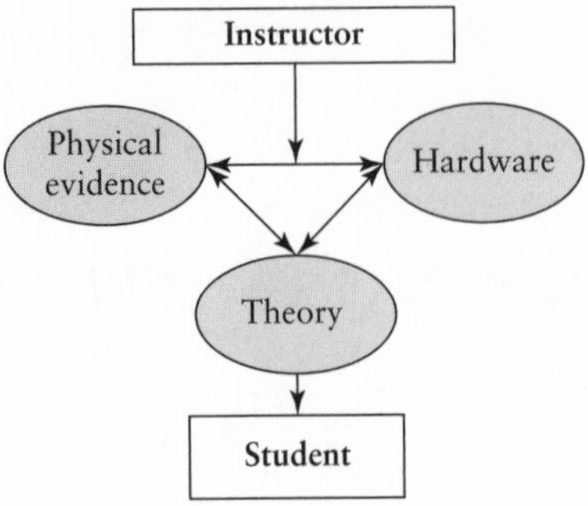

clearly defined steps. The instructor defines what needs to be done and the students' involvement is thus controlled and focused on learning the properties of a theory. Typically, the instructor's role is to guide students in their attempt to follow instructions carefully and precisely to arrive at a predicted outcome.

For example, at Michigan we observed "Signals & Systems I." In this combined lecture and laboratory sophomore-level course, the teacher introduces, in a lecture, an engineering principle or theory; defines it by using a mathematical formula or equation; and demonstrates its application to a sample problem. In the classroom, students do paper-and-pencil exercises to develop a mathematical understanding of the theory. In the lab, the students perform computer simulations intended to give them a sense of how the theory and mathematical computations relate to an observable phenomenon. For example, the instructor talks about filters and signals—concepts the students heard about in the lecture. He then draws a graph on the board for further illustration, then introduces commands, using a computer programming language that generates a graphical representation of the behavior of the concept. After this brief lecture, the instructor demonstrates a simulation on his computer, using a specialized software package, while students observe the distinct features of the theory in action.

Knowing how the graph should respond upon the introduction of filters, students attempt to perform their own simulation. They play around with the filters to get a better sense of how far the theory can be stretched, thus helping themselves become more aware of its features, if not become facile with them. This hands-on experience therefore serves as a confirmation or validation of the students' initial knowledge of the theory.

Another instructor at Michigan describes how his students, through laboratory work, develop a better appreciation for the concepts as they attempt to work with real circuits and witness the currents and voltages responding according to theory. He explains how students are thrilled to discover that Kirchhoff's laws, for example, are "valid up to the fourth digit" and actually work in reality. He notes how students consider the lab experience an opportunity to validate or confirm what they learn in lectures and to explore new ways of using the theory. The laboratory work allows students to test and observe theory under varying conditions, thus helping them achieve a deeper understanding of the concept that the theory embodies. Indeed, lab is the bridge that links the world of theory and the world of practice. It helps students see how theory operates in reality. As one faculty member puts it: "Labs make you believe it. You may not believe things until you see them."

Using the Concepts to Solve Practical Problems

When lab instructors' primary goal is helping students learn to use the concepts to solve practical problems, the instructors assign the theory or set of theories that the students will employ to solve a particular case or problem. Although students are told what concepts to use, they are often left to exercise the applicability of the theory to arrive at a result that is consistent with their expectations of the theory. They must decide how to manipulate the hardware or the physical evidence based on their understanding of the theory to address a particular case. Although the laboratory experience may involve some complex investigations, there is an element of control defined by the theories involved and the manner in which the problem is presented.

This learning experience is common in semistructured experiments, as illustrated in Figure 9.2. Students are not told exactly what to do but are given a general idea of how to solve the problem and the theories needed to do it. Instructors typically require students to use a theory or set of theories they have learned to solve a particular problem. Knowing exactly what the problem is, they apply the given theory to generate data or physical evidence needed to solve the problem and to achieve the desired outcome. Through a series of tests and the repeated manipulation of hardware, students learn to find an optimal condition for generating satisfactory results that meet their expectations given their understanding of the theory. Consequently, they develop a level of comfort with the use of the theory and become proactive in their experimental approach.

An example of this approach is the wood compression experiment in MEL II at Mines. In this experiment, the students set up a prototype fluid-powered testing system that will be used to evaluate material properties for

Figure 9.2. Semistructured Experiments

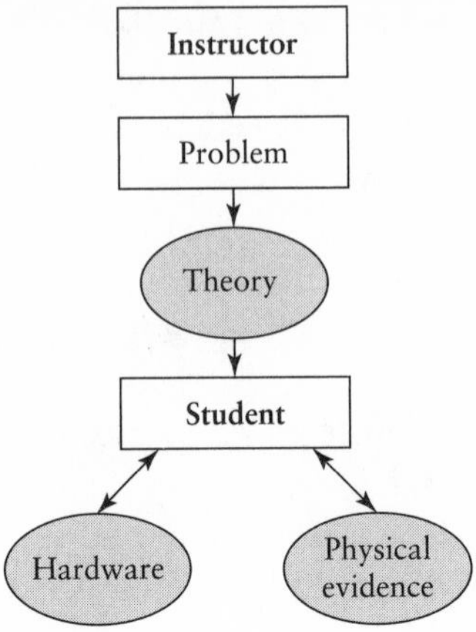

stress analysis. They must evaluate the system by performing calibrations on the displacement and pressure transducers and by conducting experiments on two types of materials.

The students are first instructed to draw a schematic of a hydraulic and electrical system for the testing machine. This should demonstrate the students' analytical modeling skills and confirm their theoretical understanding of the mechanical and electrical operation of the machinery. Once the operating procedure has been determined, students are required to calibrate both the displacement and the pressure transducer and show a graphical representation of the calibration results with an error analysis. To arrive at an acceptable calibration, students must determine the number of test samples they need to minimize the error. After exploring and calibrating the testing system, students are ready to conduct the wood compression experiment. They begin testing the wood samples and plotting a stress-strain diagram using the results.

To help students succeed in the experiment, the student lab manual includes notes and reminders about certain principles that are crucial for the analysis, testing, and evaluation of the system. Although there is adequate information in the manual on how to proceed with the experiment, students themselves must determine the details of how they ought to apply the theories they have learned to achieve acceptable results, given a concrete problem.

Students use relevant theories to solve a practical problem; in this case, to ensure the integrity of a testing system that can indicate with minimal error the level of stress or strain when evaluating properties of wood samples. Given the problem, students are challenged to apply their knowledge of the theory to generate the kind of data needed to achieve the desired outcome.

Learning to Work with Complex Systems

When the teacher's goal is helping students to deal with complex engineering systems, the prevalent model of instruction is focused on developing the students' capacity to negotiate the laboratory components and deal with the unexpected, as depicted in Figure 9.3. The instructor presents the problem and provides minimal guidance, as students take the lead in the investigation. They determine which theories to use and what physical evidence must be considered or ignored. Because of the problem's complexity, students are encouraged to think critically and make judgments. Although students may often encounter failure in these open-ended, minimally structured experiments, they eventually see it as part of the process of the investigation, during which they are expected to analyze, synthesize, and evaluate concepts learned as they apply them to complex engineering systems.

Because more open-ended laboratory experiments integrate materials from various engineering disciplines, they provide an environment that approximates professional practice. As we discuss in Chapter Eleven, because of their complexity, the experiments also challenge students to explore engineering concepts that have not been introduced in the lectures.

Figure 9.3. Project-Based and Open-Ended Experiments

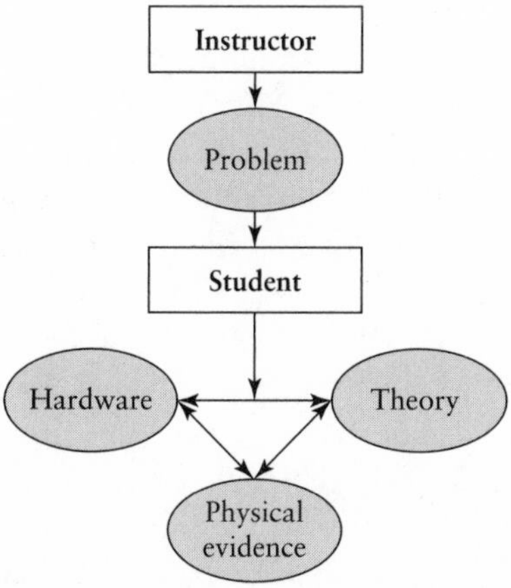

For example, in a junior-level mechanical engineering laboratory course at Michigan, students learn to work with complex systems and develop instrumentation and experimentation skills in a variety of problem situations. In one particular assignment, students conduct tests on new material using the usual hardware. Lacking familiarity with the material, they have to figure out how to run the test, given the existing tools, and how to deal with potentially unusual results. Consequently, as the faculty observe, students get a good handle on the instrumentation and become aware of the uncertainties associated with experimentation involving complex systems:

> [T]he lab required them to do tests on the material and then to fabricate the material to see what its ultimate strength properties were . . . what do you do in the presence of noise . . . Therefore the question is, how did they handle the noise? . . . So at the end, I want them to be able to understand that no measurement is perfect; therefore I have to give them a laboratory in which the uncertainty part stands out . . . I said, "You should expect the data to be noisy." But that is sort of like me telling you what an apple pie tastes like without your ever having had any pie . . . OK. I can tell you this: "You'll have apple pie, and you'll probably even like it, but if you've never had pie before or you've never seen an apple before, you don't know what's coming." . . . So they have to face up to that.

Building Communication Skills

As we discuss in greater depth in the chapter on assessment (Chapter Ten), writing is the primary communication skill taught in the laboratory. The often extensive writing assignments in laboratories are expected to help students develop and acquire the skill of communicating their thoughts and ideas in a clear, concise, and concrete way.

Students at Michigan and Cal Poly explained to us how the faculty emphasize the importance of technical communication in their preparation for practice: "Part of our labs not only reinforce what we have learned but try to prepare us for working as an engineer. You have to be able to communicate effectively to your boss and other parts of the company. So if you can't write a good lab report or convey to others what you are doing, then your work is pretty much useless. So they stress that a lot." The faculty encourage the students to recognize that writing is a critical aspect of engineering work, such that their engineering solution becomes worthless if not properly and effectively communicated to those who require it. Said one student, "They look at our writing, even our grammar, how we present our graphs. We've been graded down severely because we can't get our point across. If they don't understand our ideas because they can't get through our grammar because our sentences are too long, then they should grade us down."

Learning to Work Collaboratively

The nature of teamwork in teaching laboratories varies, depending on the learning objectives and the complexity of the experiments. In lower-level teaching laboratories, where the main objective is to reinforce theory, pairs of students run simple experiments that allow both to be actively involved in every step of the "cookbook" experiments. In more advanced laboratories, teams tend to be larger—typically between four and six students—and everyone on the team is encouraged to contribute his or her individual expertise.

Whether the student teams in the engineering laboratories are assigned by the instructors or self-selected, because students work cooperatively and collaboratively with others to achieve a common goal, the lab experience offers opportunities for students to develop their interpersonal skills.

One faculty member regularly reassigns groups to ensure that students learn to work harmoniously and efficiently with others while recognizing their individual differences. At Michigan, one faculty member organizes student teams by blind rotation so that each person will have worked with everyone in the section at least once. He also emphasizes the importance of personal responsibility by making each team member accountable for the final report that the group submits. To ensure that everyone contributes to the laboratory work, he requires each student to conduct a peer review that describes or rates each team member's degree of engagement.

Developing Persistence, Optimism, and Healthy Skepticism

Laboratory work can be very intimidating, especially if the problem being presented is something new or seems too complicated. Persistence, optimism, and healthy skepticism are personal qualities that can be nurtured in laboratory work, as we observed in the Electronics II Lab at Howard.

Students had been working on their 6-watt amplifiers, initially worked through simulation. When they began testing, one student could not get his circuit to run. First the laboratory assistant tried to help him figure out the problem. Then the student did further testing, changing, and shifting.

At this point, other students were looking over his shoulder, making suggestions. When, after several attempts, the circuit finally worked, we asked the student whether giving up on a task was ever an option. The student said, "Well, [the instructor] doesn't take no for an answer. I kept working and when I really got stuck, I had to go to him more than a couple of times. He showed me a few glitches I had and told me to come back after trying different things."

We also heard students talk about being asked to work on an experiment that may be unfamiliar to them or that requires knowledge of certain theories that have not been discussed in the lectures. Although frustrating to some students, such experiences have a strong resemblance to practice. At Mines, for example, MEL students are often challenged to work on engineering systems that may deal with unknown territory. Providing them with complex material to work on encourages them to develop the habit of boldly facing the unknown and to stretch their capacity to perform with confidence. As the faculty explain, students become better prepared professionally: "One of the things that these labs do is to develop confidence of the students to manipulate real engineering systems, as opposed to the more traditional lecture course or even canned laboratories . . . We want them to have the confidence so when they encounter a new system or machine, they will be able to work on it or design it because they have had some experience. I guess it's like experiential learning."

Instructors who seek to develop these attitudes in their students are typically very encouraging and demand a lot from the students so that they, too, will learn to demand of themselves. Although the instructors value teamwork, because they believe that students also need to learn to work on their own, they give them the opportunity to learn how to solve or deal with an engineering problem without the help of others, thus acquiring the necessary skills to support their work.

10

LAB REPORTS

FACULTY TYPICALLY USE three forms of assessment in the engineering laboratory: quizzes, exams, and lab reports. Quizzes, used primarily to track students' progress, are generally administered before or after a laboratory session, to check whether the students (1) have done the pre-lab work, (2) understand the concepts discussed in the lecture before engaging in laboratory work, and (3) know and understand what they have just done in the laboratory. Periodic exams are often based on actual experiments.

However, the lab report is the primary means that faculty use to assess student learning in laboratory courses. Whether produced individually or in teams, these are detailed accounts of students' laboratory process and findings, supported by evidence they have generated and their use of hardware.

Students may work individually on tasks that prepare them for the experiment, then write them up. If they work in teams, they are generally expected to share the same data but are required to write their own reports to show how well they understood the laboratory work. Alternatively, the students may also work in groups to generate and evaluate data and come up with a single group report that instructors assess.

What Is Measured: Content and Communication

Faculty focus on two major aspects of the laboratory report: *content* and *communication* (or as some call it, *presentation*). Because laboratory work, no matter how advanced and complex, generally follows a standard structure and is often defined and conditioned by a set of data and hardware, results are generally predictable and there is a range of right and wrong answers. Laboratory instructors look first at whether the students have a reasonable result and the mathematical calculations to support it. Instructors next check whether students are able to demonstrate their understanding of the material and explain the experimental procedure with clarity and accuracy.

Faculty told us that the students' demonstrations of content knowledge and of communication skills are interrelated. The instructors look, for example, at the students' decisions about which of the findings need to be highlighted as well as their use of graphs or diagrams to support their findings: "You can tell from the reports whether they are getting the concepts, and if they're picking up the technical writing piece. We used to have a separate grade for format and content, but we decided not to do that anymore. But someone could get the correct response in the write-up and get a low grade because they didn't communicate it clearly."

They also told us what they look for in presentation: "I look and see how their presentation of data is. So I usually put forty points for that. Half of it is on the data presentation, so that's the group grade, and the other half is on their discussion. Are they getting the point across?" Other faculty explained their assessment criteria: "[W]ork is assessed from the standpoint of how well they presented it: Did they write a good report that is concise? Did they include all the right graphics that illustrate their point? And that's assessed. But before they leave the lab, the core technical essentials have been assessed as part of the check-off process. And that stuff gets incorporated into the report and assessed as a whole."

Communication

Having the right answer, the faculty told us, is not enough. Students are expected to demonstrate that they can perform a laboratory experiment and explain the process of the experiment in writing. Further, they must demonstrate their understanding of engineering science and its application. For example, one faculty member describes looking for the students' ability to articulate the process of applying theory to practice, which is what distinguishes the engineer from the technician: "I need them to move beyond the technician level. They have to not only report numbers that make sense. They have to tell me what the numbers mean . . . Because the technician might have been able to give me a plot with . . . the cooling capacity going up, but he wouldn't necessarily be able to tell me why."

Moreover, the students must describe their laboratory work in a way that the reader is able to understand the significant components of the process. They must argue and defend their results in a concise yet thorough way and be consistent in the presentation of their findings. They are expected to be able to convey their claims convincingly. A faculty member from Michigan explained what instructors typically look for:

> They are looking for a report that has some archived value. In other words, there is enough description given and enough records are used. So somebody who finds this report five years from now might be able either to repeat this experiment or at least determine what happened … they have to get their point across quickly and easily through two things: the executive summary part of the report and their plots. They cannot count on somebody reading their report from front to back to figure out all the details. And things within a report must all be consistent. If you tell me that the answer was 27 on the first page, I better find a plot where the answer is also 27.

Strategies for improving communication. Some faculty incorporate peer assessment into the lab report assignments. In class, students or student teams swap draft reports and give one another feedback. Pairing a lower-performing student or team with a higher-performing one allows the lower performer to see examples of high-quality work and enables the higher performer to further develop skills of analysis and feedback.

In the electrical engineering department at Georgia Tech, the university's Undergraduate Professional Communications Program oversees the writing component of the laboratory courses, which is heavily integrated throughout the curriculum, beginning in the sophomore-level laboratory courses. The writing and engineering faculty work collaboratively to ensure that students learn how to write for their professional community.

According to the program coordinator, the writing component is specifically designed to help students in their laboratory writing assignments. Lectures on research process, report writing, and critique, and technical writing tips are offered to students. They are taught how to describe their research and design process clearly and accurately. They are also required to meet with a writing consultant to learn to talk comfortably about their own writing. In addition, writing workshops are offered free of charge and student support is provided through the electrical and computer engineering writing lab, in which engineering graduate students acting as tutors and evaluators make themselves available for consultation.

The Challenge of Group Assessment

Although collaborative work is an important component of the laboratory experience, the task of assessing each team member's contribution to the group effort and product poses a challenge. Typically, every member of the group earns the same grade regardless of contribution to the experiment or involvement in the development of the report. Although this practice of group assessment is not necessarily agreeable to all students, it is designed to help them realize the importance of accountability that the profession demands. As one professor explains,

> [W]hen I was with Boeing, a very unfortunate thing occurred in a Boeing airliner that had very hard landing at one of the airports in Japan, and some of the rear tail sections were damaged. The company knew that the plane needed to be fixed, so they called Boeing over and said, "Fix it." Boeing thought they fixed it. The next time the plane flew, the tail fell off and more than five hundred people died. The people who signed off on the report, that their work was done properly, are wanted criminals in Japan. I don't know if they were extradited. You put your name on the report, you get that grade. If you didn't proofread it and you put your name on it, you're sticking your neck out. So that's one of the reasons everybody who signs a report and everybody [named] on the report gets the same grade.

Group assessment can send a strong signal to students about the importance of participation and teamwork and their implications for the demands of professional responsibility. Instructors, however, realize that requiring students to work in teams does not always encourage them to be personally responsible for their work. As the faculty explained to us, some team members may simply rely on others for getting the work done and expect to be graded on the basis of what is supposed to be a team effort: "So we like the idea that they work together, but we worry about them ... sometimes one student is doing all the work and the other student is going along for the ride ..."

Because of this potential drawback in team assessment, laboratory instructors are finding ways to eliminate, or at least minimize, the opportunity for students to get a free ride. One common approach to making students responsible for their share of the work is to administer a quiz after the group has completed its work. Testing students' knowledge and skills on the experiment that the group has been asked to perform can shed some light on individual participation in the activity. However, teachers admit it is a great challenge to motivate students who are not contributing fully to do so in future experiments. On the other hand, we saw that instructors need to realize that if a group project will entail time outside of class for team meetings and other collaborative work, it may place part-time or off-campus students at a disadvantage.

Another approach, which appears to be more effective in encouraging student involvement, is creating a mechanism for students to monitor each other. At Michigan, for example, students are allowed to "fire" team members who fail to perform according to the group's expectations. In one case, a student explained, the professor played the role of crisis manager and "negotiated with the team as to what [the student in question] could do" to avoid being fired by the group. Students recognize this mechanism as an effective means for keeping team members responsible for their contributions to the project. As this student explained, introducing incentives or disincentives that are aligned with student expectations can help students take personal responsibility for their involvement in a group activity and consequently appreciate the value of teamwork and the impact it may have on their work: "[W]hat is probably the most fair is, in some of the classes you have the right to fire people and hire people ... And I think that prevents people from slacking off."

Considering Assessment

We believe that the main strategy for assessment, the lab report, is an effective one, particularly when the reports are expected to be representative of professional work and students are held to high standards of quality. Lab reports can also provide both formative and summative assessment. Timely feedback, opportunities for iteration (such as submitting a draft, receiving constructive feedback, and reworking the report), and opportunities for collaborative writing: these strategies of formative assessment increase the effectiveness of lab reports as a learning tool. Summative assessment, however, remains a challenge, particularly ensuring fair distribution of work, grading group work, and aligning the assessment with learning goals.

Assessment of lab work is an opportunity to convey the importance of professionalism: working with all the data, giving proper credit to those who have helped. Yet we saw a number of missed opportunities. For example, if instructors would give more explicit guidelines on what it means to engage in teamwork on a lab assignment, be explicit about the consequences of not practicing team skills, and offer teams some options for dealing with team members who do not fully contribute, it would be possible to hold students more accountable for their role in collaborative work.

11

MAKING A PLACE TO EXPLORE
PROFESSIONAL PRACTICE

TOO MUCH EFFORT FOR TOO LITTLE CREDIT. The constant effort to synchronize what goes on in the lab with what goes on in the lecture hall. The number of students in the lab. Keeping the lab appropriately modern, relevant, and safe. Consistently, these were the complaints and concerns voiced by students and faculty alike as we talked with them about the lab. The difficulties in scheduling and assigning credit, the challenges of teaching and grading, and the expense of equipping and maintaining the lab are very real problems. However, although it would be easy to focus considerable attention on solving any one of these knotty issues, our observations and conversations led us to see that they are symptomatic of a larger issue: the long-standing secondary role that the lab has played in the engineering curriculum as an adjunct to theory and analyses courses. In many programs, students' experience in the laboratory is a missed opportunity.

As a place to explore, to test concepts and build models, the laboratory can link the two primary aspects of practice: design and analysis. Effective laboratory experiences can greatly enhance student learning, connect theoretical knowledge and the physical world, and provide significant motivation and engagement. Like design projects, as we describe in Part Four, laboratory experiments offer opportunities for students to explore the process and dynamics of teamwork as well as their own process of discovery and creativity. Improving and expanding students' experience in the lab, engaging them in meaningful exploration, is not a matter of making more room for lab in the curriculum. It is necessary to better integrate lab into the curriculum.

The lab offers students opportunities to "acquire and integrate cognitive and metacognitive strategies for using, managing, and discovering knowledge" (Collins, Brown, and Newman, 1989, p. 480). Learning can be staged, or scaffolded, through well-designed sequences of experiments and other activities, student learning. Starting with demonstrations and controlled experiments, faculty can introduce at the most basic level the integration of expert knowledge and skills. By increasing complexity over time and introducing open-ended, highly unstructured problem-based engineering systems experiments, the instructor can move students toward "articulation and reflection" (Collins, Brown, and Newman, 1989).

"Open Lab"

However efficient, the highly structured or cookbook experiment has limitations. It focuses on helping students learn to get the "known 'right' results," which may hold them back from developing creative ways of conducting experimentation. Instead of learning the creative process of experimentation, students learn how to follow well-established procedures to solve problems that have well-known results that are unlikely to be questioned (Rosenthal, 1967). Structured experiments have the greatest value when they are designed to help students acquire experimental skills and attitudes, when the students are less concerned with getting the right results than with exploring possibilities while learning about a concept.

Learning Through Guided Discovery

Instead of being explicit about what needs to be done, instructors can guide students in discovering the appropriate experimental approach based on the material presented to them and the theory that the assignment is focusing on. The challenge that less-structured experiments and open-ended projects present may increase the level of motivation of students because it makes the task not only interesting but also personally satisfying. As one faculty member explained, "Classical mechanical engineering labs were boring; students would come in and take some measurements on an engine model and report on it."

To address the problem, the faculty member, who teaches a sophomore-level fluid mechanics class at CMU, developed what he calls an "open lab," in which students are encouraged to learn new concepts through exploration and discovery. "I spent time at science museums and watched people's reactions," he explained. "I decided it would be important to have this 'discover' mode."

The labs pertain to some concept that was recently covered in lecture or will come up shortly. Students must recognize, in the nature of the problems presented, the general domain of fluid dynamics to which the experiment pertains, articulate the problem the experiment presents or explores, bring to bear relevant principles, apply pertinent formulas, and solve the problems that have been defined.

The purpose of the lab and the procedures are not explained to the students, who work in small groups of three to four: "The students are not given any instructions. They are having lectures related to this, so they know the subject, but what they are supposed to do is not known when they come in ... The idea is to get the students involved. They look at the bits and pieces lying around, and they have to figure out what it is. [Teaching assistants] are there to only answer questions if asked."

Students are encouraged to discover or figure out the scientific principles that explain the phenomenon being observed. Although there are no recipes to guide the students, teaching assistants provide the help they need and lead them in the right direction. Hence, if a student seems to be developing unsound conclusions about the phenomena or raising flawed premises about the scientific principles relevant to the experiments, the teaching assistant raises key questions that would lead students to examine their ideas and expose their existing knowledge that may have led them to reason in a particular way. Using the Socratic approach, teaching assistants encourage students to think about and articulate their own thinking process as they tackle each experiment.

According to one TA, because this type of lab does not depend on a detailed work sheet, students work through the experiment in a purposeful way. Rather than being overly concerned about the process, which is typical of the cookbook approach, students focus on the implications of their actions as they explore the phenomena being presented by each case. Because students are forced to take personal initiative to learn by discovery through the experiments, they leave the session understanding the concepts better. Because they learn theory through direct experience, its impact on student learning can be significant. If the discovery is followed by lecture, "the theoretical development will be much more believable and would already have been partially verified" (Wankat and Oreovicz 1993, p. 181).

As the faculty observed, this course not only tries to help students learn theories using experimental methods, but also allows them to interact with complex systems as they observe the theory that might explain the phenomenon they are seeking to understand: "There is no instruction in the lab; they must discover the experiment. There are things lying around. They get help individually. They must figure what and how to measure and [to] write a report, including the lab's significance. Some get it quickly, and some really struggle to figure out what is going on. More and more professors in [mechanical engineering] are opening up labs and starting to include an experimental component in their lectures."

The approach has been successful, and the experiments are now designed with TA and student input: "This 'discover' mode is very important and exciting ... They get the sense that they made it, they moved it, they get the principle. The general reaction of TAs and students is that it is something quite exciting and different."

The open lab can promote a positive attitude toward scientific investigation and a desire for learning, encourage student engagement and autonomy, and engender in students a sense of accomplishment and responsibility. It also fosters creativity, as a faculty member noted: "The students have that 'thing' they want to do. They want to do something different. Sometimes they want to put their own touch, to show 'my style'. . . It has to be a little challenging and difficult. But you have to allow them to put their own style into it."

Open-Ended Lab in Introductory-Level Courses

Though open-ended lab work is more typical of advanced courses, as the example from Carnegie Mellon indicates, it is not unheard of for faculty members to incorporate this method of instruction in introductory-level engineering courses. They find that doing so creates opportunities for students to develop, early on, an experimental approach to problem solving while establishing a relationship between fundamental principles and elements of practice. This teaching approach can increase students' interest in scientific investigation as well as promote critical reasoning.

However, the process of discovery must be guided. Allowing students to explore or discover abstract principles on their own is unlikely to lead to genuine learning and understanding of the concepts if students do not see how their discovery relates to what it is they are learning.

Virtual Labs

Engineering's own product, technology has had an enormous impact on the way engineering is taught and learned (Feisel and Rosa, 2005). Calculations, analysis, testing, design, and building of engineering systems are now facilitated by computer software packages. Hence technology can support, but does not replace, the traditional paper-and-pencil approach; rather, it assists in complex calculations requiring quick, accurate results.

Modeling and simulation exercises serve either as a transition or as an alternative approach to a traditional laboratory experiment requiring highly sophisticated equipment that may not be readily available. Simulators, in particular, are teaching devices that mimic actual equipment and their operations. In using them, faculty find that they can offer students a learning experience that closely resembles what they might experience from actual field situations (Butler, 1983).

With a small capital investment, and without exposing students to safety risks, programs can use specialist software packages, for example, to give students the opportunity to explore the utility and limitations of a fundamental engineering concept or ideas. While working on hypothetical cases through virtual experimentation, students can play around with engineering concepts as they test the boundaries of the phenomenon being observed. As one student remarked, "When you do a simulation, you can play with it. When you do it on the board, something blows up."

Modeling and simulation are fairly common in electrical engineering courses, as they are in engineering practice. They often consist of preliminary work that offers a preview of how the concepts might be used in designing devices. Unlike force or stress, basic electrical engineering concepts like resistors and capacitors are not intuitively imagined in a physical sense. This sometimes makes the application of the concepts difficult for students. So providing students the opportunity to explore, use, and test concepts through modeling and simulation creates a gradual transition from theory to practice. Modeling and simulation offer students a demonstration of how a concept could generate an outcome that is consistent with their theoretical understanding of it. In a sense, it serves as a preparatory stage and scaffolding for the physical application of the concept. Students, however, must be supported as they internally construct their own conceptual system that relates reality to the physical and mathematical models they develop. Otherwise, the experiment becomes totally detached from reality and may be perceived as a mere testing of the theory.

With the use of high-powered computer software packages, students are able to develop and test models of complex engineering systems that otherwise could be difficult, expensive, and even impossible to do through the traditional laboratory environment. For example, students can create a model and run a simulation to observe the transfer of electricity from power plants to individual homes or to measure the parameters that would successfully launch a rocket. Because of technology, laboratory may now be extended to elaborate investigative experiments without incurring the cost associated with real-life modeling and testing. These technological innovations in teaching engineering serve as scaffolding for student thinking and activity.

With such support, students are encouraged to engage in complex problem solving and creative thinking, as one faculty member noted:

> [I]f they actually go out in private industry and work for Intel or Motorola, and they design the latest Pentium, there are four million transistors on that particular chip. One could not go to a lab and put four million transistors together and see how they function. It is required that they use computers, etc., to simulate what will go on before they could actually design the next generation computer. Without the lab, the computer simulation means nothing. However, I think we still need the combination. And in the future, there may be no computer. There may be something else that students use to emulate larger problems. But I think they still will always need a laboratory to gain understanding about the basic elements, so that they can use other systems to create larger elements that a human being sometimes can't even put together ... So I'm sort of defending the need for a computer modeling and simulation, because you can actually solve problems with computers that you could never solve in the lab. But you still need the lab ...

Although virtual experiments can stretch the imagination, both faculty and students recognize that working on real problems with actual hardware is essential. Conducting experiments with real objects keep theories well grounded in reality; as one student commented, "It's a good thing to have the simulation in hand, but it's another thing to work with the hardware. When you see it on the simulation, it doesn't show you + or −, but on the board, you have to make sure, or 'fireworks!'" The hands-on experience, students told us, is "a reality check. A good engineer knows what to neglect in modeling. This is the key, knowing when to ignore certain details. It never works the way you expect in the lab. Otherwise people will really think that the model is the reality."

Indeed, faculty who use simulation must remind students that simulation and modeling are idealized representations of the physical world and serve only as a guide for conducting engineering work. Although traditional laboratory experience will give students a better grasp of the practice, simulation and modeling could give them a broader perspective of what a good engineer could potentially achieve. The challenge, however, is being able to determine the constraints that the engineer could face in the physical world. Laboratory experience helps students be aware of the gap between the model and the physical artifact. Through repeated exercise and experimentation, students should be able to develop sensitivity towards this gap and negotiate the differences. Thus the transition between what works in theory and what works in practice is most crucial in laboratory courses.

A Place to Explore Teaching

The design and structure of laboratory experiments are critical to students' learning experience, and the effort of coordinating and teaching lab—well beyond the work of organizing equipment, supervising TAs, and managing groups of students—is considerable.

The laboratory component of an engineering program must contribute to the ultimate goal of preparing students to carry out experimental methods that can assist them in their analysis and design as they try to formulate and solve complex engineering problems. Faculty assigned to laboratories have an enormous task of developing appropriate laboratory experiments that will promote the development of varying and complex learning goals while consciously being aware of their significance to the other elements of practice, such as analysis and design. Because there is no formula for or "right" combination of laboratory experiences, faculty must plan and work creatively. Thus, we believe, the lab offers an opportunity to explore the practice of teaching.

A New Role for the Instructor

In conducting a minimally structured laboratory, the instructor plays a very different role. The teacher tries to help students discover that knowing what to do in theory may not necessarily work in practice when certain conditions are beyond their control. The teacher is a coach or guide, pointing out the critical points of discrepancies between the theory and the practice to help students appreciate the challenges of the profession. Faculty in the study explained that by acting in a more supervisory role, they allow students to be active participants in the learning process and develop the technical skills associated with professional practice.

Giving emphasis to the "purpose" of experimental work requires guiding students through thoughtful questioning of a process. Designing experiments that require students to "integrate and elaborate knowledge in new ways" (Brown and Palincsar, 1989) is highly challenging. Just as open-ended laboratory and virtual labs can serve as a good introduction to professional practice, as these encourage students to learn how to work with uncertainties and appreciate the unpredictability of the environment in which engineers work, so too do they demand of teachers new skills and attitudes about teaching and learning. The instructor does not always know what to expect. The familiar sense of control is gone. However, faculty report that the discomfort of uncertainty and the effort are worthwhile: using open-ended experiments can have a huge positive impact on student learning.

A Collective Focus on Teaching and Learning

Collectively, faculty and administration can do much to make lab truly a place for exploring professional practice. Ideally, the engineering faculty would work together to identify ways the lab can contribute to the program's goals for student learning and, accordingly, plan a sequence of experiences within individual courses, over a sequence of courses, and across the entire program. Thus faculty would design a set of laboratory experiences to support particular and immediate learning goals, such as learning theory, and ones that support more general, long-term goals, such as dealing with increasing ambiguity in problems. Faculty would work together to determine when to use structured cookbook experiments, when to use open-ended approaches, and when to use such resources as virtual labs to develop students' skills in formulating problems and solving problems.

At the very least, those faculty who teach lab must be supported in their efforts to make lab truly a place to explore the knowledge and skills of professional practice. Taking the next step—exploiting lab's potential in the curriculum as a place to approximate the challenges of professional practice—will require a professional reach on the part of faculty, and deans and department heads will need to provide leadership and support as the faculty collectively and articulate the goals of the program, creatively consider the role of the lab and the objective of experiments and assessments, and pool their knowledge about student learning.

PART FOUR

A WAY TO CREATE

ALTHOUGH FIFTY YEARS AGO design was marginal to engineering education, since the late 1980s there has been a national movement to increase undergraduate engineering students' exposure to design. As one faculty member observed, "We've added a lot of design—the pendulum has swung towards the design side." This movement acknowledges that design cannot be taught in one course, but is an experience that must parallel the student's development.

A number of factors are behind this movement, although it is difficult to know which of these are motivating factors and which are by-products. One factor is recognition that engaging students in design work, particularly during their freshman year, may reduce attrition and increase persistence through the engineering program—a connection borne out by research such as that by Knight, Carlson, and Sullivan (2007) and Bransford, Brown, and Cocking (2000) as well as positive faculty experiences in engaging students in hands-on assignments.

Industry-based or affiliated initiatives have also pushed U.S. engineering programs to include more practice-based skills. For example, in the 1990s the Boeing Corporation facilitated discussions and partnerships between academia and industry by hosting workshops between leaders in both arenas (McMasters and White, 1994) to discuss desired characteristics of graduates. In the same period ABET created enhanced guidelines that call for a significant design experience when the student's academic development is nearly complete—the senior year or capstone course—and that hold the program responsible for identifying meaningful design experiences and determining how they are integrated throughout the curriculum (ABET, 2007).

Not surprisingly, then, during our interviews we consistently heard faculty and students talk about the centrality of design activities to engineering work. It is not overstating it to say that most faculty and students see that design is "what engineers do most of their waking, professional hours!" (Bucciarelli, 1996). We heard in our interviews that guiding students to learn "design thinking" and the design process, so central to professional practice, is the responsibility of engineering education. Many engineering faculty see engineering design as central to contemporary engineering practice—stating, for example, "An engineer designs. That's what you do" and "You can't do engineering without designing; design is what makes an engineer an engineer." Faculty also see that learning to design is an important component of engineering education.

In this section we describe the learning goals that the faculty in the study identified for design, the principal methods for teaching design that we observed, and strategies of assessing student learning about design; and we consider the potential of design to prepare students for the complexities of formulating problems and solving problems in professional practice.

12

"KNOWING TO"

ENGINEERING PROGRAMS TYPICALLY distribute the teaching and learning of engineering design over four years, giving students repeated experiences in design project work. Further, several opportunities for students to develop design-related skills such as teamwork and communication are increasingly common in freshman and senior design courses; students are able to apply these skills directly in their projects and discover how essential they are to practice. These experiences with design hold the potential for approximating an engineering "clinical experience," arguably closer than any of the other components of the linear components model.

However, the programs we studied vary greatly in the extent to which these design experiences build on each another and connect to other engineering courses. They vary in the degree to which students learn to reflect on and critique their own design thinking and that of their colleagues, develop and follow a design process, engage in design from concept to implementation stages, and experience design as a very human and creative endeavor.

At one extreme is a program in which four courses (one each at the freshman and sophomore levels, and two at the senior level) are focused exclusively on engineering design, with assignments, lectures, exams, and projects building student design capacity. At the other extreme is a program without any freshman engineering courses of any sort, with design included during the sophomore and junior years as an adjunct to technology-based courses, followed by a single-term senior year capstone experience. More typical, however, are programs that have a freshman design experience, minimal design experiences during the sophomore and junior years, and a significant senior design experience. Although more electrical engineering than mechanical engineering programs couple design experiences with learning new technical material, we did not see these patterns tied to a specific field of engineering.

We would expect that the graduates of a program with significant class time devoted to learning about, doing, and reflecting on engineering design would be equipped to contribute in most phases of a design project, particularly at the problem definition and conceptual design phases. On the other hand, a student from a program with more course time devoted to learning and practicing design strategies tied to particular technologies would be better equipped to engage in detailed design work in practice. We refer to the former as "big *D*" design learning, and the latter as "little *d*" design learning. Some programs combine big *D* and little *d* learning within courses or across the engineering curriculum.

In today's professional practice, it takes big *D* and little *d* strengths to realize just about any modern artifact. Whether each individual working on a design team has little *d* and big *D* design expertise may not be important if the collective design expertise of the team yields the combination and the team members have respect for the various types of expertise and can communicate across them. It is not clear how much faculty have vigorously debated (much less articulated for public scrutiny) the roles of little *d* and big *D* design learning or mapped out for themselves and their students how the program's design experiences enact their vision of design learning. This is certainly a challenge that we would extend to all engineering faculty.

The faculty in the study did, however, describe what they called a *troika* of goals for student learning: design thinking, design process, and design skills. As they talked about them, it was apparent that they see them not as discrete goals but as an integrated whole of the three—what might be called *knowing to*.

Design Thinking

Engineering design involves a way of thinking that is increasingly referred to as *design thinking*: a high level of creativity and mental discipline as the engineer tries to discover the heart of the problem and explore beyond the solutions at easy reach. It involves divergent-convergent questioning, making estimates, conducting experiments, reasoning with uncertainty, and working with a team (Dym and others, 2005).

Explains Danny Saffer: "[D]esign thinking is creative, innovative, and focused on problem-solving ... a focus on customers and users, finding alternatives, ideation and prototyping, wicked problems, a wide range of influences, and emotion." He continues, "Other disciplines, I'm sure, do one or more of these at any given time. But I think it's the *combination* of these that people mean—or should mean—when using the phrase 'design thinking'" (Saffer, 2005).

The faculty and students we interviewed described design thinking as defining the problem, generating candidate solutions, and evaluating and implementing those solutions. To be able to formulate the essential problem, define constraints and requirements necessary for any proposed solution to be viable, and organize the problem, students must learn to formulate and ask many questions, seek out information, and sift through data.

Defining the Problem

Students and faculty explained the importance of learning how to go about defining the problem, offering that "Once you've got the problem formulated correctly you're more than half way to solving it . . . But that action of posing it—what are your assumptions, what are you trying to do, what should you be trying to do?—that's the central aspect." This might be called *problem spotting* or *need finding*.

Defining the problem includes questioning of how the problem is framed and whether it can be restated to allow a wider range of solutions. In teaching design, faculty can help students learn to think more broadly about the problem statement. For example, if—using an anecdote from practice described by Adams (2001)—faculty ask students to design an automated tomato picking machine that would be less damaging to tomatoes, they might point out that the solution in practice was to reframe the problem as "make less-damaged tomatoes," leading to a redesign of tomatoes so that they are less fragile—a biological solution to a problem initially perceived as an engineering problem. The problem formulation of "make less-damaged tomatoes" is closer to the *essential problem* than "making a less damaging tomato picker," yet it raises important questions about the larger consequences of a solution.

The engineer establishes the characteristics of any acceptable solution: the constraints, criteria, requirements, goals, and standards that a solution should meet and the values that it should embody. Although some of these reflect physical reality, others reflect cultural, corporate, and personal values and goals, including such diverse factors as aesthetics, environmental sustainability, equity, and return on investment. Still others are the constraints faced by individual engineers as they undertake their engineering work amid multiple demands and finite resources.

Defining the problem includes breaking it into subparts. As a faculty member noted, engineers "take problems and divide them into smaller problems and find solutions ... This is an important skill." Ideally the solutions to the subproblems will be independent of one another, so that the solution to the larger problem is created by simply assembling all the subsolutions. However, the complex nature of technology is making division of problems into subproblems increasingly difficult. As described by Dym and colleagues, "[A] hallmark of good system designers is that they can anticipate the unintended consequences emerging from interaction among the multiple parts of a system" (Dym and others, 2005, p. 106). Designers must anticipate both technical and nontechnical consequences of the design.

Much as an engineer might be focused on creating a product, process, procedure, or service that solves a problem, so design courses and activities focus on the students—on helping them understand and implement the processes and methods of realizing an artifact. Indeed, the quality of the student-created artifact may be of secondary importance in the learning process. In our observations, we saw that to help their students understand how to identify and spot problems, generate design specifications, and go from these specifications to a final artifact, faculty give them opportunities to practice establishing objectives and criteria and generating, synthesizing, analyzing, selecting, constructing, testing, and evaluating alternatives.

Generating Candidate Solutions

Generative thinking is "divergent thinking" (Chaplin, 1989; Eris, 2004; Hudson, 1966). Starting with the assumption that there is no ready-made solution, that a solution will need to be compiled or invented, the engineer dreams up possible—or impossible—ways of solving the problem. Some faculty identify this as the highly creative phase of the work, offering, "There is also a creative aspect. There isn't a formula for doing these things. You have to ... try to generate ideas on your own, continually asking ... 'Can this be done in a better way?'"

In professional practice, to generate solutions, engineers draw on such tools as brainstorming and synectics, sketching, and thinking techniques involving fantasy, lateral thinking, inversion, and analogy. These tools of professional practice are increasingly used in engineering education. For example, TRIZ (pronounced *treez*, a Russian acronym for *teoriya resheniya izobretatelskikh zadatch*), the theory of inventive problem solving developed by Genrich Altshuller and colleagues in 1946, provides tools and methods for an algorithmic approach to the invention of new systems (see, for example, Altshuller, 2005).

Students and faculty described the importance of learning to create candidate solutions. They explained that generating a number of ideas increases the likelihood that an acceptable solution will be created, and they noted the value in using tools and strategies to aid in generating possible solutions. A student described the experience of learning to not be satisfied with her first idea: "[A] lot of us were ready to use a solution the first week. And [the professor] really slowed us down and showed us that whenever you're approaching a design problem, you have to see everything that's out there before you reduce it; that the final product is a long way off."

Evaluating and Implementing Candidate Solutions

At some point, an engineer must step back and see whether the solution is reasonable. To winnow candidate solutions in order to arrive at the best one for the current situation, engineers use "convergent thinking," involving analysis, judgment, critique, and decision making (Chaplin, 1989). To help in deciding which solution to develop, engineers use informal and formal tools and strategies to create physical or analytic models of the proposed solutions. The tools may be based on, for example, scientific principles, business practices, or heuristics, including rules of thumb. As we describe in Parts Two and Three, engineering students learn some of these tools in the analysis and laboratory courses.

These tools allow the engineer to predict behavior and performance, then compare the predictions against criteria and standards. At times, it may be appropriate to use first-order tools, such as back-of the-envelope calculations or simple physical mockups; at other times advanced simulation tools such as finite element analysis or stereo lithography are required.

In some situations, interpreting the predictions relative to design requirements is straightforward, particularly when requirements, such as weight and speed, are quantitative. Often, however, interpretation is not straightforward: aspects of the criteria and requirements may not be quantifiable. As a faculty member described it, "There is no question that the engineers work on [the] quantifiable using quantification tools. At the same time, the decisions that need to be made are not always purely quantifiable. The nonquantifiable stuff—we still deal with it. We have a basic difficulty in that at some level the results of engineering decisions have to be also measured by and against the immeasurable. How we deal with that is an ongoing battle." A particularly "nonquantifiable" aspect of engineering decision making includes issues of professional ethics, which we discuss at greater length in Part Five.

To be able to evaluate and implement candidate solutions, students need to learn how to explore through modeling and simulation; identify and use the appropriate tools for creating these models; create models when many details of the solution have not yet been defined; interpret model predictions against requirements and criteria; and define appropriate actions based on the interpretation.

Design Process

The design process is not linear: at any phase of the process, the engineer may need to identify and define subproblems, then generate and evaluate solutions to these subproblems to integrate back into the overall process. The engineer may return to an earlier stage at any time. The engineering design process can also be described as mindful and intentional iteration, looping back to generate additional ideas—when, for example, an unanticipated requirement is introduced. The process also involves the awareness and discipline to move forward toward implementing a solution.

A faculty member explained the iterative and intertwined nature of defining, generating, testing, and evaluating ideas: "If the first thing you try doesn't work, you try a different attack and you keep going at it until you solve it, because for most problems there are many different ways of solving or approaching it, but one that actually works best. And you have to be, well, stubborn enough to keep at it. I would say [engineers rely on] persistence ..."

As Figure 12.1 illustrates, revisiting, revising, and solidifying prior thinking spirals out from the start of a project.

Engineering faculty and students alike described engineering design work as process. They described organizing, structuring, and coordinating the work that helps the engineer and engineering organization keep an eye on creating a timely and relevant solution. A student's comment captures how her understanding of process has matured with her education: "There are an infinite number of ways to solve a problem—it is just about finding the most efficient way."

Design Skills

Faculty and students described a wide array of skills necessary to design. Brainstorming and synectics support concept generation; application of numerical modeling tools supports the evaluation of these concepts. Among the broader professional skills, we frequently heard the terms

Figure 12.1.   Spiral Model of Product Development

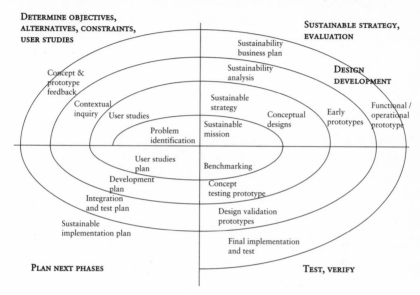

Source: *Adapted from A. Agogino, 2006 and 2008.*

communication, teamwork, time management, and *project management.* Although sound technical knowledge remains a core of engineering work, we heard resounding acknowledgment among faculty and students that these professional skills are also critical. We look at each of them in more detail.

Communication

The oral communication skills that professionals need range from being able to give formal presentations about design solutions to managers and clients, to being able to debate the merit of proposed solutions with colleagues in a constructive and productive manner, to reaching out to a broad community of people who may have knowledge and insight into—and stakes in—the design problem being worked on, but limited nontechnical vocabulary or understanding.

In addition to these, faculty noted the array of written communication skills the students need to learn: documenting solutions in ways that codify requirements and intent, form (for example, dimensions, materials, geometry), function (for example, description of behavior), how the solution meets required goals, and alternatives explored. Whether writing reports, memos, digital files composed of tables, drawings, narrative descriptions, or math models, the engineer employs communication skills both during the work (status reports, for example) and at the culmination of a design project (final project reports). Even informal written communications, such as e-mail and blogs, play an increasingly important role, particularly in work that is geographically distributed.

Teamwork

Designing all but the simplest of devices requires a number of engineers working together in a coordinated and integrated manner. The team members that today's students will likely encounter may have varied disciplinary and cultural backgrounds and experiences, and they will work together on site or may be scattered across multiple continents and time zones. Thus teamwork involves a wide array of skills, from trust building to negotiation to conflict resolution. Because design work includes being able to organize time, monetary, and physical resources so that individual and team efforts meet the demands, requirements, and milestones of the overall project, students must also develop personal, group, and project management strategies.

Faculty and students alike told us that teamwork is an essential component of engineering practice, because professional projects are generally beyond the capacity of a single individual. Many of the students we talked with told us that communication skills are critical to successful collaborative project work: "Part of the learning that goes on [is] how to communicate your ideas as fast and as efficiently as possible so that all your members of your group can be on the same page, so you are like a well-lubed machine in your design process."

The Missing Dimension of Design

We did hear some faculty and students talk about societal and ethical implications of engineering design work, expressing it as "Once you mess with the world, you are responsible for the mess you've made." However, learning to incorporate these implications into design thinking in specific ways was not a learning goal mentioned by faculty in talking about design-related coursework.

There are a few exceptions. For example, in a senior capstone class we observed at Michigan, a professor challenged his students with questions about design decisions related to environmental sustainability; he had them work through several case studies in real time. In the capstone course at Cal Poly, students must use an ethical framework to assess the ramifications of their projects.

Recognizing and working with the societal and ethical implications of engineering design in a systematic and consistent manner is a key aspect of professionalism. The ethics of design encompasses responsibly creating new products and services, as well as creating responsible new products and services. That this is not an explicit or dominant goal of the design-focused project-centered learning, which we describe in the next chapter, is troubling. It certainly is an untapped opportunity.

13

PROJECT-CENTERED LEARNING

LARRY LEIFER OFFERS THREE AXIOMS of engineering design education: design education is a social activity, learning to design requires becoming comfortable with ambiguity, and all education is re-education (Leifer, 1995). The dominant pedagogy we observed in our study schools—project-centered learning (PCL), which is typically found in freshman design courses or senior capstone courses—is consistent with these axioms. PCL is "design-oriented project-organized education which deals with the practical problems of constructing and designing on the basis of a synthesis of knowledge from many disciplines and is therefore having students learn to *know how*" (Dym and others, 2005, p. 109. Note that Dym and colleagues use the term *project-based learning* [PBL]; PBL is also the acronym for the older pedagogy of *problem-based learning*—described in Savery and Duffy, 1995—that was used broadly across the undergraduate curriculum and other professional schools. We use *project-centered learning* and *PCL* to avoid any confusion.)

A senior affirmed the effectiveness of this approach: "Instead of just talking about how you might design for manufacturing ... I just did it. It's more than just what you learn in the books. Really, in engineering, you can't just read about engineering; you have to do it."

The centerpiece of PCL, as we observed it, is a design problem, often referred to as a *design project*. By working through this design problem, students practice a way of thinking and using the design process, and they exercise a set of design-related skills. Although we saw variation in the extent to which the design process, design thinking, and design skills are formally and explicitly taught as a complement or adjunct to PCL, we observed, in general, that faculty use PCL in stand-alone design courses, though it is sometimes incorporated into more theoretically oriented courses.

For example, a freshman-level course may include a design project as a means to motivate and inspire the new student's interest in engineering as a major, while providing a contextual foundation for subsequent engineering science courses. In a senior-level design course, in which students' commitment to engineering is a given, design project work provides an opportunity to synthesize prior learning and apply this learning to solving a more open-ended problem.

The Power of Project-Centered Learning

Faculty and students alike told us that they value design projects as a vehicle for learning. For one thing, they are effective for motivating students. As a veteran design educator reflects, "[P]rojects are easily assigned which are exciting, entertaining, glamorous, and attract favorable and national-level press" (Adams, 1971, p. 1). The motivational power of projects is expressed by one student: "Classes where you have something tangible that you want to strive towards, will keep people motivated [and] working together. A real-life application really helped us work together and communicate with each other, and strive for a goal."

Because design projects allow—and often require—students to synthesize and apply techniques and knowledge learned in other courses, they help mature the students' thinking. As one senior shared about a senior design course, "I'd say what ME 450 does for us is bring together all the different elements I've acquired over the years, combining them into one."

In addition, design project work allows—if not forces—students to lead and direct a large portion of their own learning. In a lecture-based course, even one employing cooperative or collaborative learning strategies, the teacher is the architect of the learning experience and knows or is able to readily find the solution to any assigned problem (Smith, Sheppard, Johnson, and Johnson, 2005; Felder, Woods, Stice, and Rugarcia, 2000). The teacher is seen as *the* expert. As the students and faculty in our study described PCL, they consistently referred to the teacher as a "leader," "mentor," "coach," "advisor," "consultant," "time keeper," "*an* expert," and "manager." Students not only learn to define what types of information they need to navigate the design problem, but also discover where they might find it: "[I]n our projects, definitely knowing when to ask the professor for help and even when to go to other people, saying 'I know you've got sort of a background with this. Do you have any idea what we could do to try and get past this problem?'"

Design projects can also help students develop confidence in their problem-solving abilities. As one student commented, in design you "cannot be afraid to step where you've never stepped before." This sense of confidence is described by a veteran design teacher: "And there's this 'can do' attitude ... the student sees this mountain of a problem and says 'My god, I can't do this' and then at the end of the semester they've sort of climbed through it, maybe topped the mountain in the process ... they learn how to cope with failure and recover from it."

Students also learn to deal with ambiguity. By their very nature, design problems are both multi-answer and ill-defined. As a faculty member noted, "There's not a single solution to a design problem. That's just what design is about." The student who is used to "right answer" problems will struggle at first: "It may be a pain to them, they may be frustrated by it, but they have to really get that experience," noted a faculty member. In time, the students appreciate that the ambiguity of school-based design projects approximates the ambiguity in practice, and that they are learning to work through it by using the theories they have learned, as well as a set of work practices.

A Safe Place to Fail

At the same time, faculty point out that design project work in an academic setting does not (and maybe should not) mimic practice in at least one important way: "This experience is done in a relatively benign environment, a guided environment. It is not the same as in industry. There are people [who say] 'Why don't you do this when you get to work? You learn how to design when you get to work.' It's not the same; the stakes are different." Another colleague added that there is "less pressure here ... you can afford more failure here, you learn from the failure here."

PCL and the Learning Goals of Design

In an educational setting, where the lessons learned from a failed design approach may be more fruitful than those from a successful one, PCL is a powerful pedagogical strategy. Students become skilled in design thinking, design process, and design skills. Grossman and colleagues remind us that any classroom-based pedagogy for learning professional practice such as PCL will always be an "approximation of practice" (Grossman and others, 2009). However, through a variety of approximations of design practice, PCL can be "tuned" to highlight or focus on various aspects of engineering practice. It is flexible enough to allow the teacher to frame the project to intentionally draw out aspects of professional practice for instructional purposes. For example, by integrating industrial-grade computer aided design (CAD) software tools in a PCL experience, even if the particular design task is fairly simple, students are able to focus on the visual communications used in design.

McMasters (1997) offers a number of practical issues faculty should consider in "tuning" design projects, including how much time students can realistically spend in formulating and solving the problem, how well the faculty member understands the problem and its context, how much time faculty can give to students in support.

By making PCL team-based, faculty give students a way to develop the ability to working on teams. As one student described it, "Working with others is how it is when you get out in the real world. You're never just off in a closet by yourself. Being able to bounce ideas off your team members, you come up with so many more ideas."

Team members must learn to communicate with one another and with a broader group of stakeholders. Some courses extend the challenge by grouping students from different fields or disciplines on a single project. With explicit instruction on effective teamwork and communication strategies, along with timely feedback from faculty coaches, students' competencies in working as productive members of an engineering team can improve.

Starting Out: Freshman Design

The last fifteen years have seen an increase in the number of freshman-level design courses. Many, using process orientation and team-centered learning, engage students in multiweek design projects. Dym and colleagues (2005) refer to freshman-level courses with a focus on design as "cornerstone courses," as they serve as a student's foundation in designing, leading eventually to the senior-level design courses referred to as "capstone courses" (p. 103). These freshman-level courses are also complements to the engineering science foundation courses in mathematics and sciences.

Freshman-level design courses commonly take a holistic approach to design education by having students experience that design is more than a project, more than teamwork, more than an oral presentation, more than analysis, more than creativity: it is a comprehensive and professional endeavor that is both fun and hard work. Accordingly, we noted three categories of course objectives associated with freshman design courses:

1. *Providing an encouraging, interactive learning environment.* The course is focused on the creative aspects of design, such as learning

to exercise imaginative and intuitive instincts and flexible thinking, and learning that design is a creative enterprise that involves imagination, risk taking, working with ambiguity, and a willingness to value the need to make decisions in the absence of complete knowledge and certainty.

2. *Developing an understanding of the profession.* Students are encouraged to define, formulate, and solve open-ended or underdefined problems, using modern engineering tools such as Gantt charts, QFD, need-finding; and to find information and use a variety of resources in support of solving a particular problem, which helps develop the habits and skills of staying abreast of changes and advances in professional practices and available technologies in general. In some cases the course is also a recruiting tool: "Design turns students and potential students on . . . lets them do something in a field and helps [us] recruit."

3. *Developing skills for team-based problem solving.* The students have opportunities to work effectively in a team, learning about communicating, negotiating, and persuading, and learning to use graphic and visual representations and thinking.

Freshman courses at CMU, Mines, Michigan, and Howard offer useful examples of different approaches to freshman design. These courses share a goal of introducing first-year students to the open-ended and creative nature of engineering design, but they differ in the extent to which design is taught as an activity tightly tied to a body of field-specific knowledge or as an activity in its own right with its own body of knowledge.

CMU. Through seven introductory freshman engineering courses, each with a field-specific framework, students are exposed to the basic concepts in an integrated and contextualized manner, to illustrate a logical way of thinking about problems and their solutions, and to convey the excitement of the profession. Students are required to take two of these courses during their freshman year to gain hands-on design experience with key field-specific concepts and inform their choice of engineering major. Field-specific knowledge and skills are thus tied to the design projects, which are formulated by the instructor and supported by locally created resource materials.

For example, in "Fundamentals of Mechanical Engineering," students explore structural analysis, mechanism design, fluid flows, and thermal systems. Using principles and methods of analysis presented in lectures, students complete two major design projects, the first of which emphasizes the modern practice of "paperless" engineering design, analysis, and manufacture, and the use of industry-grade engineering software supported by faculty-created self-paced online tutorials. "Fundamentals of Electrical and Computer Engineering" is organized around twelve core electrical and computer engineering topics that are then connected to designing, analyzing, and building an electromechanical system, such as a robot. In both courses, while planting the seeds for future field-specific coursework, the students are engaged in a hands-on design-and-build experience using key technical concepts in close approximation to the way a mechanical or electrical engineer would use them.

Mines. The "Engineering Practices Introductory Course" focuses on the engineering design process. Student teams work on one project for the semester. At the end of the semester, the teams present their solutions in a competitive, trade-show type event, with faculty judges determining the best design solution. While designing, for example, playground equipment for handicapped children, mountain trails for persons with disabilities, high-altitude weather balloons, and earthquake kits and seismometers for K–12 education, the students learn the basics of AutoCAD and drafting and how to present and promote their design solutions as if in a corporate setting. A faculty-made reader provides background materials and exercises on topics ranging from project management and teamwork to written and oral communication.

Howard and Michigan. Both programs offer "Introduction to Engineering," in which freshmen engage in semester-long design projects without field-specific distinctions. At Michigan, approximately a thousand students (five hundred per semester) take the course, developed in late 1990s to give freshmen an experience on the engineering campus, which is separate from the main campus. Intensive writing assignments are anchored to an intellectual focus on engineering.

At Howard, the goal is for freshmen to experience design as a general problem-solving strategy, so that they can begin to learn the skills of formulating problems and solving them, as well as to work on teams. The course, with its emphasis on general engineering tools, skills, and strategies, is followed by a second, freshman-level, field-specific course tied to the major, which students select before matriculating. Some of the field-specific courses maintain design as the central educational focus; others focus on introducing the key conceptual principles of the discipline.

Comparing the approaches. Tying engineering design to a particular field-specific body of technical knowledge constrains the design problems and the potential size of the "idea space" for students to explore, limiting students in reframing the problem and exercising a high level of creativity. Students can, however, dive deeply into the implementation of a solution because they have at their disposal particular knowledge resources for realizing it.

In contrast, when engineering design is the focus, students have greater opportunity to explore the nature of the design problem and think broadly about possible solutions. There may be less emphasis on implementation of the design, though prototypes of key components of the proposed design solution may be required. With these courses it is challenging to provide students with the necessary technical resources, for even if they are all working on the same problem, their solutions may vary widely. Students may also have the opportunity to seek input from a broader community of experts and resources.

Senior-Level Design

As required by ABET, all undergraduate engineering programs culminate in a major design experience (ABET, 2007, p. 3). Often called the *capstone experience*, it represents an opportunity for students to synthesize techniques and knowledge that they have acquired over their first three years of study. That the capstone experience associated with engineering majors is focused on design suggests that design is considered a pinnacle activity for engineers.

At our study schools, the senior design experience is generally embedded in a one- or two-term required senior-level course, with varied titles such as "DVLSI Design I," "Biomedical Instrumentation and Design," "Modern Control System Design," "Design and Manufacturing III," "Senior Design I & II," or simply "Engineering Design."

Organization of Capstone Experiences

Most capstone design experiences involve teams of three to six students working on a single project for the duration of the course. Other models include the ones at Mines, where students specializing in electrical and mechanical engineering work on multidisciplinary teams; at CMU, where mechanical engineering seniors are teamed with industrial design and business students; at Cal Poly, where seniors generally work on their capstone project individually; at Georgia Tech, where electrical engineering students work on teams of three to five on subsystems of a larger, class-based project, such as building a "future truck"; and at Michigan, where electrical engineering students work for part of the course on a major project that is closely tied to a particular technological subfield within electrical engineering, such as designing VLSI circuits.

Types of problems

The design problems given to students as part of their capstone experience are more open-ended than any the students are likely to have encountered up to that point in their academic careers. In some cases students are given specific design criteria that must be met, so they are challenged to exercise creativity amid stringent requirements. For example, a senior engineering student described the challenge of her capstone project: designing for an external client a surgical helmet to protect surgeons by filtering air that might carry tuberculosis and other air-borne diseases, optimizing for weight, comfort, cooling ability, and air movement.

Other capstone design projects are even more open-ended, engaging students in defining requirements and criteria. The students may be working on multidisciplinary design teams: "We have two artists and three engineers working together . . . building a piece of kinetic sculpture with a control system . . . you trip sensors and different crank shafts will respond in kind of an organized but chaotic way."

Still other capstone design projects have students working on improvements to existing products, requiring that they coordinate closely with existing, well-established technologies to ensure that their design contributions will work within a larger system, as described by another senior: "We basically took all their numbers on the way the process works right now and designed a new section to it to meet their requirements . . . It was a fun project."

Integration and Ownership

Most apparent in the senior design projects is the difference in student-teacher relationships. Although the professor may still give lectures to teach about new technical and process-related materials, much of the student-teacher interaction is focused on the work of the projects. This interaction commonly takes place in scheduled weekly, small-group meetings. For example, at Georgia Tech we observed a one-hour meeting of seventeen students and two faculty members about the team's "future truck." The faculty members served as facilitators, initiating and moderating discussion, highlighting relevant issues, requesting updates, and raising economic and safety issues. Students' project updates resulted in short student-teacher and student-student discussions about particular aspects of the design work.

We also observed students in teams of four meeting around a conference room table for their weekly forty-five-minute session with their capstone course instructor. The faculty member used the students' weekly assigned task as the jumping-off point for discussion, asking the students about their process to complete the assignment. He offered suggestions (along with his reasoning) and commented on their answers in a manner that left final decision making up to the students. The students asked several questions and shared design and research problems they needed help with. The students were very engaged in the discussion and aware of the technical problems they were likely to confront, and they seemed to be fully prepared for the meeting. (Unfortunately, we were not able to see any of the numerous out-of-class meetings of the team members, in which much of the important design thinking is going on and students are relying on one another as fellow engineers.)

We learned about frequent, informal, and spontaneous student-initiated student-teacher discussions. For example, at Cal Poly students working on "power projects" have twenty-four-hour access to a laboratory space where they work on their capstone design projects. The space is equipped with six workbenches, each with an oscilloscope, computer, and AC/DC power. There is a specific time each week when the faculty member overseeing these capstone projects is in the laboratory, but it is up to the students to set up times to meet with the instructor for weekly updates or demonstrations. Students and the teacher do not meet formally in class, and the faculty member acts as a project advisor.

In addition to these informal meetings, we also observed students' end-of-term presentations, in which student teams present their final design solutions in a public setting. These ten- to fifteen-minute presentations, often PowerPoint-based, generally include demonstrations of working hardware or prototypes. Many of the students dress in professional attire, and often the presentations are made in spaces that enable visitors and fellow students to attend. Each team's presentation is followed by brief Q&A. The role of the faculty member in these sessions is mainly as host.

Major Outcomes of the Capstone Experience

On all of our visits, the seniors' high level of engagement with and excitement about their capstone design projects was evident. They told us that project work helps them develop confidence and brings many pieces of their education together, and that the work is fun. It was common for us to hear that the capstone "made me more excited about the major" or "made me want to take more classes to learn all that I still don't know." We heard that it was "what I had been waiting for"; "what we are here for"; "one of the few times where you actually apply, hands on, the theory that you learn all through school."

BUILDING SKILLS FOR PROFESSIONAL PRACTICE We heard many specific messages from students about the importance of the capstone design experience to their learning skills they expect to take into practice. The consistency of these messages, irrespective of the particular details of the capstone experience, strongly suggests that the capstone implementation of PCL realizes several of the attributes of this particular teaching strategy. We heard from seniors that the capstone experience is highly effective in giving them experience with working in groups and helping them develop the associated professional skills. Many of them talked about learning to communicate and coordinate with fellow team members, as they learn that in the engineering workplace "you are never working alone. Every project has something and someone else hooked to it."

Seniors also talked about learning to manage time and project milestones as part of the capstone experience, reflecting that "this course gives you hands-on experience about how long it will take ... You must learn to integrate your own team's efforts with other teams. This means developing a timeline." The importance of learning to manage time is underscored by a faculty member who teaches a capstone course: "Most students, it's their habit to wait until the night before and then pull an all-nighter. It may work in other classes where they can write down answers out of the book, but they can't do it in a design class ... they start to learn, due to feedback, that it doesn't work."

INTEGRATION AND APPLICATION Capstone design experiences require that students identify critical technologies and approaches, stay abreast of change in professional practice, use analysis in support of synthesis, appropriately model the physical world with mathematics, build up real hardware to prototype ideas, and troubleshoot and test hardware. In other words, to solve the design problems they are assigned, students must appropriately, flexibly, and adaptively apply their technical knowledge to the task at hand.

The senior capstone experience involves students in integrating and applying knowledge and skills that they may have learned separately. Said a faculty member, "The design courses represent a synthesis of the other courses and materials. It is a chance for them to put it all together."

Another faculty member noted that this ability to synthesize across fields is critical to design work. When they enter the senior year, he commented, students are skilled at solving individual problems for which there is an answer at the back of the book. However, he continued, "When it comes to open-ended problems they have to choose: What am I going to design? What are the disciplines that are needed to make that design?

How detailed do I go into each of the disciplines? They're not good at that, and so there is this certain natural evolution we see in them during the capstone experience."

Students, too, see the integrative power of the capstone experience, offering that the experience "is important because you learn all these theories in school. This is one way that we can actually apply the things that we learned and put all the pieces together." A senior describes that the application of prior learning to a new situation is not always as straightforward, as one's attempts to map theory to a physical object: "It is kind of shocking because you took a refrigeration class but this is a real refrigerator. You know, it looks a lot different in a book than it does in real life ... it kind of bridges that gap. I think once you can do that you are truly into engineering levels ... you can take this jargon of equations and engineering methodology, and begin to apply it to real-world problems."

A Transitional Moment

Faculty and students talked about the capstone experience being a major transitional experience for students, representing a transition critical to their professional development. One faculty member offered, "Before people take the senior design course there is a sort of fear of the unknown. And after, they have an ability to synthesize the material together. I think that without it the program would seriously suffer."

Students seek information from a wide variety of sources. They take greater responsibility for and ownership of the direction of their work because, in the words of two seniors, "It is kind of our own thing, teachers not telling us exactly what to do. It is like we are trying to solve problems that we pose to ourselves," and "We have a say in what we want to do."

Although there is clear evidence that the capstone experience is transformational for students in and of itself, it is likely that the transformation started during the freshman year and progressed through the senior year. The capstone experience represents a culmination of that progression and an opportunity to put into action a maturing that happened over years.

14

ASSESSING DESIGN

ENGINEERING DESIGN EXPERIENCES encourage students to learn a way of thinking, a process for going about design work, and a set of design-related skills. Individual courses may emphasize one, two, or all three of these goals. In this chapter, as we describe how faculty go about assessing students' learning of a way of thinking, a process, and a set of skills, we ask the reader to consider the extent to which the assessment is aligned with these goals.

For example, we noticed that the closer student work gets to professional practice, the less willing or able faculty are to grade it. We also noticed considerable tension between what matters to the design faculty (teamwork, communication, efforts, and process) and what is ultimately graded.

What Is Assessed

Whether it is a prototype of a final design solution or a computer-based simulation; whether the team produces reports, makes presentations, or gives demonstrations, the teams' "products" are used as measures, proxies, or indicators of design learning.

For example, many projects call for a final engineering report and formal technical presentation by the team. The report typically describes the final design solution and rationale for arriving at it, as might be done in a professional project review meeting, in which the high-level features and attributes of the final design are showcased.

An individual student's final grade in a capstone or cornerstone course is often based on his or her team's final report and presentation, along with interim items, such as the proposal, project notebook, and documentation. An industry-sponsored design project may also incorporate client input into the final grade.

Individual work assignments that complement the team project work include homework assignments, quizzes, and examinations in which students must individually exercise and demonstrate newly learned design skills. Faculty explain their motivation for assigning individual work as ensuring that every student learns a set of skills. For example, in the freshman design class at Mines, an individual exam determines student competency with the drafting software AutoCAD.

Faculty also explain that they assign individual work to discourage "freeloaders." With design projects "one loses somewhat the ability to 'grade' individual performance and some students coast at the expense of others. This coasting is often due to the daily nature of assignments from lecture courses, which contrasts with the longer time scale usually accompanying a project . . . It can be solved with structure and with proper project choice and timing" (Adams, 1971, p. 1–2).

Individual assignments requiring demonstrable participation and accountability are used as a means to minimize "coasting." For example, in the early stages of design work, team members are often required to come to meetings with lists of individually generated design ideas; these lists serve not only as a launching point for a group brainstorm, but also as a means to promote individual accountability and participation, particularly if they are turned in to the instructor for review and grading.

What Matters

We talked with the faculty about what aspects of design learning they are hoping to see in these products—with some surprising results. We expected that most, if not all faculty, are looking for technical merit in these measures: Does the solution work? Does it meet constraints? Is it clever or novel? Is the client pleased with the result? However, this was not what faculty talked about when we asked about assessing students in design PCL situations. The three consistent goals of assessment that we heard were ability to work in a team, to communicate, and to put forth a concerted effort.

Teamwork

Faculty described the importance of students' demonstrating that they can work productively over an extended period with a group of "colleagues"—their fellow students—and that they can work through rough spots, whether technical or interpersonal. Said one faculty member:

"There's the design process and all that side of things, but there's the team aspects of it and how the team manages itself. I will tell my students, 'You may have problems and there's any number of different ways that you'll have problems. I want to see that you guys recognize that you have problems and are trying to deal with it.' And I tell them at the end, 'If I felt like you guys were not managing your situation and trying to struggle to come to a resolution, I probably will hold that against you.'"

Peer assessment as part of teamwork. A design course may use peer assessment for summative or formative purposes, and may focus on students assessing one another's work products (presentations, reports) or their processes, including teamwork. One reason for using peer assessment, faculty noted, is that they believe teammates can provide valuable feedback to one another on teamwork—perhaps better than can faculty, who generally do not observe the team as it is going about its work. The faculty also noted that giving peers feedback mimics professional practice (for example, 360-degree performance review), and they believe that the use of peer review minimizes the incidence of freeloaders.

One faculty member describes his use of formative peer assessment and its power to identify team problems:

> I have students do self-grading as well as grade each other within their teams, with fairly extensive justification of their grading. And I take that very seriously. And I tell them I don't share that with each other unless I ask their permission to do that. If there is a remarkable difference between what I think and what they think, we have to deal with it. I do this three times a year, every semester, and in fact when there is a discrepancy it has been very interesting. This usually helps with the student who was getting dumped on, rightly or wrongly, to uncover team dynamics; some of the group thinks this fellow doesn't perform, that fellow feels that the group is not appreciating him so he doesn't perform, so it spirals down into nothingness. And if you capture that early enough you recover. [Otherwise] you get this snowballing effect.

Although some faculty use peer assessment as part of the summative assessment, others stress the importance of using peer review for formative purposes only, not including it in the grade. In all cases, however, faculty who make use of peer assessment note that it must be honest, well structured, and anonymous. However, faculty and students alike voiced concerns about the legitimacy of having students grade one another ("Isn't this the faculty's job?"), the reliability of student assessment, and the possible effects on team cohesiveness. They ask whether peer assessment can be done in a manner that is consistent with other course goals. Research on developing and validating peer assessment tools and strategies is ongoing, both within and outside the engineering community (see, for example, Dominick, Reilly, and McGourty, 1997; Sheppard, Chen, Schaeffer, and Steinbeck, 2004).

Communication

Faculty told us that a student's good solution will not necessarily earn a good grade if the student is unable to communicate it to others (though we assume that a technically poor solution that is well communicated would not earn a good grade either). Both written and oral communication skills are given significant emphasis and account for a large portion of the students' final grade.

Through both these modes of communication students are required to convey their final solution, the need that it is addressing, the rationale and process for its creation, and alternatives considered. Doing this effectively requires that students have a command of text, visual, and graphic tools and can use quantitative or qualitative data and evidence to tell a coherent story about their design process and their artifact. It is not unusual for students to turn in draft reports or give dry-run presentations to get formative feedback. We note that periodic informal design meetings with faculty also play an important role in students' learning to convey their design work to others.

Effort

Faculty noted the importance of recognizing students who put forth a concerted effort. Although the technical merit of the final design is important, faculty say that the amount of effort the student puts into the process is equally important. They believe that students must learn about working hard. However, trying to grade effort creates challenges:

> You're really stuck, to some extent, in the grading that you can give them and the differentiation you can do, because you can't give someone who has put that much time and effort and work into it a very poor grade. I mean if they have met . . . the requirements—our baseline requirements—if they have met that, you almost feel compelled to get them a pretty good grade (even better than you would in a normal 400-level nondesign course). That's not really a problem because they have put the time and effort into it, but all that does is scrunch up the

grading. So the grading is quite, quite different than a sophomore-level class and even different than another 400-level class that's not a design class.

Assessing Progress

Many faculty to use a grading scheme that also accounts for the various stages of a student's progress throughout the project. We observed that assessment of mid-term project proposals and oral presentations can be formative, providing feedback to students on improving their work, and summative, in that it is a component of the final grade. Another way that faculty make progress a component of the final grade is through assessment of student's development and growth evident in the weekly meetings between the faculty and student project teams.

What Counts: It Comes Down to a Grade

At the end of the term, faculty must combine their assessment of the quality of the student-created products and the quality of the work that informed the products—teamwork, communication, effort, and process— to give each student a grade in the course. A few faculty present this as a straightforward process:

> They're graded on their professionalism. A "C" says they've done what they said they were going to do. They have to submit monthly reports about their progress. If they use proper grammar, style, and convey real information to me about what they and the team [have] done, then that's acceptable. If they attach a data set I wasn't expecting, then that's more than acceptable. And that's "C," "B," and "A." I don't have to evaluate them other than that, and I think that's pretty realistic for the work world. They are evaluated by their peers for their team-work. I look at whether they are acceptable, outstanding, or barely there. They are evaluated by the client. Did they meet expectations? Did they do what they said they would? Was the result or report profes-sionally done? The client's evaluation does figure into the final grade.

However, many others find it difficult to connect assessment of skills such as teamwork and communications to a grade. As one faculty member explained, "Grades are measurable, and this goes back to being uncom-fortable dealing with things that are necessarily unquantifiable. You know as much as you know. It may be heresy to say grades and learning are not perfectly correlated—I think we all know that at some level. And because we tend to emphasize grades and we have such things that are measurable, we don't always hit the things that are not measurable and make for a good design."

Faculty work to map between learning, products, performances, and grades in various ways. For example, one faculty member described how he and colleagues who are coteaching the capstone design course wrestle with assigning grades to design project work by remaining true to the minimum learning factors they can all agree on.

Another professor, admitting that evaluating design projects is heavily subjective, attempts to quantify his subjective assessment by assigning value to the different categories that should make up the final grade. With the help of the teaching assistant, the faculty member goes through the different categories for assessment and defines the observations that support each category. He also looks into the complexity of the problem that the team had to solve and how well they managed to achieve their goals. However, he makes it clear that failing to achieve their goal does not necessarily mean failure in the course, because it is possible that students achieve something else in the process of failing. His constant interaction with the teams also gives him additional information about who does most of the work. He describes all the complexities to assigning grades:

> Working with them, getting the coffee, you see what's going on. You could see who's working hard and who's not. One of the worries ... I've never had a project fail. Once in a while, we have to redefine success, but they've always gotten through it. I try to tell them that failure's OK, too; they are not going to fail the course because they did not quite meet their goals ... They're out there reaching and they don't know, [that] this is the good time to fail. So if they try real hard and achieve something in the process of failing, that counts, too. So grading is really hard. It's quite subjective. You've got midterm and you've got homework and you've got labs that are all graded, too. And so all that has to come in, but generally everybody does try hard. That's probably one of the reasons for the spread on grades between A– to A+. Between A+ and A– on a project is that some of them don't work as hard, some of them don't reach as far. You have to put some spread on them. If everybody seems to do spectacularly, you give them all A+, I guess. You know it is subjective. I don't know what else to do.

Some students expressed appreciation of grading practices that incorporate faculty-student interactions: these allow the faculty member to have a better idea of their learning, and consequently inform his or her judgment of their work. Students appreciate the fact that they are graded on how their work reflects what they know and not on how their work compares to that of others. They say it has a positive effect on their learning: faculty seem to focus their attention on what they are learning rather than to how they can do better than their peers.

As one student explained, "How my capstone design course is graded is good, because the teacher meets with us twice and he gets a better sense of how to grade us, because he sees how our group is interacting, and that's a better basis for a grade, how we're interacting." Another student observed, "In some classes, you do the homework, you have the midterm, you cram for it, you get a good grade. Two years later, you try to remember some of the thermal that you took—good luck! The things that you learn in classes like 450 [a capstone design course]—where you're not specifically graded relative to each other, and you're graded on how you're performing—helps people retain a lot more of the information."

Assessing Design Thinking

Through faculty-student team meetings, reports, and presentations, faculty can begin to assess whether students, individually and collectively, are learning to define and follow a design process and acquire oral and written communication skills. Adding in peer-assessment strategies also gives greater insight into students' abilities to work effectively on a team. However, none of these various measures gives much of a window into how individuals are learning to engage in design thinking.

Some evidence of individual students' progress in design thinking may come out in faculty-student team meetings, if the meetings allow for times of "free thinking." However, the faculty member must provide models for articulating design thinking, use prompts for eliciting students' thoughts, employ skill in drawing out students who are hesitant to speak up, and, above all, have a clear idea of what student progress looks like.

Some faculty have found student design logs and portfolios to be useful. Not only do these instill a habit that the students will need to take into professional practice, but they allow for the faculty member to see the individual student's process of developing and exploring ideas (Yang and Cham, 2007). To be sure, there are a host of challenges associated with logs or portfolios. They must be collected, graded, and returned in a timely manner. Beyond the practical questions are the philosophical: Does logbook or portfolio work represent a place to develop ideas or a venue for presenting mature ideas? How does one assess someone's raw thinking? How does one extract meaning from messy log-book scribblings? Is the assessment formative or summative?

Despite these challenges, there is an active and growing community both within and outside of engineering that is studying how logs and portfolios can serve as a useful tool for both learning and assessment. This community is developing grading rubrics and experimenting with how various models of logs and portfolios work in particular course settings (see, for example, Hebert, 2001). Digital media are increasingly playing a role in the creation, sharing, and grading of logs and portfolios. Some useful and new methods for "seeing" individual student's design thinking may emerge from these efforts.

15

MAKING A PLACE TO CREATE

CAPSTONE DESIGN EXPERIENCES provide excitement, motivation, and synthesis—too late. One course at the end of the student's program is not sufficient time for the iterative process of learning and actively integrating knowledge, building skills—preparing for professional practice.

Project-centered learning (PCL), whether promoting little *d* or big *D* learning, is an effective, flexible, and robust strategy for helping students learn to design. It promotes student activities and actions that are more representative of engineering practice than the problem sets and exams typically used in theory-based engineering science classes. It can also be highly motivational for students and allows for synthesis of knowledge and skills. Like fully developed laboratory experiences, PCL can put students into learning situations that require that they confront ambiguity and uncertainty as an expected and integral part of the work.

PCL is not a perfect pedagogy. Based on our discussions with faculty and students, the challenges of using PCL include defining projects appropriate for the skill level of students at the various stages of their development, ensuring that faculty serve as effective coaches to student teams, and coordinating teaching among a group of faculty. A more important challenge, we believe, is fairly and consistently assigning grades when product, process, effort, and improvement—as well as willingness to take risks—are valued and valuable components of the learning experience.

Nor is PCL the sole way of teaching design. Other design teaching strategies include case-based instruction, using design cases in which particular aspects of the design process are highlighted. Examples of this approach include Rose-Hulman Institute of Technology and Carleton University case studies (http://www.civeng.carleton.ca/ECL/) and multimedia cases and games by Agogino (see, for example, Agogino and Hsi,

1994; Richkus, Agogino, Yu, and Tang, 1999); reverse engineering or dissection exercises, in which students literally and intellectually take apart common and not-so-common devices to tease out relationships between form and function (Sheppard, 1992; Wood, 2000); and role-playing games such as Delta Design by Bucciarelli, in which team members take on the roles of project manager, heat transfer analyst, structural engineer, and architect to design a 2D house for the planet Deltroid (Bucciarelli, 1999). These types of exercises can complement PCL projects within a single design course, highlighting particular aspects of design, or they can enhance more theory-oriented courses to put concepts into a practice context.

The project-centered learning we observed in a variety of freshman- and senior-level design courses simulates, in a studio experience, the process of problem formulation and problem solution that is the core of engineering work. Importantly, in PCL the teacher is less the revered authority and more the guide and coach as students work their way through a process of collective problem discovery, collaborative problem definition, and attempted solution. Because so much of the responsibility for learning and for the project's success falls on students, PCL often provides students with valuable experience in how to find knowledge as well as how to apply it.

The Challenges of First-Year Design

Faculty teaching design to first-year students noted that they face two particular challenges: the students' degree of knowledge, particularly in science and mathematics, and their hands-on skills with technology. Faculty often must deal with this challenge at the same time they are teaching large classes—groups of students that number in the hundreds.

Students Start from Scratch

When students enter an undergraduate engineering program, although they are expected to have a solid, albeit limited, understanding of mathematics, the physical sciences, and technology, they do not, some faculty observed. Incoming students' modest understanding of math and science severely limits faculty's ability to engage students in design; as one instructor observed, "It's extremely hard to teach design if they barely know the math, they barely know the field, they know nothing." In addition, faculty perceive that many students enter college with different experiences with technology than did students of previous generations: "The students have changed. Twenty years ago we used to see students from farms ... who had hands-on experience. They had worked on their cars. Now few have had real hands-on experience. This hampers the design process—you need to take it apart and get your hands on it."

As we discuss later, creating successful design experiences for students at any level requires that faculty formulate appropriate design tasks and compile necessary resource materials. For freshmen engaged in design projects, this may require that faculty create custom resources, tailored to the backgrounds of their students; we saw this at CMU, where online tutorials support them in learning to use professional-grade software, and at Mines, where a locally produced manual provides students with information on a variety of professional skills.

Project-Centered Learning for Large Courses

The demands of teaching freshman design go well beyond working with the limits of students' knowledge and finding appropriate projects for students to work on. They also entail supporting teams in a variety of ways, including advising and assessing performance. Faculty noted, "You don't grade a design project report in fifteen minutes," and that "there are lots of faculty-student engagement and team meetings. It goes beyond what the credits might indicate. There is coaching and mentoring, both of which take time."

Although these challenges may be manageable when the number of students in the course is small, they take on new proportions when it comes to large courses. At several of the schools we visited, the number of students taking the freshman design course may be five hundred to six hundred per term. As a faculty member reflected, "We have nine sections, three hundred students per term—we have to be able to scale things. The size also means that the faculty does not necessarily talk much with one another. We are also spread over several buildings."

Is it possible to create meaningful design experiences for such large groups of students? Although facility issues are a matter of resources, we saw creative solutions to the issue of faculty time, all of which involve dividing students into smaller groups or sections and having a lead course coordinator of a single course. Successful implementation requires commitment of resources at various levels, from individual faculty members and faculty teaching teams up to the department and broader institutional levels.

Design in the Sophomore and Junior Years

Most students have some design experience during the middle years, but concerted attention to design is rarely a part of students' coursework in the sophomore and junior years. As we describe in this section, we saw three approaches to design in these middle years. The most prevalent is using design projects in a variety of ways in courses that are mainly focused on acquiring technical knowledge.

Another approach, less common, is a set of connected courses that, as part of a focus on technical knowledge, teach specific design skills; understanding of design process, thinking, and skills is an explicit course goal. A third approach, the least common but most promising, is a sequence of courses over all four undergraduate years; the primary focus is engaging students in design work. Students must acquire field-specific technical knowledge in other course or independent study. To be sure, more research would help educators understand current strategies for teaching design and how they might be improved, and new strategies might be explored (Atman, Kilgore, and McKenna, 2008; Dym and others, 2005). However, our study suggests that there is no other place in which the nature and fascination of engineering work becomes so apparent for students as in design courses.

Developing Usable Technical Knowledge

Sophomore and junior design projects are sometimes used to support students' learning to apply technical knowledge. For example, a faculty member explained, "In the dynamics course, which is traditionally just equations, we have a semester-long substantial design project. The idea is that a subject like dynamics should not be offered simply for the betterment of the student. The course is designed to solve problems. And design problems require them to use their skills and theory learned in dynamics to solve the design problem." In this way, qualities critical to engaging in design are also being developed and nurtured, giving students additional opportunities to develop and practice design-related skills and attitudes.

When design is used to augment student learning in upper-level technical courses, the students may spend one or more weeks applying the technical concepts to solve a design problem. As one faculty member noted, "[T]hey're learning how to apply the theory and the equations and the things they have learned [about signals, systems, and microprocessors] to something real ... as an example, a controller for a vending machine. So they know what the process is, how to define the input and output based on the education that they have, and they know the systems theory and so forth. Based on that, they design something, they simulate it, then they build it and demonstrate that it works."

The students must grapple with multiple viable solutions (some or all of which are unknown to the instructor at the time the problem is posed to the students), the problem is ill defined, and students are required to seek out knowledge beyond what is being taught in the class. These design exercises require that students apply concepts in a more authentic situation, which challenges them to conceive of the system on which to apply the concepts. The outcome of the assignment may be a computer simulation or physical model of the design concept or a design report and presentation (which describes assumptions, alternatives considered, the final solution, and validation that the solution meets requirements). For example, in a sophomore-level engineering mechanics course, students could be assigned a project to design, analyze, build, test, and document their creation of a truss-style bridge that meets specified size, weight, cost, and material requirements. If these requirements are not too constrained, students are able to design something that is uniquely theirs.

However, it was not clear to us how students connect design exercises embedded in advanced technical courses to other more explicit design work, and how faculty hold students accountable for knowing something about design processes. One barrier is the division of labor among faculty, especially in large programs.

Developing Design Skills

Some programs offer a connected set of courses to develop the student's understanding of the design process, design thinking, and associated skills, in the course of learning technical knowledge. These courses, which might be called design-supported courses, serve as prerequisites for those that follow in the sequence in the program's course catalogue and have been identified in the program's ABET self-study as contributing significantly to a student's understanding of design. These courses introduce new field-specific technical topics and more general design-related topics, such as design process and technical writing, in conjunction with multiweek design projects. The students have weekly problem sets, project proposals, hardware demonstrations, and final reports and presentations, and the work may be individual or team-based; team-based work is becoming increasingly common.

Although the idea behind design-supported courses is good, we saw that in operation, the experiences are rarely staged or scaffolded, so that students and faculty alike are not focusing on students' progress in becoming skilled designers.

Building Students' Design Experience

Nationally, a few programs offer a sequence of courses whose primary, if not sole, focus is engaging students in engineering design work, giving them needed field-specific knowledge. Lecture time (if any) is used to present advanced design approaches and strategies, or specialty material needed for a particular class of design problems. Some of these lectures may be given by outside experts. Rowan University, for example, offers the Rowan Engineering Clinic, a sequence of eight semester-long design courses (Chandrupatla and others, 2001). Each semester of a student's engineering program includes a significant design experience. Each course is multidisciplinary, involving students from the schools' chemical, civil and environmental, electrical and computer, and mechanical engineering departments. Faculty from these departments, in addition to those from English and communications, are responsible for teaching the courses. During the first four courses, spanning the freshman and sophomore years, students develop design-related skills and practice problem-solving strategies through homework assignments and design project work. Project work includes engaging students in mechanical dissection exercises, which challenge them to define and understand the design solution embodied in existing artifacts, such as hairdryers or radios (Sheppard, 1992). By the junior and senior years, students are engaged in year-long projects.

In 1995 Purdue University created a multiyear design experience, the Engineering Projects in Community Service program (EPICS): "[U]ndergraduates earn academic credit for their participation in the design teams that solve technology-based problems for not-for-profit organizations in the local community ..." (Coyle, Jamieson, and Oakes, 2005, p. 139). The teams are multidisciplinary, drawing students from across engineering and around the university; vertically integrated, maintaining a mix of freshmen through seniors each semester; and long-term, as each student participates in a project for up to seven semesters. The continuity, technical depth, and disciplinary breadth of these teams enable delivery of projects of significant benefit to the community (Coyle, Jamieson, and Oakes, 2005; see also DeRego, Zoltowski, Jamieson, and Oakes, 2005).

Although developing and maintaining these programs takes considerable effort, they yield significant student learning: students are able to take on fairly sophisticated design and technical challenges and work within complex environments.

Through the use of design, courses can complement each other, offering students a way to integrate and synthesize knowledge and skills. A student explained, "We start out small, we have 250 [design-supporting course the sophomore year], 350 [design-supporting course the junior year], then finally senior design [450]; you have all these classes and you learn stuff." When the conceptual connections between courses are obvious, students gain the opportunity to build the powerful connections that lead to deep knowledge.

A Place to Create Connections

Weaving design experiences throughout the curriculum in this way helps students make connections among disparate areas of knowledge and skills, integrating these at various stages of their education as their knowledge and skills develop. The intellectual requirements and pedagogical processes involved in the teaching of design integrate engineering education's central goals, and involve students in the kind of thinking that engineers use in professional practice. Thus, we believe, design activity provides the most commodious and stable bridge between learning the basics of engineering knowledge, skill, and judgment and entry into actual practice.

We believe that design's networking function, along with the special kind of engineering thinking it engenders, argues for placing design in a more central position in engineering curricula from the first year through to the end. As students progress through their program, the sophistication of the design assignments, including both the technical and contextual complexities encountered, should escalate. This involves concurrently supporting and measuring students' growing technical and professional development. Studio-based teaching practices enable students to see professionalism issues, including ethical concerns, as integrally related to the technical and communicational challenges of particular design projects.

PART FIVE

AFFECTING THE WORLD

IN A 2000 PLENARY ADDRESS to the NAE, William Wulf reflected on the Academy's selection of the twenty greatest engineering achievements of the twentieth century, observing that the achievements were selected not for their technical marvel but for their improvement of people's quality of life.

However, although engineering creates products that have a beneficial influence on the meaning and convenience of everyday living, Wulf noted, the inherent unpredictability of technology's impact, citing information technology and biotechnology as examples. Complex systems pose the risk of product behaviors that are, in principle, impossible to predict. Even though these products will most likely run "to spec," engineers are not in a position to anticipate every situation (Wulf, 2000).

How to engineer ethically when the objective risk of complex systems is a given? This is one of the central ethical challenges for engineering in the twenty-first century. The new century's most pressing ethical challenges concern the public commitment of the profession as a whole. The inherent unpredictability of technology's impact does not absolve the field of engineering from responsibility for the results of its creations.

Its public purposes, its contribution to human welfare, and its meaning in the context of the contemporary world are core commitments that define engineering as a profession. Out of these come a commitment to protecting public safety and the environment; acting with integrity in negotiating multiple, often conflicting, loyalties; and upholding standards of honest and responsible practice. Professionalism, in this comprehensive sense, is the foundation for engineering practice, the understanding and commitment that informs the engineer's use of knowledge and skills.

How do engineering programs prepare students to enter practice ready to draw on a solid understanding of professional concerns and behaviors—to use, in daily practice, honesty, responsibility, and fairness; to draw on solid understanding of and commitment to larger issues like environmental protection, safety, and the broad human impact of engineering work? As we describe in this part of the book, this dimension of professional preparation is the least realized, most outsourced, and least connected component in the linear components model so prevalent in U.S. undergraduate engineering education.

However, this condition of understanding and commitment—variously called *professionalism*, *professional responsibility*, and *ethics*—is what ABET requires accredited engineering programs to educate their students toward. ABET's general statement of the goals for education in ethics, developed in 1997, reflects the kind of broad conception of this domain that we believe is needed: graduates must have "an understanding of professional and ethical responsibility, broad education necessary to understand the impact of engineering solutions in a global and societal context, recognition of the need for and ability to engage in life-long learning, and knowledge of contemporary issues" (ABET, 2007).

In this section, we invite the reader to consider a set of goals for preparing engineering students to become responsible professionals, with understanding and commitment central to their concept of practice. Along the way, we introduce examples of effective practice from a variety of engineering programs—some among those we visited, others elsewhere in the United States. As we describe the kinds of education for professionalism and ethics that we saw in our site visits, we ask the reader to consider how this central aspect of engineering practice can be made a more central component in engineering education.

16

A FOUNDATION FOR PROFESSIONAL PRACTICE

THERE IS NO DOUBT that faculty understand that ethical behavior is part of an engineer's work. For some it is synonymous with engineering practice. As one faculty member explained, "What it means to be a professional engineer includes at least two things ... One, to recognize that engineers are members of a community, that they just can't act alone... There are boundary conditions on making money, and as a professional you don't just do everything that you're asked to do; you're not just a hired gun. The second thing is that you're not just a lone hired gun; you have a responsibility not just to the professional society, but to society as a whole. And that the professional organization as a whole has an obligation to society."

Some faculty affirmed their responsibility to make students aware of ethical issues, as reflected in the words of the following professor: "Leading engineers within the profession and the professional societies and ABET have increasingly seen the importance of professional ethics; public responsibility; the priority of public health, safety, and welfare in the engineering code of ethics. And within the profession, that's more and more important, and it's our job, it seems to me, as educators, to help students see that."

In our surveys and conversations, both faculty and students talked about engineers' need to design products keeping in mind potential benefits to humanity and the environment. As students told us, "An engineer uses his or her skills to benefit mankind. There are lots of ethical decisions involved, including how close to cut the factor of safety and using this steel beam that costs less versus another one that costs more" and "An engineer must be able to think inside and outside of the box. And must think beyond now and about the future and everyone around you. Sustainability is important. An engineer must address broad concerns."

In spite of the importance of ethical behavior and reasoning expressed by those we interviewed, the ABET requirement related to ethics has probably been the most difficult for engineering faculty—and students—to come to terms with (see Herkert, 1999; Shimmel, 1999; see student outcome requirements at ABET, 2007, p. 2). Engineering educators do not dispute the importance of acting ethically. However, they face difficulties related to (1) defining the academy's role in promoting ethical responsibility and (2) figuring out how to effectively design and integrate ethics into the engineering program.

Macro- and Microethical Dimensions of Practice

Like a number of people in the field of engineering ethics who have adopted an expansive conception of professionalism and ethics in engineering, Joseph Herkert has called for engineering ethics education to address a broad range of concerns. Acknowledging the importance of individuals' exercising moral responsibility in their professional decisions, Herkert suggests that this essential *microethical* dimension should not cause us to lose sight of the *macroethical* dimensions of engineering practice—issues that relate to the responsibilities of the profession and individuals in their roles as members of the profession: public policy questions, the institutional and political dimensions of engineering practice, and problems of "collective professional responsibility and the role of engineers as ... citizens" (Herkert, 1999). Even if graduates are not expected to move into positions that involve policy formulation or other direct macroethical decision making, the larger perspective provides an important context that should play a role in shaping many aspects of microethical professional responsibility.

Similarly, Nicholas Steneck argues that engineered products should be considered not abstractly, but rather in terms of their relationship to people and the environment, which give those objects their social and economic meaning and human relevance. Engineering is thus the process of designing and producing objects or systems that "affect the ways humans live and interact" (Steneck, 1999). In this view, engineering professionalism is central to the meaning and purpose of the discipline and its everyday practice.

How salient the various aspects of professionalism will be at any given time and their significance for the engineer depends on the kind of work, the institutional context, and the engineer's role within that context. The relevance of larger issues of public safety or environmental impact, for example, varies. Engineers in the first stages of their careers will likely be in roles with little autonomy or responsibility for decision making. Yet personal integrity, honesty, and reliability are very important in every situation and role.

Providing a Broad, Solid Base

Despite these limitations on most recent graduates' decision-making responsibility, engineering students need to be prepared for the full range of issues within a broad conception of professionalism. It is not possible to predict the roles they will assume over time, so it is best to provide a background that will support many different positions. Some will eventually assume leadership roles in industry, government, the military, or professional organizations. In fact, many engineering schools are quite vocal in claiming that they educate future leaders, though surely they do not expect their graduates to step into institutional leadership roles immediately on graduation. This focus on leadership has implications for the teaching of professionalism, because the full array of professionalism issues, from personal integrity to a grasp of the broad social implications of engineering work, is crucial for responsible and inspiring leadership.

Other graduates become entrepreneurs at some point in their careers. For these individuals, an understanding of the social, historical, and cultural contexts of their work, as well as the technical and business contexts, is essential for fostering the imagination and vision they will need to become successful entrepreneurs. Among other things, entrepreneurs need the ability to understand social trends and the complex, interlocking social, economic, and political forces that yield both opportunities for and challenges to new ventures. This requires a rich education that extends well beyond the technical.

"Citizen-Engineers"

Even those students who will not become institutional leaders or entrepreneurs can benefit from exposure to macroethical perspectives as well as microethics. Bella and Jenkins (1993) stress the important role of engineers who are employees of large organizations in helping to protect against misdirection. They observe that when engineers define their identities and responsibilities almost exclusively in terms of their immediate organizational roles—in which they focus all of their attention on completing the assignments immediately at hand, with no time or inclination for reflection—they can become functionaries who abdicate moral responsibility to the organization and are vulnerable to subtle pressures that can lead to distortions in judgment, potentially contributing to serious negative outcomes. Bella and Jenkins argue that the best safeguard against this common (and, in their view, dangerous) situation is to prepare students to become "citizen-engineers" who maintain a serious concern for the health, safety, and welfare of the public, even if these larger issues seem rather remote from their day-to-day work.

Identifying Learning Goals for Professionalism

ABET's guidelines do not specify particular curricular or other strategies to meet the requirements related to professionalism, except to say that there should be a general education component that "complements the technical content of the curriculum" (ABET, 2007, p. 3). How then might educators specify goals for this important dimension of engineering education?

There is a shared code of ethics for professional engineers (Engineers' Council for Professional Development, 1978), and many engineering specialties also have particular codes. Despite the differences among these codes, which reflect the issues that are most salient in each field, they share a set of central tenets or values: understanding the public purposes of engineering, its contribution to human welfare, and its meaning in the context of the contemporary world. These serve to organize more specific injunctions for responsibility to the public, competence, and accountability, such as commitment to protect public safety and the environment; to act with integrity in negotiating multiple, often conflicting, loyalties; and to uphold standards of honest and responsible practice.

We believe that codes of engineering ethics offer useful guidance in this task of defining goals for undergraduate engineering programs. Because ethics codes originate from within the profession, they outline the kinds of professional and ethical issues that practicing engineers in various specialties are likely to confront. For that reason, they can inform engineering educators about the kinds of issues and dilemmas that graduates should be prepared to handle, providing a useful template for educators who are designing and assessing programs that support professional responsibility and ethics in engineering.

However, the codes can be a valuable framework for helping educators think about educating for professionalism only if educators look below the surface of each provision, asking how students could be prepared to live and work according to that provision, what capacities and qualities are needed, and how engineering schools might educate toward them.

Core Values of the Profession: Competency, Responsibility, Accountability, and Fairness

All of the codes acknowledge the overall mission of the profession as contributing to human welfare. Accordingly, they articulate the overriding importance of competence, responsibility, accountability, and fairness. Stressing public safety, health, and welfare and protection of the environment, they call for engineers to be proactive in reporting violations and in working for the well-being of their communities.

The codes stress the responsibility to be competent in one's work, to be careful not to misrepresent one's competencies, and to continue building one's competence through continuing professional development. Other provisions extend honesty to all of the engineer's professional activities and call for loyalty to both employer and clients or customers, which includes acting in their best interests (as "faithful agents or trustees") and maintaining their confidentiality. Fairness includes respecting the intellectual property of others and avoiding conflicts of interest; discrimination based on race, gender, or religion; and unfair competition, which includes actions such as soliciting employment from clients who already have engineers under contract for the same work or offering gifts or other payments in order to secure work.

The codes thus specify numerous standards for ethical engineering practice, summarized as follows:

○ Understanding of the mission, social context, and policy implications of the field

○ Thoughtful and knowledgeable consideration of the potential impact of one's work on the environment and the public

○ Personal responsibility for the outcomes of one's work

○ Commitment to public welfare, even when it conflicts with one's economic interests

○ Substantive knowledge of the kinds of ethical challenges likely to arise in practice

○ Capacity to identify ethical issues that are embedded in complex and ambiguous situations

○ Judgment to understand and resolve conflicting loyalties and obligations

o Appreciation of the multiple perspectives on an issue and to negotiate a common understanding

o Wise judgment in the face of considerable uncertainty

o Creativity to develop win-win solutions when core values such as honesty and loyalty conflict with each other

More generic versions of many of these capacities are important for one's personal and civic life as well as for good engineering practice; helping students develop these qualities will serve them well, and their families, communities, and nation will also benefit from their preparation as thoughtful, responsible, and ethical people.

The first provision in virtually all codes of engineering ethics refers to the profession's responsibility to the public, which prominently includes the responsibility to contribute to human welfare and to protect public safety and the environment. This emphasis on public responsibility suggests that engineering schools should engage students in thoughtful discussions about the meaning of engineering and technology, including its social meaning and context. Most students arriving at college to study engineering have never thought about the place of the profession in the world, the history of technology's impact, its potential for human benefit and harm, and the field's complex relationships with other social processes and institutions. These issues relating to the broad public mission of engineering constitute an important cluster of goals within the broader rubric of professionalism.

Central emphases within the broader category of human welfare are the overriding values of public safety and protection of the environment. The American Society of Mechanical Engineers stipulates, as the first of its "Fundamental Canons," that "Engineers shall hold paramount the safety, health, and welfare of the public in the performance of their professional duties" (ASME, 2006, p. 1). Codes of engineering ethics make it clear that responsibility for public safety and welfare takes precedence over other obligations. For example, IEEE's code requires engineers to "disclose promptly factors that might endanger the public or the environment" (IEEE, 2006). Acting according to these priorities is seldom straightforward, though, because the public risks and benefits are unclear in most situations, and the immediate risks to the individual's career of "informing the proper authority" may be all too evident. The codes do not specify what kinds of responses are required, who the proper authority is likely to be, or when engineers, especially those who are not in leadership positions, are obliged to act. All of these issues need to be worked out within the particular situation and context in which the problem arose.

Teaching the Core Professional Values

Being prepared for engineering practice that is aligned with the spirit of these standards entails a wide array of abilities and qualities. Engineering education cannot, of course, fully prepare students to handle successfully the most difficult situations in which their work seems to entail risks to the public, but helping students to understand and deeply internalize the core values of safety, welfare, and environmental protection sensitizes them to these issues and flags the kinds of situation in which action may be necessary.

To be prepared to enter professional practice that embodies these values, students need a keen awareness of the potential risks of their work, both immediate and long-term, and experience grappling with trade-offs that often arise between safety or environmental protection and other considerations, such as cost. Toward that goal, they need help thinking about whether and how their responsibilities regarding safety and human welfare vary depending on their particular role in their workplace, and they need support in developing personal qualities like the courage needed to make and carry out difficult decisions.

The codes also make it clear that engineering competence is inseparable from the ethical dimensions of the work. Central commitments are to develop and maintain one's competence, to never claim competence one does not have, and to contribute to others' competence by providing opportunities for professional development of the engineers under their supervision. Thus it is important for faculty to convey to students that truly excellent work in engineering must include both technical and ethical dimensions: quality *is*, in essence, an ethical dimension of engineering, for the two are inseparable. As one faculty member we talked to said, "To do engineering is to undertake an ethical activity. I mean, you could sort of ignore it, but it's not possible to remove it. That's like saying, 'What if we just remove gravity?' Can't do that, right?"

Other aspects of the codes are similarly rich in implications for engineering education. The codes point out the engineer's accountability to various interested parties, including employers, clients, and the public. Given the prevalence of team projects in professional practice, students also need to develop a sense of responsibility, fairness, honesty, and loyalty toward their teammates and other coworkers. Managing these various loyalties and accountabilities is not always straightforward, however, because fidelity to and trusteeship for the individual's employer, teammates, or clients can conflict with each other and with the engineer's responsibility for public safety and welfare.

Understood in this way, the educational goals for preparing students for responsible professional practice are extensive and challenging, even if we acknowledge they cannot be fully achieved during the undergraduate years. An appropriate overarching educational goal, we believe, is to develop students' understanding that, as engineers, they affect the world; and because they affect the world, they must therefore be committed to developing and maintaining professional competence, exercising responsibility, being accountable, and acting fairly. With that goal in mind, we turn now to a description of what engineering schools are doing to support students' ethical-professional development.

17

FINDINGS FROM THE STUDY: AN UNEVEN BASE

AS WE HAVE NOTED ELSEWHERE, the teaching strategies, curricular arrangements, and assessment employed in a program carry powerful messages about what the faculty and, by extension, the profession consider important. For this reason, we focused particularly on the "how" as well as the "what" of attention to professionalism in undergraduate engineering education. In this chapter, as we discuss our findings, we ask the reader to consider students' current opportunities to develop a base of understanding and commitment that guides them as they enter practice and whether they are sufficiently prepared to continue deepening that understanding and commitment throughout their careers.

Curricular Strategies

Although engineering programs vary in the extensiveness and depth of their attention to professionalism and ethics, they share a small set of curricular strategies, from planned or spontaneous classroom discussion in engineering courses to modules on ethics as part of an engineering course, stand-alone courses in the engineering program, and required courses in the liberal arts.

In engineering science and technical courses, design courses, and labs, faculty incorporate discussions of professionalism and ethics, most often references to public safety, whenever they arise naturally in connection with the topic at hand. These discussions range from a brief mention of a well-known case of engineering failure to classroom or homework exercises in which students grapple with trade-offs between potentially conflicting values such as cost and safety.

Some programs provide modules on engineering professionalism and ethics, typically consisting of two or three class sessions, most often in the capstone design course. Ethics modules are sometimes included in other design courses and freshman "introduction to engineering" courses; they provide more extensive coverage of ethics and professionalism than the relatively brief references to these topics in engineering science and technical courses.

Stand-alone courses in engineering ethics offered as part of the engineering curriculum by the engineering faculty may have a concentration-specific focus ("Ethical Issues in Electrical Engineering" or "Engineering Ethics and Public Policy") or general focus ("Ethical Issues in Engineering" or "Technology and Contemporary Society"). Some programs require students to take broadly focused courses on ethics or moral philosophy through the college or university's philosophy department. Students might choose one course from several options in philosophy or another discipline that offers courses relating to ethics.

Key Issues in the Classroom

Whether as part of courses or modules or through spontaneous attention to ethical issues, we noted that discussion of the broad public mission of engineering and the profession's ethics codes is an element of most, though not all, of the programs we studied. However, the depth of teaching about professionalism-ethics and the codes varies a great deal, and unfortunately it appears to be fairly minimal in most programs. In one program we studied, for example, the IEEE code was distributed at an orientation lecture along with other program-related materials, with no evidence that it received any comment. In another program, students were referred to codes of ethics on the Web sites of professional societies.

Faculty who introduce the codes generally comment on their importance and (particularly those faculty with industry experience) point out the potentially disastrous results violations can have for individuals' careers, for their firms' credibility, and for the public. One student, a senior who had already begun working, told us, "A few classes, less than five, touched on ethics. I think this topic should be worked into the program more. The consequences were not apparent to me before going into the work environment. You can really ruin your career."

Although fairness is represented in engineering codes of ethics, this important ethical principle is seldom addressed explicitly in engineering education. Discussions of academic integrity offer an opportunity to talk about fairness as well as honesty, but our study indicated that few faculty make this connection. Fairness can also come up in the context of team projects, which are commonplace in design courses. If handled well, team projects and the teaching of teamwork skills can highlight, in an immediate and compelling way, the importance of reliability, a sense of responsibility, loyalty to and concern for the group, fairness in distribution of burdens and rewards, and mutual respect and consideration among team members. These issues are often implicit in team-based activities, but they are seldom raised to a level of explicit concern.

Although most faculty members we spoke to acknowledged that they do not introduce codes of ethics in their own courses, they were confident that students learned about these codes in other courses. Sometimes faculty members identified the course in which they believed the code was covered, but in a number of cases we learned that, in fact, ethics codes were not covered in that course. Even in those programs in which students are not routinely exposed to ethical codes, many faculty thought that they were.

Notably, engineering codes of ethics are almost never presented in the courses outside the engineering department that are used to satisfy the engineering ethics requirement. If a department relies entirely on those courses for coverage of ethics, its students could graduate without having been exposed to an engineering ethics code.

At the other end of the spectrum, we saw programs in which students applied codes of ethics to case studies in graded assignments. For example, students might be required to write a paper identifying the relevance of one or more professional codes to a specific situation or to present a case focusing on the ethical issues involved, as represented in the code for that field. We observed mechanical engineering student teams at Mines, for example, presenting cases that explored the conflict between commitment to consumer safety and loyalty to one's employer. At Georgia Tech, mechanical engineering students grapple with real-life cases involving violations of the engineering codes. These types of cases often generate considerable interest and trigger lively discussions among students. As one senior observed, "A lot of times people changed their minds after the discussion and decided they were wrong. I think that is important and shows that [the decisions] are not all common sense. It makes you look into the problem in more depth, and realize that the answer is not obvious." As the students began to examine the subtleties and complexities of the cases, they began to see that the obvious answer, often based on common sense, is not always the appropriate response for the situation.

Some faculty members make a particular effort to convey to students how important it is for the practicing engineer to maintain firm connections with the basic mission and broad impact of the work. As we discuss in the final chapter of this part of the book, when taught with this goal in mind, both domestic and international service learning and extracurricular service projects reinforce students' desire to use their work to contribute to human welfare. These experiences can also expose students to the complexities of contemporary social problems and policy issues, if the supervising faculty use reflection to connect the service projects to these issues.

This conception of professionalism is what we refer to earlier as the macroethical dimension of engineering. Herkert points to the challenges of supporting students' learning of macroethics and advocates the integration of engineering instruction with curricular programs in science, technology, and society (STS), when practically feasible, to integrate technique with the social meaning and broader ethical context of engineering practice (Herkert, 2002).

However, this does not seem to be a common practice. Although we encountered some attention to macroethical issues in the engineering departments we studied, few engineering schools or departments have instituted systematic programs to educate for this broad sense of professionalism. Most engineering students do not participate in STS programs or service learning, and engineering ethics is seldom taught with this kind of scope.

Our impression that the broad public purposes and implications of engineering receive relatively little attention in engineering education is consistent with other published reviews of teaching practices in engineering ethics. Kipnis (1981), for example, surveyed the literature on engineering ethics and found that most texts limited the scope of "concern for public welfare" to the important but narrower concept of the public's immediate safety. Other studies (for example, Little, Hink, and Barney, 2008) have reported similar findings.

The level of attention given to ethics in the engineering curriculum and classroom points to a general lack of attention to students' professional formation. Through our site visits, surveys, and study of the literature, we found that faculty touch on a wide range of professional issues but give significant attention only to three: public safety, environmental impact, and honesty.

Public Safety

The engineer's responsibility for ensuring public safety is universally acknowledged as a key issue and is the topic most likely to be mentioned by faculty who incorporate ethical concerns into their analysis, lab, and design courses, as well as by those who teach courses or modules specifically addressing engineering professionalism and ethics. As one design professor said, "I spend the first couple of weeks in graphics lecturing on design and the process and safety, which from an engineering standpoint ... safety is 50 to 60 percent of ethics."

A faculty member described how he draws students' attention to the implications for human safety of precision in solving analytical problems:

> I stress loss of life. I say to them not to fudge the numbers. Two periods ago about 75 to 80 percent of the students got the wrong answer on a problem ... What happened was that the answers in the back of the book shifted over one column. It was a typographical error. But the students took the answer (which was wrong) and worked backwards to figure the problem. So of course they were wrong. I gave them all a zero. I told them, "Solve the problem your way. If you're wrong, you're wrong. Don't rely on someone else's answers. Otherwise, you're going to kill someone." That always gets their attention. It happens so much in industry.

Students affirm the emphasis on safety: "This is one thing I could say about being a student here: from the beginning, from freshman year, they've always stressed ethics and public safety as two very key factors you must consider as an engineer."

Environmental Impact

It is increasingly common for courses in design to address energy conservation, alternative energy sources, use of hazardous materials, and recycling of materials from obsolete products. Attention to these issues helps students understand that their work has real consequences for the world. Understanding that their actions and designs have consequences for others and for the environment increases students' awareness that in becoming engineers they are taking on important responsibilities.

Honesty

We noted some particular examples of how faculty introduce the issue of honesty. As academics, many faculty, when asked about ethical issues, think first of academic integrity, and many say they incorporate ethical issues into their classrooms by talking with students about the academic honor code, plagiarism, and other kinds of cheating. As one electrical engineering department chair pointed out, referring to the university's honor code and what it means to comply with it provides an opportunity to talk about ethics in every course. Research that shows the high prevalence of cheating among engineering students and the predictive value of that cheating for dishonesty in the workplace underscores the importance of this set of issues (McCabe, 1997; Harding, Carpenter, Finelli, and Passow, 2004; Finelli, Harding, Carpenter, and Mayhew, 2007).

Questions of academic integrity for students often lead naturally to ethical issues that arise in professional academic work, such as questions of authorship in publications and other aspects of intellectual property. These issues are close to the actual experience of many faculty, and they often feel better qualified to speak about them than about topics from industry, which may be remote from their experience. In addition to questions of honesty and fairness that arise in publishing and other domains of intellectual property, faculty can discuss their sense of accountability to the university and the students, describing (1) occasions on which they have confronted situations of potential conflict of interest in consulting work, and (2) conflicts between personal loyalties and larger concerns that arise in university business.

The same or related issues can arise in industry, and faculty who have experience working in those settings often connect academic integrity issues with related issues that come up in industry. Students need to understand, as one design professor said, "that you give and take credit where it is due. Being from industry, I talk about the ethics of patents and disclosures."

Other faculty stress the importance of honesty as a precondition for high-quality engineering work. For example, a laboratory instructor points out the role that scrupulous honesty plays: "The most obvious way it works ... is the issue of data entry and reporting the result that they actually get. [The students] want to get the textbook answer, and they don't get the textbook answer with a real system and real setup. 'So, this is what you really got, and that is what you want to report. Now it's time, as an engineer, to talk about why you got the results that you did and to reflect on what caused your system to behave that way.' That clearly has implications in terms of ethics."

Observed Pedagogy: The Case Study

For the teaching of engineering ethics, the dominant pedagogy is the case study, whether used in a stand-alone ethics course in engineering or philosophy, an ethics module within another course, or a brief, spontaneous reference to ethical or professionalism issues in the context of an analysis, lab, or design course (Herkert, 2001). We saw that in addition to cautionary cases of well-known disasters, faculty use real cases from practice as well as hypothetical cases to present moral dilemmas as problems for students to work through.

Cautionary Cases

Historical cases such as the Hyatt Regency walkway collapse and the space shuttle *Challenger* disaster are often discussed briefly in the context of lectures in analysis and design courses. These cases illustrate the importance of care, technical precision, and honesty; what can go wrong when these standards are compromised; and how serious the consequences can be. When examples like this are threaded throughout the program, they impress on students the value of public safety and the connection between technical competence and human consequences.

Because safety is mentioned frequently in many programs, students come to see it as a central concern or core value of the field. If the cases are vivid and well told, they can be emotionally engaging and powerfully memorable. As one student said, "In our dynamics class we had an incredible section on ethics. We were talking about SUVs and rollover and all that. That had a big impact on me." Because analysis faculty understand the technical dimensions of these cases and because they are accustomed to working examples into their lectures, this approach to using cases is accessible to a wide range of faculty, including those who know little or nothing about ethical theory.

A limitation of this approach is that it does not require students to struggle with the kinds of trade-offs that engineering decisions require or with the fact that the consequences of those decisions become clear only in retrospect, so these cases may not show how difficult judgment and choice can be. For that reason, they are not sufficient for helping students learn to identify potential issues and problems before they become obvious or to sort through conflicting priorities.

New Points of View and Moral Dilemmas

Some faculty use both real and hypothetical cases, along with more active pedagogies, to take on these challenges. Howard University professor Taft Broome uses hypothetical cases to show students how much they take for granted. In one exercise, he asks students to think about how to design products for small, undeveloped villages where electricity is not available.

In others, he integrates questions about values into hypothetical analytical problems to show how different values assumptions can affect numerical results. As he explains, "I've got some hardcore problems where a student has to make a value judgment—both answers can be correct—but the student has to make that ethical choice before he or she chooses what equations to use." He offers this example:

> You work for a company that has a fleet of trucks that are going to carry loads. You have to find a braking system for the trucks. You have two choices: brakes that will stop real fast, very uncomfortable, or brakes that stop slowly and smoothly, comfortably; they cost the same. If the driver of a truck using the first set puts on the brakes at sixty miles an hour, the load will shift, break his back, and kill him, costing your company $1 million. If they use the slower brakes, the shifting load will not kill the driver, but will break his back and put him in a wheelchair and cost the company $3 million. Which braking system do you use? Before you answer that problem, you've got to make that choice.

As Broome explains, "forcing the student to talk about it in public is the educational part of that process ... It's a classical problem in every textbook, but it doesn't put the broken back and the insurance costs in there."

Hypothetical cases like this are usually short on details and context and thus much simpler than the problems students will actually encounter in their work. Although faculty using them would be well advised to address this directly with their students, active engagement with simple cases like this, despite their evident artificiality, does help students experience conflicts between values such as safety and affordability and the challenge of making this kind of trade-off.

Wrestling with cases framed as moral dilemmas—either real or hypothetical—is also a staple of ethics courses offered through philosophy departments. A philosophy course at Georgia Tech, "Ethical Theories," is typical in its emphasis on teaching classical ethical theories, such as utilitarianism and deontology, and on asking students to apply those theories to contemporary problems. Students are required to demonstrate their facility in applying these frameworks both in class discussions and on quizzes. In part because the course is offered at an institute of technology, the professor places particular emphasis on issues of concern to science and technology. However, in colleges and universities that are not centered on technology, this substantive relevance to engineering is less likely to be present.

Developing Professionalism Through Service Learning

Although the case study is the primary mode of teaching engineering ethics, in recent years service learning has become an increasingly important pedagogical approach in engineering. Like their colleagues in other fields, engineering faculty have begun to use service learning to foster a number of important professionalism outcomes, including a sense of social and professional responsibility, ethical awareness and sophistication, and skill in negotiating the contexts of engineering work, including intercultural contexts both domestically and internationally (Tsang, 2000).

In service learning, students participate in organized, sustained service activity that is related to their classroom learning and meets identified community needs. Students then reflect on that experience through activities such as class discussions or journal writing, articulating what they have learned about the social issues connected with their projects or the cultural, economic, or policy contexts of the work. A number of studies have shown that students who participate in high-quality service learning benefit both academically and civically (see Eyler and Giles, 1999; Pascarella and Terenzini, 2005; Sax and Astin, 1997).

In engineering education, service learning is essentially an arrangement and context for design experiences. In a typical service-learning project, students design a product to meet an identified need in a low-income community or to help individuals in special populations. For example, these projects might create products for the disabled, such as improved wheelchairs or page-turning devices for quadriplegics. This often involves establishing collaborative relationships with local non-profit organizations that serve a variety of community needs.

International Service Learning

A growing number of engineering schools sponsor international service-learning programs, with student projects serving communities in developing countries around the world. These international experiences can be very valuable introductions to global issues such as economic development and intercultural differences.

At Harvey Mudd College, for example, students in the freshman engineering design course create products for poor rural villagers in Central America. In 1995, Harvey Mudd developed a relationship with a humanitarian group that has been working with a village in Guatemala for more than twenty years. This group acts as a liaison between the students and the village, teaching students about the needs of the local community, the nature of locally available materials, and other design constraints for their projects.

Using readily available, inexpensive materials, students create simple devices to ease the burden of carrying supplies along rugged mountain paths, to store and distribute potable water, and to improve the energy efficiency of cooking, heating, and lighting. Students in the course not only learn the basics of design, but also experience a compelling example of how their work as engineers can contribute to human welfare. As one student said, "This course really gave me the impression that I'm doing something that has the potential to change something, as opposed to just memorizing the following ten equations."

Students can learn a great deal from experiences like this, particularly as globalization escalates. However, international service-learning programs have some serious pitfalls that need to be addressed from the outset. Faculty who facilitate cross-national service have long been aware of the risks entailed in short visits to or engagements with poor countries by middle-class American students who have little real understanding of the local culture. In engineering, the risk of unintended consequences may be even greater than in some other disciplines, because projects may introduce technologies with significant impact on the local way of life. Developing long-term relationships with communities and liaison organizations can help mitigate these risks. In the Harvey Mudd course, students' interactions with the Guatemalan village are guided and informed by the intermediary humanitarian group that has come to understand the local situation well, having worked in that particular village for a long time.

Preparing for Service

Whether the site is domestic or international, students must be well prepared prior to their community engagement. Recognizing how acutely important this is, some institutions require students to take a course or mini-course that addresses the many complexities of community engagement before they participate in service learning.

At Smith College, Professor Donna Riley prepares students for international work. Her project-based course introduces students to the technological, cultural, and policy aspects of international development (Howe and others, 2007). Students discuss the promises and limitations of technology for development, along with related issues concerning globalization, the legacies of colonialism, and the relationships between privileged American students and the recipients of their work. Such preparation increases the chances that the service projects will be mutually beneficial and is also, in itself, an extremely valuable learning experience.

Service learning can be used at any point in the undergraduate engineering curriculum. Clearly, the projects in the freshman course at Harvey Mudd are technically much simpler than those carried out in senior design courses, the typical site of service learning. Some programs even provide participating students with a long-term, sustained service-learning experience over the course of their undergraduate years.

The best-known multiyear service-learning program is EPICS, mentioned in Chapter Fifteen, which is now a national program with eighteen participating universities. EPICS emphasizes a wide array of design, management, organizational, and communications skills, as well as community awareness and professional ethics. Student teams carry out long-term service projects over as many as seven semesters. Each project team, charged with delivering a system to a partnering community service agency, must field a prototype, train community partner representatives in use of the system, collect feedback, and make any reasonable changes requested by the partner.

Both students and faculty receive course credit for participating in EPICS. In addition, these programs require support personnel, laboratory space and equipment, and hardware and software (for prototype development and use off campus). Participating institutions see this significant investment of resources as cost-effective because the program has such a powerful impact on many valuable learning outcomes, including technical, design, teamwork, and communication skills, as well as understanding of the social contexts and meaning of engineering work and a commitment to engineering for the public good.

18

PREPARING FOR NEW-CENTURY PROFESSIONAL PRACTICE

ALTHOUGH WE SAW EXAMPLES of effective teaching for ethics and professionalism in the engineering programs we visited and reviewed, we also became aware of some important limitations on the effort to make the ethical dimension a central part of professional practice. Chief among these is faculty skepticism and misunderstanding, reflected in the piecemeal approach to ethics in the curriculum and the way in which student learning is assessed—which, we believe, supports student skepticism and apathy toward ethics. In our view, these represent notable opportunities for growth in programmatic effectiveness with regard to professionalism and ethics. Thus we close this part with a look at a variety of ways in which engineering programs approach the understanding of and commitment to professionalism. As we describe them, we ask the reader to consider how professionalism in practice might be made central, rather than peripheral to engineering education.

Faculty Attitudes About Ethics

Perhaps the most glaring weakness of the current state of education for engineering professionalism is the widespread lack of enthusiasm for this agenda among faculty and students. Our research makes it clear that many engineering faculty have not thought much about their program's responsibility for ethical-professional preparation, and many are skeptical of the feasibility and legitimacy of the undertaking.

Skepticism

When asked whether they believe it is important to teach for ethical development, faculty often reply that ethical choices in the profession are driven primarily by the individual's underlying moral character, which they assume is established in childhood, mostly by family experiences, and quite fixed by the time students reach higher education. This leads them to deny that professional ethics can be learned in the course of higher education, except in a fairly trivial sense. Many believe that it cannot be taught in any real sense at all, as this faculty member argued: "As far as ethics, I don't know what is taught here. And I don't remember if I had a course in ethics. Even if I did, it would not have altered that much. Ethics comes from inside."

Engineering students often share the faculty's skepticism about the importance and feasibility of educating for ethical development. We heard sentiments like these on a number of campuses: "Ethics is something you have to have on your own. You really cannot teach ethics," and "I don't want to have a class that I have to pay for and sit there and talk about how to be a decent human being or a decent employee for a company. . . . I think that's kind of a waste of units." Another student commented, "Our degree is about the technical stuff. Someone in industry on the job will tell us if something is an OK thing to do."

Misunderstanding

Misunderstanding of what it would mean to educate for ethical maturity is also widespread. Some faculty wish to stay away from teaching ethics because they see it as punishing students who exhibit poor character. As one said, "I am not a policeman, finding out their sins. I emphasize safety . . . [but] I don't consider that we, as professors, should have to act as police. I don't feel that this is my responsibility."

Another common misunderstanding (one also shared by educators in a number of other fields) is that educating for ethical development is nothing more than preaching a simple view of the difference between right and wrong. Granted, "preaching to students" is unlikely to result in the important qualities of professionalism we have outlined here. However, "preaching" is far from the only option for fostering the broad array of abilities that engineers need—as professionals and as citizens. The maturity, expertise, sophistication, and wisdom needed for true professionalism are neither established, for better or worse, early in life nor teachable through preaching. They require education for deep understanding, along with practice, experience, and the ongoing ability to learn from experience.

Social science research supports our conviction that these capacities can be learned in late adolescence and early adulthood. In fact, the undergraduate years are a prime opportunity to foster students' ethical development, especially—though not exclusively—for those who enter college right after high school, as do most engineering majors. All of the major developmental theorists point to this period, which is often considered to represent the transition to adulthood, as a time of great moral exploration, ferment, and consolidation (see Erikson, 1968; Perry, 1968; Kohlberg, 1973). As we note in Chapter Three, it is a moment for important cognitive development.

At this time in their lives, young people question their ethical, social, and personal assumptions, make critical career and other life choices, and rethink their sense of who they are and what is important to them. There could hardly be a time more ripe for ethical growth. If engineering schools are to take advantage of this developmental opportunity, they will need to help faculty understand better what teaching for professionalism means, why it is important, and how to do it. The faculty can then work to dispel the misunderstanding and skepticism of students regarding these important developmental opportunities.

The Powerful Message of Assessment

Adding to the powerful message sent by faculty skepticism, we noted, is an equally powerful one that learning about ethics does not count. Outside of stand-alone courses and modules, assignments related to the ethical dimensions of engineering are less likely to be graded than other assignments, and students often are not held accountable for learning this material. This is a problem. The practice of not grading this work, or treating it as pass/fail with little effort required to pass, sends a message that ethical issues are not important and that standards of quality do not apply to the explication of those issues.

Because many engineering faculty perceive the work involved in ethics modules and courses as essentially subjective and personal, they are baffled by what it would mean to establish standards of quality against which it can be assessed. In fact, it is quite possible to do this, as indicated by the fact that humanities faculty routinely assess this kind of student work, offering evaluations and feedback on how to strengthen the work. This does not mean that there is one clear set of right answers to ethical questions. Just as with design, there are many possible good solutions to an ethical problem, as well as many poor solutions. When students are writing papers or making oral presentations, their work can be evaluated: Have they demonstrated an understanding of multiple factors to be considered? Made a credible case for their position? Spelled out the likely consequences of several alternatives? These and similar questions can form the basis of assessments.

The Powerful Message of the Curriculum

Given the misunderstandings about education for professionalism and the limited enthusiasm for it shown by both faculty and students, it is no wonder that this dimension of students' preparation is weaker than others. Some program leaders carefully think through their strategies for supporting student learning in this area and carry them through during the entire duration of undergraduate study. However, that kind of broad, intentional approach to teaching for ethics and professionalism is relatively rare. Few departments establish explicit goals in this area or monitor and coordinate coverage. In only one case that we observed, a design course, are faculty members required to present their proposed ethics coverage to a departmental committee for approval.

It is commonplace for faculty, even department chairs, to be unaware of whether or how their program supports its students' ethical development. Nor is it especially unusual for programs to claim more coverage in their ABET self-study documents than is evident on a closer look. In one program, for example, ethics is described in the ABET document as among the course objectives for freshman and senior mechanical engineering courses, but when we interviewed the professor who teaches the courses, he said that he does not cover ethics.

From our campus visits, a picture emerged of rather spotty and unsystematic attention to students' professional or ethical learning. In two programs, ethics coverage seemed to be almost entirely unplanned. The program assumed that ethical issues would arise spontaneously in some courses, but there was no effort to ensure that this happened. In five programs, we noted, students encounter sustained consideration of professionalism and ethical issues only once, most often in relatively brief modules or in an ethics course taken outside the department. Four programs made education for ethics and professionalism a higher priority, addressing them in a planned way in more than one course or module. Even for these, ethical-professional learning was likely to be present only in the first and last years. Serious attention to ethics in the freshman year was unusual, and many efforts to provide some early exposure to these issues were fleeting—typically a single lecture, with no accompanying assignment.

Taken as a whole, courses that address engineering ethics in some way touch on many of the issues represented in the professional codes of ethics, whether or not the codes themselves are discussed. Unfortunately, most students experience a rather small subset of those issues. Only a few of the programs we reviewed ensured that students experience comprehensive coverage of the many issues that are represented in the aggregate. Furthermore, since most departments do not track ethics coverage, they have no way of knowing how comprehensive their students' ethical-professionalism education is.

A National Issue

Empirical studies of education for ethics in engineering suggest that the programs in our study are not unusual: students often fail to receive strong support for their development in this domain. Robert McGinn, professor of engineering at Stanford University, reports survey data that indicate significant gaps between the ethical realities of engineering practice and preparation for those realities in engineering schools. Participants in his survey of practicing engineers say that they regularly face ethical issues in their work, but most feel they were not adequately prepared to handle those issues. There is virtually unanimous belief among the practitioners that meaningful discussion of ethical issues should be integrated into formal engineering education. McGinn concluded that "practicing engineers 'in the field' apparently feel more strongly about the desirability of such integration than do most engineering faculty or engineering school deans" (McGinn, 2003, p. 528).

In an accompanying survey of engineering students, McGinn found that almost all students expect to face ethical issues in their future practice, but fewer than one third say they have discussed an ethical issue in an engineering course other than those devoted specifically to engineering ethics. Most students who said they encountered ethical issues in nonethics courses did so within the university's program on science, technology, and society. Many students report that they believe it is as important to be "professional" as it is to be technically expert, but only a small percentage said they had learned anything specific from their engineering courses about what this entails (McGinn, 2003).

To our knowledge, no studies directly measure undergraduate students' growth toward the specific dimensions that define professional-ethical maturity, as we have described it here. However, research on the impact of college more generally suggests that studying engineering at the under-graduate level does not seem to foster these qualities. In fact, this research shows that on several relevant outcomes engineering students look quite different from students in other majors.

The most comprehensive research in this area has been conducted by the Higher Education Research Institute at the University of California, Los Angeles. In his highly regarded book, *What Matters in College? Four Critical Years Revisited*, Alexander Astin (1993) reports the results of a study that followed students from freshman through senior year. After reviewing the effects of various college experiences, Astin concludes that "engineering produces more significant effects on student outcome than any other major field" (p. 371). Majoring in engineering is correlated with students' achievement on the GRE quantitative test and their self-reported growth in analytic and problem-solving skills and job-related skills, for example. Not surprisingly, it is also correlated with the likelihood of pursuing an engineering career.

These positive correlations come at a cost. Engineering majors express the least satisfaction with their college experience. They are also more likely than any other majors to graduate believing that (1) the chief benefit of college is to increase their earnings potential, (2) individuals cannot change society, and (3) it is not important to develop a meaningful philosophy of life. Relative to other majors, being an engineering major is also correlated with being less committed to promoting racial understanding and less likely to describe oneself as socially concerned or altruistic.

A More Effective Approach

These data suggest that undergraduate engineering programs would be well advised to increase the priority given to students' professional-ethical development. Although not consistently realized in most programs, many valuable elements of a more effective approach are already present. To reach the next level of impact, these elements need to be expanded, connected with each other, and implemented more systematically.

Further Integration of Ethics with Practice Experiences

Throughout this report, we have argued that organizing undergraduate engineering around professional practice would enhance the usability of the knowledge students gain as well as strengthen their design and other engineering skills and integrate their knowledge and skills. Our review of attention to ethics-professionalism has convinced us that increasing the emphasis on professional practice could also lead to deeper, more transformative development of students' understanding of the social and ethical dimensions of engineering.

Almost all of the programs we reviewed include ethical considerations in the capstone design courses, through ethics modules. Thus the coverage of ethical issues is immediately useful in helping students think about their own design projects. However, modules of this kind vary a great deal in the degree to which they lead to a thorough integration of ethical-professional issues with students' design and other practice experiences. The more thorough this integration is, the more likely the experience is to result in greater sensitivity to ethical issues and ingrained habits of ethical behavior as well as shifts in the way students understand engineering work and their own roles and responsibilities as engineers.

Ethics modules within capstone design courses are not the only way to integrate ethics into engineering practice, however. If structured carefully, many activities that address technical learning goals can also support professionalism and ethics, as they do in EPICS and other high-quality service learning programs. Both curricular and extracurricular activities can support this integration as long as they entail engagement with complex tasks that require technical skills, interpersonal capacities, and multiple dimensions of professionalism. Wherever engineering students are engaging with the practice of engineering—whether it be design courses, co-op experiences, summer or part-time engineering work, or project-focused extracurricular activities—they can progress in professional and ethical development as well as technical ability if these are made explicit goals that receive serious faculty attention.

Effective Use of Ethics Courses

Although ethical issues can and should be integrated into a wide range of courses on other topics, it is important to complement this integrative approach with courses that give sustained attention to ethics and professionalism. Engineering ethics courses can deepen students' understanding of ethical issues they are likely to confront, especially when faculty use active pedagogies. Often these courses cover a wide array of issues that may not otherwise be addressed, including the kinds of ordinary conflicts and challenges that can come up in the daily life of practicing engineers.

Courses in moral philosophy outside the engineering program can also contribute to students' ethical development as well as to their intellectual breadth and sophistication more generally. These courses teach students useful ethical concepts such as principles of justice and human welfare and how to apply them to cases. They also give students practice thinking about moral conflicts: seeing that there are multiple considerations in these cases; that positive values often conflict with each other; and that, although there are no easy answers, some formulations and rationales are more credible and better argued than others.

Despite these benefits, relying on general philosophy courses as students' only systematic exposure to ethics also carries risks. Especially when these courses are taught outside the school of engineering, students may not know how to connect what they learn to their own work, even if they do practice applying the theories to cases. If students are to take advantage of what they have learned, they have to be shown how to apply what they are learning to engineering problems and encouraged to practice making those applications themselves.

Another risk of relying on general philosophy courses to foster professionalism and the capacities needed for ethical and socially responsible engineering practice is that moral philosophy courses tend to focus more on learning philosophical theory than on teaching the skills of ethical problem solving. The process of ethical problem solving in real situations is usually quite different from working out what one or more theories would dictate when moral values or principles conflict. For example, classical approaches to teaching ethics tend to center on what has been called *quandary ethics*, the seemingly irresolvable conflicts that are of particular interest to many philosophers. To illuminate moral theory, philosophers' formulations of these very tough dilemmas tend to close off any possible loopholes so that the essential conflict of values cannot be avoided. In contrast, real-life ethical problem solving starts with serious and creative efforts to find solutions that will resolve the quandary without sacrificing either set of values—in essence, to create a win-win solution or find some common ground on which the contending parties can meet. For these reasons, we do not believe that general moral philosophy courses provide a strong enough basis for engineering professionalism and ethics to satisfy the ABET requirement in that domain. This is so in spite of the important contribution they can make to liberal learning for engineering students as well as for students in the arts and sciences.

Use of Heuristics

Analytic frameworks, or heuristics, to structure case analysis support the development of more mature thinking about cases that raise complex ethical issues. Learning to use heuristics can help students apply what they learn in class to cases they encounter in professional practice; even simple heuristics can be useful if students are guided in applying them to cases in a thoughtful way. In the ethics module of a capstone design course in the electrical engineering and computer science program at Michigan, for example, the module included a graded assignment in which students apply a heuristic that involves literally drawing the line between ethical and unethical behavior. The students discuss a wide range of ethical issues, including intellectual property, safety, and obligations to the employer. For example, the class debates the ethics surrounding hacking and the use of Napster to download free music. In a line-drawing exercise, students draw points on a spectrum between ethical and unethical behavior as they discuss the issues surrounding a case. Then the professor modifies the behavior being evaluated so that students need to rethink their judgments about where this new behavior falls on the spectrum, redrawing the point on the spectrum at which it falls.

The line-drawing exercise is just one of several heuristics this module uses to help students think about cases. The module culminates in oral presentations by student teams and a written assignment, "the ethics case study," in which students apply several of these heuristics. The students must summarize the scenario or case study assigned to the team, evaluate the situation from the perspective of two of the ethical theories presented in the module, apply the line-drawing technique discussed in class, and show how IEEE or Association for Computing Machines ethics codes apply to the scenario.

In the mechanical engineering program at Michigan, case studies built around engineering failures are introduced in a sophomore-level course and discussed in the context of another heuristic, a checklist of ethical concerns developed by Nicholas Steneck (2007). The checklist asks students to apply several ethical frameworks, a cost-benefit analysis, and decision-making standards in the areas of technological advancement, economic development, public health, public safety, and the environment. In their senior year, students revisit the same checklist of considerations and use it as a framework for thinking about historical engineering failure cases and about their own industry-sponsored design projects. Students weigh the importance of each criterion and then discuss, in a paper, the trade-offs they made as they carried out their capstone design projects.

In addition to Steneck's checklist, students in this and other courses practice applying codes of engineering ethics to historical cases and to their own design projects. Combining case discussions with consideration of the relevant codes is a useful way both to give students a structure for thinking about the cases and to bring the codes to their attention in a vivid way. When students actively work through the cases themselves, attempting to confront choices and consider the applicability of the ethical code, they come to a deeper understanding and appreciation of both the codes and the ethical issues that arise in engineering work.

Several students we interviewed said that applying ethical codes to real cases made clear to them that the codes cannot be applied in a mechanical way to solve ethical problems; that ethical questions and the guidelines for addressing them that are encapsulated in the codes are not just "common sense," as some students had assumed; and that many people reconsider their initial responses to ethical questions when they are given the opportunity to think them through more fully and to discuss them with others.

Faculty remarked that when students apply professional codes to historical cases, both the cases and the codes come to life in a more compelling way: "In an ethics module in a junior dynamics class that I taught, we went over professional codes of ethics, ethical responsibility of an engineer. We looked at case studies ... We looked at a [1967] B.F. Goodrich brake design in which the engineers falsified test data to get a government contract. And there was an engineer who was faced with being fired. This is the kind of situation an engineer could be faced with. We talked about 'What would you do?' ... we went over the ASME code of ethics, which some students didn't know existed."

Institutional Intentionality and Attention

Although strong curricular continuity in ethics coverage does not appear to be typical in engineering education, some programs do achieve a notable degree of coherence in this domain (see, for example, Gharabagi, 2007). We encountered several programs that introduce ethics modules and other means of paying attention to professionalism and ethics as early as the freshman year and that maintain continuity of emphasis on these issues throughout the undergraduate years. This is clearly a more powerful way to influence the development of students' professionalism than relying entirely on a brief module in the senior year. Ethics coverage in these programs typically begins with freshman-year introduction to engineering courses and continues with courses that stress ethical issues in the context of analysis, laboratory, and design.

One of the strong freshman-year courses with a focus on engineering professionalism we encountered is "Nature and Human Values" at Mines. This course is intended to help students learn to identify themselves as professionals with responsibilities to society and the environment. The instructors, from different engineering disciplines, each bring different strengths. From these multiple perspectives, all of the participating instructors address questions of how nature affects humans and how humans affect nature. This four-credit course represents both ethics and technical writing in the curriculum. The connection of these two learning goals is significant. Faculty we spoke to at Mines talked of their efforts to thread ethics throughout the curriculum in a way that parallels their earlier work in weaving writing through the curriculum.

Michigan also introduces its first year students to a broad range of ethical issues through its freshman introduction to engineering course. This is followed by courses in subsequent years that pay particular attention to ethics, culminating in a fairly extensive ethics module in field-specific capstone design. The mechanical engineering capstone course we visited gives significant attention to fostering a sense of social responsibility. As already noted in Lee Shulman's foreword, we observed the professor challenging his students to consider a product's total life-cycle and bring to bear all of their engineering knowledge to design with that life-cycle in mind. The instructor had students consider two contemporary products—a six-year-old coffee maker and a six-month old cell phone—and struggle with the questions "Now that these two artifacts are past their useful lives, what will we do with their constituent parts? Even more important, how might they have been designed to leave fewer dangerous or unrecyclable pieces when they were retired?" He gave them time to inspect and handle the component parts of the devices and asked them to devise answers to those questions (or in engineering parlance, design solutions). Their problem solving strategies involved more fully defining the questions, seeking out information, thinking creatively, and exercising judgment, all while working within a team setting. In other words, he held them accountable for acting like engineers.

The students in the class seemed to have taken to heart the message of this exercise. As several students told us in response to questions about their vision of what made an engineer: "An engineer is someone who uses mathematics and the sciences to mess with the world by designing and making things that other people will buy and use." They quickly added, however, "Once you mess with the world, you are responsible for the mess you've made." This was indeed the principle the instructor had been illustrating in his lecture in this senior design course. The way the instructor posed the issue, and the way the students grasped it, presents responsibility as the logical and practical continuation of the design process itself, not something added on. Properly understood, figuring out what to do with "the mess you've made" is simply an extension—albeit one often overlooked—of the task of design itself. In such an approach, ethical considerations are an essential component of basic engineering knowledge, pervading the design process.

Another example of connecting freshmen-to-senior course experiences around professionalism is at CMU, where students are prepared to think about ethical questions throughout their undergraduate years. A freshman-year course includes case studies and discussions of professional ethics as well as analysis and design problems, and two junior-level analysis courses include ethics-related modules. This culminates in senior-level courses that incorporate sophisticated ethical analyses, often within the context of case presentations.

In mechanical engineering at CMU the senior level course is "Engineering Analysis." This course is designed "to develop in the student the professional method of solving engineering problems in analysis and design through application of the fundamental principles of the engineering sciences" (unpublished syllabus). Along with its focus on advanced analysis, the course also prominently includes a faculty directed ethics module, case studies, graded group assignments, and technical analysis to highlight engineers' ethical dilemmas and responsibilities. Course objectives include "an ability to analyze engineering decisions, both other people's and their own, for technical and ethical quality and support their evaluation with reasoned arguments." In analyzing technical and non-technical aspects of engineering failures, students in the course grapple with the complexity and interconnectedness of such considerations.

In our visit to a class session of "Engineering Analysis," we observed four students presenting a case study of the well-known Quebec Bridge failure, including analyses that addressed the history, the design issues and problems, and the responsibilities of the various participants, along with the resulting legal judgment made by the Canadian court. The polished, thirty-minute presentation relied on detailed historical data and articulation of the engineering principles that had been violated, ultimately resulting in structural failure. The team led the class in a lively discussion of who was to blame, and they articulated their own positions on that question along with supporting arguments. To bring the case directly into the class, one presenter explained that graduates of engineering programs in Canada still wear iron rings, which used to be made from the metal of the failed bridge, as a reminder of their obligation to the profession and society. The student had one of these rings, which he had borrowed from a Canadian friend. No doubt, a key to the high quality student work we saw in this course is that, by the time they began working on the case presentations, these students had already had years of experience thinking about ethical issues.

Consistent and cumulative learning for professionalism and ethics, as demonstrated in this class session on the Quebec Bridge failure, does not happen without sustained effort. It requires systematic attention to what issues students are engaging with and where and how this engagement happens. This kind of self-conscious and intentional approach enables many faculty to contribute important, albeit partial, elements to a fuller picture, while ensuring that students are engaged with enough of these elements to constitute broad coverage of the important issues. This kind of intentional approach is needed if we want the whole to be more than the sum of its parts. In such an approach, ethical considerations are an essential component of basic engineering knowledge, pervading all engineering processes.

PART SIX

BRINGING PROFESSIONAL PRACTICE FORWARD

WE BEGAN OUR STUDY of undergraduate engineering education guided by an overarching question: do the components of the undergraduate curriculum work together as cohesive, effective preparation for today's professional engineering practice?

In the course of the study, as we examined both the strengths and the weaknesses of engineering education, we refined our questioning: does the current engineering curriculum and pedagogy support the integration of knowledge, skills of practice, and professional values necessary for today's professional practice? Knowing that many of those who complete engineering programs go into other, often related, fields, can we say that the undergraduate curriculum prepares them to bring that engineering perspective to the policy and other problems they might work on as professionals?

We concluded that today's engineering education is strong on imparting some kinds of knowledge but not very effective in preparing students to integrate their knowledge, skills, and identity as developing professionals. This lack of integration also weakens the transfer of the engineering perspective to other areas in which engineering graduates find employment.

Thus the central lesson that emerged from our study is the imperative of teaching for professional practice, with *practice* understood as the complex, creative, responsible, contextually grounded activities that define the work of engineers at its best. We use the term *professional* because we insist that engineering is and should be understood and taught as a profession rather than a bundle of technical skills for sale. This means, as its codes state, engineering claims or *professes*—as do medicine and law, for example—to serve the public with specialized knowledge and skill through commitment to the field's public purposes and ethical standards.

Engineering education, then, rightly aims to develop more than technicians. It attempts to form future professionals who can be entrusted with responsible judgment in the application of their expertise for the good of those they serve. Professionals act for others' benefit, not simply their own. They are, in this sense, ethical sense fiduciaries, bearers of the trust of those who depend on their knowledge, skill, and judgment. We propose that teaching for professional practice should be the touchstone for future choices about both curriculum content and pedagogical strategies in undergraduate engineering education.

In this closing part of the book, we move from questions of analysis to thoughts about action: how might undergraduate engineering education move toward this goal more effectively, especially in light of the profound changes to professional engineering practice in our global era? As do the authors of *The Engineer of 2020* (National Academy of Engineering, 2004) and *Engineering for a Changing World* (Duderstadt, 2008), we base our suggestions for improvement on the premise that the overriding purpose of engineering education is to prepare future engineers who are both competent and attuned to the full range of demands and possibilities inherent in the professional practice of engineering.

To accomplish this goal, both curriculum and teaching strategies must be carefully crafted to enable aspiring engineers to move from thinking like students to thinking like beginning professionals. Effecting such a change in engineering education is, in essence, a design problem. To that end, we take our line of questioning yet another step: as stewards of the engineering profession, what role does the engineering faculty play in framing the curriculum to prepare students to enter the professional practice?

We begin by reemphasizing the challenges that today's global engineering world poses to the assumptions underlying the prevalent model of engineering education. To meet these challenges, to educate the new-century engineer, we argue for moving away from the historic *linear components* model while updating the assumptions that guide engineering education. Such an educational model, which we call *networked components*, breaks with many of the key assumptions of the received linear model. To illustrate these points, we describe (1) developments in medical education that provide a useful comparative perspective, and (2) contemporary findings about how people learn, both of which strengthen the case for moving toward a networked components model that can bring professional practice forward as the constant focus of engineering education.

We close by offering a vision of what education for the new-century engineer could look like, noting promising developments that we observed in the course of our study. After presenting a set of design principles for networking the components of engineering education so that they focus on professional practice, we conclude with a map, if you will, for how the field might get from here to there by engaging the academy and its stakeholders in the profession.

19

A DESIGN FOR ACTION

THROUGHOUT THIS REPORT, as we have described undergraduate engineering education in the United States and the limitations of the linear approach that has long shaped the curriculum and teaching strategies, we have done so fully recognizing that the acquisition of technical knowledge that is the primary focus of engineering education—fostering both ways of thinking rooted in mathematics and the natural sciences, and competence in contemporary technologies and procedures—is crucial to professional practice. Engineers must be able to apply math, science, and engineering concepts and to use modern engineering tools (Lattuca, Terenzini, and Volkwein, 2006).

However, acquiring technical knowledge cannot be the only goal if engineers are to be both competent and attuned to the demands and possibilities inherent in the profession of engineering. Although the use and acquisition of technical knowledge is central to engineering work, it does not represent the full range of knowledge, skills, and understanding and commitment needed by students who enter today's engineering profession. Indeed, employers cite as the qualities they most seek in new engineering hires the ability to work on teams, to communicate effectively, to engage in lifelong learning, and to apply engineering program-solving strategies (Lattuca, Terenzini, and Volkwein, 2006).

Although effecting a delicate balance among the traditional linear components might seem the most expedient solution to addressing these deficiencies, continuing to focus primarily on technical knowledge is increasingly unrealistic. To date, defining what is the core or key knowledge to be learned as part of a four-year engineering education has been a difficult and perpetual task, and the impulse has been to simply keep adding. However, the knowledge that underpins engineering work is continually expanding. Some of this expansion stems from a deeper and more sophisticated understanding of science and mathematics; some from engineering's habit of bumping, moving, and merging into new problem domains, such as biological systems, earth systems, security and wealth, and developing countries; and some from recognition of the utility of knowledge and practices in heretofore seemingly unconnected fields such as sociology, anthropology, and business.

To be sure, some knowledge becomes obsolete—or seems to become obsolete—with new discoveries and inventions, but there is every indication that growth in knowledge seen as critical to today's engineering endeavors will continue to increase rapidly. It is less possible than ever for an engineer to know everything; the more important skill now is to know how to learn. Thus the faculty must be highly selective in choosing what conceptual and technical knowledge to focus on. Although we fully recognize that identifying a core knowledge set is important, though challenging, we are convinced of the wisdom of Hoover and Fish's advice that "a curriculum may be practically effective even though far short of being theoretically complete" (Hoover and Fish, 1950, p. 451).

Engineering work is integrative at its core. As described in Part One, engineering work is not simply a body of knowledge or a set of work processes; it is the purposeful and thoughtful integration of knowledge and process to create a solution to some particular problem. This is in contrast with engineering education as it is currently framed—the preparation provided by formal education being largely segregated into separate, linear components. Technical knowledge acquisition is expected to occur primarily through a series of lecture-based courses and problem set assignments that, when combined with required science and mathematics courses outside of engineering proper, make up the great bulk of the curriculum. In contrast, introduction to and preparation for practice takes place through a small number of laboratory courses—often taught simply as adjuncts to engineering science courses—and a few design courses, often at the end of the program. The concerns of professional identity and purpose may receive significant attention, either incorporated within some design experiences or as stand-alone ethics offerings, or they may not.

Knowledge, practice, and professionalism do not, however, figure separately in the actual practice of engineering. Because the engineer integrates these resources, habits, and attitudes, engineering is more than just the application of technical principles; rather, it is the art of identifying and solving problems with technically based ideas and strategies. Skilled engineers are integrative thinkers. What is needed for more effective engineering learning are ways of teaching that better connect the component parts of engineering work.

Expanding the Vision of the Profession

Today's world further demands that engineering education be intentionally aligned with the best emerging understanding of the nature of engineering work and professionalism. To prepare students who are ready to enter the profession as new-century engineers, engineering programs need to enlarge and reconfigure their goals. Undergraduate engineering education might fruitfully align its purposes with the broader goals of undergraduate education, regardless of major or discipline, described by six of the most influential national education associations as "the ability to think, write, and speak clearly; to reason critically; to solve problems; to work collaboratively; to acquire field-specific knowledge; and to acquire the judgment, analytic capacity, and independence of thought to support continued, self-driven, lifelong learning and engaged citizenship" (American Council on Education and others, 2006; the other five associations are the American Association of State Colleges and Universities, American Association of Community Colleges, Association of American Universities, National Association of Independent Colleges and Universities, and National Association of State Universities and Land-Grant Colleges).

This holds true for undergraduate education, which was the focus of our study, but it is equally true for preparation of engineers at the master's level. At both levels, engineering education needs to start with a vision for engineering work that recognizes that engineering practice has entered a more demanding era, in which engineers must function as responsible participants in networks of interaction that include social and cultural as well as technical and scientific dimensions.

Aligning Engineering Education with Professional Practice

This new vision of engineering work holds, we believe, five key insights for rethinking the education of engineers:

- Engineering work is inherently interactive and complex.
- Formulating problems and solving problems are interdependent activities.
- Engineering has many publics.

○ Engineering incorporates many domains beyond the technical.

○ Engineers affect the world.

Engineering Is Inherently Interactive and Complex

We noted in Part One that professional practice can no longer be described as arriving at technically competent solutions to problems set by others—the familiar picture of engineering work in large industrial organizations. Increasingly, doing engineering entails working with various parties with different perceptions and assumptions to formulate and solve problems. According to technology historian Thomas P. Hughes, the complexity of contemporary technological systems, together with their sometimes unanticipated effects on human and natural environments, is pushing engineering work in the direction of "interdisciplinary interactive groups sharing perspectives and information needed to create and control" such systems (Hughes, 2004, p. 78).

Given these trends, it is, at the least, unfortunate that the linear components model of engineering education presents students with a picture of the field as largely applied science. The problem with this view, as embodied in the overwhelming emphasis on engineering science courses in the typical undergraduate curriculum, is that it needlessly restricts the development of students' expertise to solving problems that have been largely formulated in advance. By placing so much weight on the acquisition of theoretical knowledge outside of context, the prevailing conception of engineering education has long retarded the development of the wider range of expertise that graduates will need to draw on in actual engineering work. Indeed, it has never been an efficient means of preparing students for the world of practice. However, the problem has become more acute as professional practice has developed toward greater interactive complexity, both among the different parties involved and within the technological systems themselves.

Formulating Problems and Solving Problems Are Inherently Interdependent Activities

Engineering education needs to confront directly, in both its curriculum and its teaching practices, the challenge of teaching what Gary Downey has called "problem definition and solution" as correlative and interdependent goals (Downey, 2005). Unlike the older model of technical problem solving, this expanded conception of pedagogical purpose requires a rethinking of how, for example, engineering science is taught in relation to what students are learning about carrying out design projects.

Engineering Has Many Publics

In the new world of engineering, in which global competition and cooperation are becoming increasingly common, engineers find themselves immersed in complex human and organizational environments that they need to understand in order to function effectively and responsibly. Because engineers' solutions have effects in the world, the ability to understand others, whether other specialists or lay publics, and the ability to participate with them have become core competencies for engineers, as reflected in the ABET standards for engineering program accreditation (see ABET, 2007, p. 2).

Engineering Incorporates Many Domains Beyond the Technical

Recognizing that engineers participate in what Williams calls the "hybrid world"—in which human values, embodied in technological design, affect and "feed back on" both the physical and social aspects of this environment in which the two dimensions are intertwined (Williams, 2002, p. 31)—expands the dimensions of what is understood as core knowledge and competence for engineering programs. Physical and information systems can no longer be presented innocently, in abstraction, separate from the human and natural environments with which the technology functions and whose future it helps to shape. Concretely, this means that the social sciences and humanities disciplines now have specific roles in the engineering curriculum, as key tools for the understanding of the context of engineering problem formulation, but also as necessary means for thinking about the place of the engineer in the new hybrid world.

Engineers Affect the World

Engineers are inescapably participants, interacting with many others to develop and deploy technologies. A sense of responsibility for their interventions in the world they share with others must shape future engineers' understanding of who they are and of their place in the world; this demands that consideration of the ethical and professional responsibilities of engineers be given a radically more central place in the curriculum. The worst outcome would be well-trained technological experts who lack the understanding and the interest to concern themselves with how that expertise is used. The discouraging finding, reported in Part Five, that engineering programs typically *reduce* rather than expand students' concerns with the social consequences of technological expertise gives urgency to this reorientation.

To give substance to these insights, we turn to a discussion of how engineering programs might organize so that students' learning experiences develop such an integrated base of professional knowledge, skills, and understanding and commitment.

20

USABLE KNOWLEDGE

THE EMPHASIS OF UNDERGRADUATE ENGINEERING EDUCATION needs to be on teaching for *usable knowledge*. By this we mean the concepts, tools, and procedures of the field, organized in ways that enable learners to deploy them to both formulate problems and solve problems. Centering engineering education on professional practice does not mean abandoning the central and critical role that learning and applying theoretical, technical, and contextual knowledge plays in engineering. Rather, it means reframing and teaching this knowledge in ways that more directly connect it with engineering thinking and action. Accomplishing this, however, will require moving beyond the linear model of instruction.

Engineering practice is rarely linear in the way engineering education has historically presented it. Indeed, this has always been true, but its significance for educational preparation is now heightened by the changes occurring in the world of professional practice. Engineering problems typically require multiple iterations and usually demand taking account of multiple points of view. Such work places a premium on habits of thought that few educational programs emphasize: integrated thinking in which the scientific, technological, contextual, and ethical dimensions of engineering become routine aspects of increasingly sophisticated professional thinking. The alternative model of an engineering program, the kind we call *networked*, incorporates the iterative aspect of professional learning through problem formulation and solution.

Engineering educators can look to two sources in particular—medical education and the learning sciences—to understand how and why undergraduate engineering education might be redesigned to teach for integrated, professional thinking.

The Example of Medical Education

We fully recognize that the transformation we are proposing would be a profound one. However, it can be done. Medical education has been making such a transformation over recent years, and we offer the story as an example of what is possible.

Medical education has much in common with engineering education, and the profession has had similar, profoundly changing needs. Though engineering and medicine differ in important ways, each field is heavily invested in the understanding and use of science to accomplish its own ends. Indeed, aside from engineering, no profession is more involved with science and applications of modern technology than medicine.

Medicine is not so much a science as what one commentator has termed "an intensively science-using" profession (Montgomery, 2005, pp. 46, 52), calling attention to the distinction between the cognitive tasks involved in scientific discovery and explanation on the one hand and the actual practice of clinical diagnosis and treatment on the other. Because of the great cultural prestige of science, physicians have wanted to draw the mantle of science over their practice as completely as possible. In this, the history of medicine parallels that of engineering, which has sought the same prestige and drawn on similar scientific metaphors to describe the work of the profession. There is insight to be gained, we believe, from considering how medicine has begun to reconfigure and reconceive the core of its educational preparation.

The standard medical curriculum, established early in the twentieth century at about the time the modern university engineering program was being organized, began with heavy doses of basic sciences and only then proceeded to clinical training, typically in the teaching hospital. Today, however, in order to improve learning, medical education is introducing clinical experience or its simulation earlier and earlier in the medical school curriculum. Further, medical educators are giving increasing attention to the value of integrating the teaching of basic sciences with experience with practice, starting from the students' very first encounters with medicine. One can observe the implications of modern learning theory carried out in concrete form.

As David Irby, vice dean of education at the University of California, San Francisco School of Medicine, explains, medical education "has taken to heart the results of the learning sciences and the research on physician expertise to redesign curriculum, instruction, and assessment." He describes the four major themes emerging from The Carnegie Foundation for the Advancement of Teaching's study of medical education:

1. Integration. Physicians must learn to connect formal knowledge with clinical experience. This is best advanced through early clinical immersion and by connecting basic, clinical, and social sciences throughout training.

2. Individualization. Recognizing the diversity of background experiences and rates of learning of each student, medical education should establish clear competencies or learning outcomes, assess performance comprehensively, and allow individuals to graduate at different rates and with greater elective options in order to develop added areas of expertise.

3. Insistence upon excellence. Medical education should inculcate the importance and value of relentlessly pursuing excellence, life-long learning, innovation, scholarship, and discovery as a moral imperative for practice.

4. Identity formation. The professional and moral development of physicians-to-be is an important part of the learning process and needs to be explicitly taught, modeled, and assessed. [Irby, 2008]

We believe that engineering students' overall learning trajectory is likely to be similarly enhanced when experiences in engineering school replicate the essential characteristics of the best of learning in and from professional practice.

"Circular, Interpretive Procedure"

In actual clinical decision making and therapeutic interventions, physicians do not proceed by deducing what to do from general principles. In a recent study of physicians' ways of reasoning, Katherine Montgomery argues, "Despite medicine's appeal to the canons of physical science as a model for its work, physicians do not reason as they imagine scientists do." Faced with a patient, physicians do not "proceed as they and their textbooks often describe it: top-down, deductively, 'scientifically.'" Instead, they reason from cases (Montgomery, 2005, p. 46).

Note the parallel here to the current understanding of the relationship of "engineering science" to the practice of engineers. In the received model, as we have seen, students are taught that engineers work mostly by making deductive applications of general scientific principles. In the case of medicine, however, Montgomery's study as well as other research indicates that actual clinical decision making follows a different logic. That is, it is neither deduction from general principles nor induction from the particulars to a universal concept. Instead, doctors form hypotheses about the possible causes of a particular patient's situation, then test those possibilities against details revealed by closer examination of the patient.

This "circular, interpretive procedure," as Montgomery calls it, moves between "generalities in the taxonomy of disease and the particular signs and symptoms of the individual case." This intellectual movement proceeds "until a workable conclusion is reached" (Montgomery, 2005, p. 47) and a plan of treatment is developed. This is the medical equivalent of formulating problems and solving problems in engineering. The thinking at the center of clinical reasoning in medicine, then, shows significant similarity to formulating a design problem. In both clinical reasoning and engineering design, the narration of cases and their development is essential to the process. In fact, Montgomery argues, the case narrative is "the principal means of thinking and remembering—of *knowing*—in medicine." The case narrative represents nothing less than "clinical judgment . . . in all its situated and circumstantial uncertainty" (Montgomery, 2005, p. 46). It enables practitioners to make sense of the contingent unfolding of a disease or medical situation by setting up a kind of conversation, a back-and-forth, between the patient's particular story and general analytic knowledge.

Analytical modes of explanation alone simply cannot achieve the integrated forms of understanding that medical professionals produce through this kind of narrative sense-making. Could not something similar be said about the unfolding process of formulating problems and solving problems in engineering?

Into the Guild of Practitioners

The chief accomplishment of medical education lies in its ability to bring novices gradually into the guild of practitioners who practice these complex and demanding skills. The chief pedagogical means to this end is an ongoing, back-and-forth conversation between the particular situation of the patient's narrative and the general principles of analytic, scientific knowledge. To be effective, medical education works hard to provide a foundation in both kinds of learning. Thus one cannot become a doctor in any responsible or meaningful sense without proper induction into the scientific knowledge and frameworks upon which medical practice depends. Abstract, analytic representations of scientific knowledge provide useful scaffolding for physicians who must deploy large quantities of knowledge about human anatomy, physiology, and the like. However, doctors must also be able to integrate, or reintegrate, this analytic knowledge in ongoing situations in which the final question is always *what to do, for and with this patient, at this time.* This is the essence of professional practice in medicine.

It is not hard to see the parallel to the education of engineers. Engineers, too, are faced with the challenge of bringing to bear on often vaguely defined problems a large body of complex knowledge, much of it scientifically based. However, the application of this knowledge is rarely deductive. It requires the effective use of scientific principles and knowledge to support the formulation and solution of an engineering problem. That in turn depends on the use of skills and understanding that can be learned only in practice-like situations, whether simulated or actual. Like developing physicians, engineering students need experiences in which they can observe and imitate more expert practitioners who guide the novices' progress through feedback and coaching. In this sense, they need to become apprentices as they gradually move toward the understanding, skills, and sensibilities of competent and responsible practice. In the process, engineering students need to see repeatedly, as do developing physicians, how theory and practice can enhance each other as they interact in the actual work of the field.

Guidance from the Learning Sciences

Another source of guidance in transforming engineering education comes from the learning sciences. As we noted in Part One, recent research has produced a remarkable consensus as to how learning takes place. The principles of learning identified by this research are implicit in the apprentice-like interactions between clinical teachers and students that we have just surveyed in medical education. Among other things, those guided engagements with clinical practice help medical students develop the ability to move back and forth between concepts and practice, a capacity that lies at the heart of medicine as a science-using practice.

In our visits to engineering schools, we saw examples of similar pedagogies, in which students are guided and coached toward more competent performance as they engage in activities that represent important aspects of engineering practice. This kind of teaching was especially evident in the areas of design and laboratory, but sometimes also in the teaching of engineering science. It is striking that these pedagogies in engineering education embody the central idea emerging from recent research on how people learn: the idea, derived from the study of a variety of fields, that all complex learning resembles what researchers call the *development of expertise.*

As we noted in Chapter Three, what distinguishes experts from novices is not so much the amount of knowledge they command but the organization and ready usability of that knowledge. They can identify significant patterns in contexts of application. Their facility in reading situations and retrieving and deploying their knowledge is useful for thinking, judging, and acting in their fields. In other words, more than just knowing a lot about their area, experts possess well-structured, usable knowledge. This well-structured, usable knowledge allows experts to solve problems in their domains efficiently, effectively, and creatively.

In sum, learning represents a process of growth toward the complex abilities that mark expertise in a field. The central task of educators is helping novices move toward the capacities of expertise in the field for which they are being prepared. Engineering educators are thus faced with the challenging design task of developing curricular and pedagogical strategies to start their students on this process of growth toward expertise. The learning sciences provide guidance in this task.

"Cognitive Apprenticeship"

The clear implication of research into learning—as evident in the theories of John Seely Brown, Allan Collins, Susan Newman, Paul Duguid, and others—is that faculty-student interaction associated with effective learning involves some form of "cognitive apprenticeship" through which intellectual development occurs (Collins, Brown, and Newman, 1989, pp. 454–460; Brown, Collins, and Duguid, 1989, pp. 39–41). Such an "apprenticeship of the mind" allows the learner to enter the world of the expert in carefully staged and monitored steps. This is the "learning in context" we describe in Chapter Six, and it is the focus of clinical medical education, in which what is being learned is understood in ways that connect with the practice to which the learner is, in effect, apprenticed.

The rich body of research on learning provides a number of key concepts that attempt to capture the essential features of this learning process. A grasp of these concepts enables educators to observe and articulate the often subtle dynamics of classroom practice. Four such fundamental concepts seem especially important for developing ways to critically examine and improve engineering study (see Collins, Brown, and Newman, 1989, pp. 480–483):

1. Modeling—providing representations of practice.
2. Scaffolding—providing support for students' efforts to imitate the teacher's performance.

3. Coaching—giving deliberate, planned feedback that guides learners toward more competent imitation of expertise.

4. Fading—removing the scaffolding as student performance strengthens.

In effect, these principles suggest that robust learning of complex practices depends on experiences that enable learners to observe and then imitate the knowledge and skills of experts. The best learning happens as experts model performance in such a way that learners can imitate the performance. And this process is greatly facilitated if the experts provide feedback to learners about their performance. This feedback guides the learners in making the activity increasingly their own. Seen in this perspective, to learn a complex practice such as engineering requires mostly learning by doing. It requires practice and feedback on that practice, followed by learner response to the feedback and recurrent attention to the goals and procedures that make up the field.

Each step of this iterative process raises a host of questions that warrant educators' attention. First, students need to see what expert performance looks like. They need clear representations of expertise in the various aspects of performance that are central to the field. Moreover, these representations of expert performance have to be offered repeatedly, at higher levels of complexity and skill, during the years of training, because novices are not in a position to appreciate the many aspects of expert performance when they first see it.

Modeling

The requirement that educators model or otherwise represent expert performance points to the importance of clearly identifying the forms of expertise that students ought to gain during the years of their training. Presumably, these forms of expertise should map onto the capacities that graduates will actually need when they enter practice. A key principle of effective teaching and learning is "teach what you want students to know or be able to do." Yet it's surprising how often this apparently simple maxim is violated.

Because expertise is always shared among members of a community who have mastered certain practices, the process of modeling, imitation, feedback, and correction typically takes place within such communities. Pedagogy, in its core sense, is the community's organized practice for shaping this expertise in aspiring new members. This raises the question of what kind of expertise the community of professional educators in a field represents and how closely the expertise at the center of induction into the field connects with the expertise needed by practitioners of the profession.

Sometimes this connection is not as strong as it could be. We have written in another context, for example (Sullivan and others, 2007), that, to a large extent, legal educators are helping students gain the expertise of legal scholars rather than that of practicing attorneys. Our formulation of engineering education as preparation for professional practice makes this same point: educators need to be intentional in preparing students for forms of expertise that will support competent, creative, responsible, and evolving engineering practice. Engineering educators therefore need to foster not the expertise of scientific research but the expertise of this science-using practice.

Scaffolding

Once engineering educators are clear about the expertise to be developed and have found compelling ways to represent that expertise to students, the next step is to help students to perform the practices themselves. This is assisted greatly if the learners' performance is guided and supported by what has been likened to the scaffolding used in the construction of buildings. In this terminology, students' efforts to perform the practices they see must be scaffolded, to help learners better understand the important features of the performance and to provide a guiding structure for their efforts to imitate those aspects of more expert performance.

In clinical medicine, model or typical cases, along with assignments that help students identify the most relevant concepts in human biology, serve as scaffolds or templates to guide student understanding of the unfolding disease process in a patient. In much the same way, assignments that guide engineering students in connecting basic physical concepts with real engineering problems can function as scaffolds for them as they learn to think and perform like engineers. This can take place in laboratory settings, in design projects, or even in well-crafted analysis courses. This kind of scaffolding, which supports students' performance of rudimentary aspects of expertise, is an apprentice-like situation even if it is not literally an apprenticeship with a master practitioner.

Coaching and Fading

Once students have ventured to undertake their own novice-level performances, they need feedback and guidance—coaching—on where they are on the right track and where adjustments in performance are needed. The scaffolding is withdrawn as students become more competent, and the teacher-expert "fades," stepping aside to allow learners to exercise more discretion in their own thinking as they approach higher levels of mastery in their field of practice.

It is important to note that the cycle of representing expert practice, scaffolding student performance, providing feedback on performance, and fading or removing the scaffolding is repeated at new levels of challenge as students advance toward greater expertise. In this process, scaffolding and guidance is provided for the next level in the learner's development toward competent performance, the learner practices, receives feedback, and the scaffolding needed at that stage fades. In this way, the learning process keeps moving forward.

Adapting the Apprenticeship Model

The applicability of this coaching or apprenticeship model to the learning of observable skills such as craft and athletic performances is clear. In engineering schools, however, the kinds of expert-learner interactions visible in areas such as clinical medicine can be harder for both teachers and students to discern. Particularly in the analytic core of engineering science courses, the complex cognitive patterns used by the teacher-experts often are not explicit and thus are difficult for their students to observe. Likewise, it proves difficult for teachers in the typical analysis course to notice students' accumulating misunderstanding (Streveler, Litzinger, Miller, and Steif, 2008). These misunderstandings, if left uncorrected, can often derail the best intentions of instructors. This is important, because when students do not have the opportunity for immediate feedback on their efforts to imitate correct thinking, such misconceptions can continue to fester, undermining future learning. These difficulties are especially pronounced in large classroom settings such as those in which the bulk of engineering science is taught.

Fortunately, contemporary learning theory addresses, in its articulation of the *cognitive apprenticeship*, cognitive or intellectual development as well as the development of more concrete skills.

Making the Invisible Visible

How can the process of modeling, scaffolding, feedback on performance, and fading be applied to intellectual capacities, which are not visible in the same ways that physical skills are? First, the representation of expertise: teachers have to make their own intellectual processes (their performances) visible. This means that the teacher-expert has to make visible to learners the otherwise invisible processes of thinking that underlie complex cognitive operations at the heart of engineering thinking. Teachers have to articulate and demonstrate, rather than simply assume, the thought processes they want students to learn.

Then students' efforts to replicate those thought processes need to be made visible so that the teacher can see where the learner is on and off track, in order to provide appropriate coaching and feedback. This need to make the invisible visible points to the importance of formative assessments that reveal students' underlying thought processes. In fact, learning theory's emphasis on the key role played by feedback is the core of the important discovery that assessment can work effectively to *develop* learning as well as to measure it. To complicate matters even further, cognitive capacities and technical skills are not the only things that students are, or should be, learning. Engagement in the process we have described—in essence, engagement in practice—is also *formative*. That is, the process of learning a complex practice such as engineering necessarily shapes the perception, imagination, and deportment of anyone who undergoes it.

Professional Formation

The formative aspects of engineering education are important complements of the explicit features of curricular learning and contribute to the students' emerging professional identities. As we have spelled out in earlier chapters, students need to develop engineering intuition of various kinds, a sense of salience that brings into focus the significant features of complex and ambiguous contexts and tasks, the subtle wisdom required for making collaborative work maximally creative and productive, and a host of personal qualities like persistence, open-mindedness, and tolerance for ambiguity.

Too often, however, educators pay little or no direct attention to the implicit formative influences of educational experiences. This means that those influences shape students in ways that are haphazard and largely unnoticed. The formative influences of education can be beneficial in many ways but can also yield unintended, sometimes counterproductive, results. Because the systems in which engineers must operate are inherently loosely bounded and open, questions about the contexts of work and the outlooks and purposes of other participants need to be as much a part of students' learning processes as the more traditional technical knowledge and skills of mathematical modeling and understanding of materials and physical conditions. The formative features of professional education bear directly on the degree to which students become sensitized to the full range of work contexts and the varied outlooks and purposes of those for whom and with whom they work.

Reflecting on their assumptions about "the way things are" can help students and faculty alike become more aware of the ways in which particularities of their experience have shaped their understanding of reality. This kind of reflection helps them see that what they take for granted is not necessarily the nature of reality; that people trained in other traditions and cultures may not share their perspectives. Downey's work on intercultural communication in the formulation of engineering problems illustrates the ways in which greater reflective awareness facilitates effective communication across national and other cultural differences, a capacity that is increasingly important in this global era (Downey and others, 2006).

Opening Professional Practice

Educational activities that open professional practice to learners— through experience and reflection on that experience—support learning in many ways, some less immediately evident than others. Students acquire not only abilities but also sensibilities that expand their repertoire of habitual interpretations and responses beyond what it had been previously. They are learning in and for the contexts defined by the professional practice itself, as that practice is represented in the professional education they are experiencing. When students are engaged with professional practice as a central part of their training, the experience influences their understanding of what the world is like, what is possible and worth doing, and their sense of who they are and might become (Bransford, Brown, and Cocking, 2000).

Seen in this way, professional schools are, and should be, complex organizations for initiating the next generation of practitioners into the important dimensions of the expertise that defines a given profession. This conception of professional education underlies our conviction that learning in engineering schools should be guided by thoughtful, carefully chosen representations of engineering—what we call *professional practice*, in its full sense of knowledge, capacities, and a strong identity rooted in the defining purposes of the profession.

In this sense, the overall trajectory of professional education begins with learners who think like students and aims to develop them toward thinking and performing like professionals—in this case, professionals in the field of engineering. This educational arc, from prereflective toward reflective thinking, involves movement away from learning to do competent academic work (and to get high grades) toward involvement of the whole learner in appropriating the ways of thinking, performing, and understanding that characterize the expertise and identity of a beginning engineer.

Our hope is that engineering educators rise to the challenge of realizing these aims more effectively. To that end, we offer a set of principles to guide the design of engineering education that seeks to prepare students for professional practice.

21

TOWARD A NEW MODEL FOR ENGINEERING EDUCATION

HOW MIGHT ENGINEERING EDUCATION move students from student thinking to engineering thinking, reflective judgment, and analytic problem solving? Developing the expertise of professional practice is an iterative process. The ideal learning trajectory is a spiral, with all components revisited at increasing levels of sophistication and interconnection. In this networked model, the traditional analysis, laboratory, and design components would be deeply interrelated: engineering knowledge remains central but is configured to include both technical and contextual knowledge; competencies of practice, laboratory, and design experiences are integrated into the whole, as are professionalism and ethics.

Integrated Goals for Learning

In a networked approach, the goals for student learning are integrated under the overarching goal of professional formation, positioning students to continue the development toward being new-century engineers or new-century professionals in related fields. Moreover, the faculty would make these goals explicit to students and follow their progress toward them.

This would not be difficult to effect. Consider the learning goals of technical courses, lab, and design, which we identify in Parts Two through Four. As we noted, some goals are explicitly acknowledged by the faculty, ABET, or the profession. Others are implicit, evident through the faculty's curricular and pedagogical choices. Most striking about the lists of goals is that they are so similar. They can be resolved into the following four cross-cutting goals:

○ Developing a robust base of substantive knowledge of engineering science

○ Developing robust skills for using knowledge to interactively formulate and solve problems: creativity, engineering intuition, practical ingenuity

○ Developing the attitudes necessary to interactively formulate and solve problems: persistence and healthy skepticism, dynamism, agility, and flexibility

○ Developing the skills and attitudes for effective leadership, teamwork, and communication

A networked program would be designed so that learning in one area supports learning in another, always with the understanding that, because engineers touch the world in far-reaching and profound ways, the aim is to develop professionals who can act in the "hybrid world" (Williams, 2002, p. 31) in which the engineering is for "us."

Students and faculty alike would understand that these cross-cutting goals for student learning are in service of the core values of the profession—commitment to being competent, responsible, fair, and accountable. The overarching goal of the program would be to position students for a lifetime of continuous learning and growth.

In other words, to draw on Shulman's encapsulation of a professional, undergraduate engineering programs would be designed to position students to begin providing a worthwhile service in the pursuit of important human and social ends. They would begin a lifetime of pursuit of knowledge and skills as they continue to develop the capacity to engage in complex forms of professional practice, learning to make judgments under conditions of uncertainty, learning from experience, and creating and participating in responsible and effective professional communities.

Imagining the Networked Model

With learning proceeding in a spiral rather than a linear configuration, concepts and tools are revisited with increasing degrees of sophistication in order to make sense of the puzzles of how things work. Concepts and tools are nodes in an interactive network in which the various components of engineering science, laboratory, and design, as well as professional identity are understood to influence one another. They also influence how each is taught. Instead of proceeding in a single linear movement from theory to application, the new model allows for and encourages,

Figure 21.1. Networked Components Model

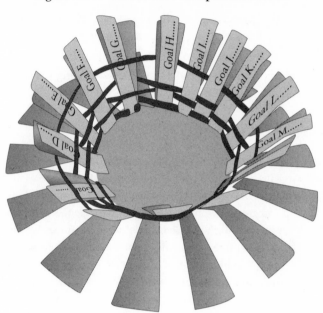

for example, issues from design practice to influence what concepts are taught in engineering science courses and by what means. Indeed, perhaps the greatest advantage that a focus on professional practice can bring to students is to promote, throughout their undergraduate training, the habit of moving fluidly back and forth between particular situations and general principles, which is characteristic of engineering—and professional practice—at its best. The curriculum and teaching strategies are structured by the demands of professional practice. The student would move back and forth among the components, pursuing ever-deepening competence in core knowledge, skills, and commitments. The curriculum would entail weblike patterns of interaction, in which students' development in one component is used to frame and spur progress in the others. Hence the networked quality of this approach, which we illustrate in Figure 21.1.

Designing for the Future of the Field

We do not claim to have a detailed plan for transforming engineering education from a linear model that focuses on acquisition of technical knowledge to a networked model that has, as its core, the knowledge, skills, and understanding of professional practice. Nevertheless, to help engineering educators meet the challenge ahead, we offer four design principles, illustrated with some promising examples: (1) provide a professional spine; (2) teach key concepts for use and connection; (3) integrate identity, knowledge, and skills through approximation of practice; and (4) place engineering in the world, encouraging students to make connections.

Provide a Professional Spine

As the integrated goals we offer suggest, requirements associated with what today are ancillary components of the typical program would instead be the major concerns around which the program revolves. During each year of their program, students would have experience with and engage in reflection on the meaning and demands of professional practice.

This emphasis on professional practice, the spine linking theory and practice, would give coherence and efficacy to the primary task facing schools of engineering: enabling students to move from being passive *viewers* of engineering action to taking their place as active participants or *creators* within the field of engineering. In this process, the student would begin to develop an identity as an engineer: a professional whose work is about providing worthwhile service in the pursuit of important human and social ends, who possesses fundamental knowledge and has the capacity to engage in complex forms of professional practice, able to make judgments under conditions of uncertainty.

The professional spine would be the engineering equivalent of the clinical dimension of medical preparation. Thus engagement in increasingly practice-like experiences would be a central feature of engineering education. These practice-like experiences can point toward both analysis and design as central tasks of engineering work, with laboratory courses and attention to professionalism and ethics contributing heavily to that goal—a thoroughly integrated approach to engineering education.

A PLACE TO EXPLORE PROFESSIONAL PRACTICE Lab and design courses, for example, could be reconceptualized to form this spine; the key is creating connections so that the focus is on professional practice and the integration of technical knowledge, skills, and understanding and commitment.

Laboratories already serve as a powerful tool for helping students learn to work with real hardware and systems, often collaboratively, so they are well suited to a practice-based approach. In some laboratory courses, students are challenged with designing, building, and demonstrating hardware that has some specified behavior, applying key technical concepts in all phases of the design-build-demonstrate cycle. Although the teacher generally specifies the particular behavior the system must display, in charting their course through the cycle students have greater autonomy than they might in engineering science courses. This kind of experience affords students the opportunity to learn that to become an engineer means explicitly joining a community of practice that draws flexibly on a variety of forms of knowledge and skill to formulate and solve problems of technological design. Science and mathematics then function as tools for disciplined thinking as well as ways of testing and improving imagined solutions.

Clearly, laboratory experiences in which students must master concepts to formulate problems and solve problems of increasing degrees of complexity have a critical role to play in the professional spine of the networked model. Weaving design experiences throughout all of the undergraduate years provides further opportunities to explore professional practice, connecting analysis and professional issues. As we note in Part Four, design has become more and more central to modern engineering work. Design experiences in the curriculum can lead students to draw upon conceptual, scientific knowledge while learning the skills of working with real materials. At the same time, students can be coached in design processes and in how to communicate and cooperate effectively with other parties to achieve a goal. These "other parties" include not only other students but, in an increasing number of programs, actual clients who bring to the experience a host of different perspectives and kinds of knowledge.

Done well, design courses enable students to recognize that engineering involves much more than following a fixed process or methodology; it involves ways of thinking (Neeley, 2007). The teaching practices cultivated by the studio settings of design courses exhibit the modeling, feedback, and close interaction between student and teacher, as well as student and student, that is known to produce effective learning. Well taught, design experiences also enable students to glimpse themselves as engineers at work and therefore have the potential to offer repeated and varied experiences that support the development of professionalism. This continuing attention to shaping students' sense of responsibility and purpose is essential to making the undergraduate years a powerful formative period with long-term positive impact. Helping students develop strong habits of professional thinking and acting are both, of course, central goals of the entire engineering curriculum.

EXAMPLES FROM THE FIELD In our field research, we encountered several powerful examples of how design can be used to give spine to programs. At Rowan University, for example, students undertake multi-disciplinary design-project work each semester. As the students' technical and professional competencies mature, the sophistication and complexity of the assigned design projects grow from reverse-engineering existing consumer devices in the early courses to designing and prototyping leg-powered, stair-climbing, electro-mechanical robots systems in the later courses (Chandrupatla and others, 2001).

Some integrated design experiences also pay significant attention to the social context of the work and the nature of professional interaction with clients. EPICS illustrates how useful project-centered learning can be for supporting this kind of learning, as students engage in long-term, community-based design projects to develop solutions that not only have technical merit but also are sustainable and viable for real clients. In connection with these projects, the program assesses and gives credit for student work in the area of ethics and professionalism, which signals the importance of these ethical and professional aspects of learning—and of engineering work (Coyle, Jamieson, and Oakes, 2005; DeRego, Zoltowski, Jamieson, and Oakes, 2005). Because the EPICS projects serve pressing community and individual needs, participation in the program enables students to appreciate the personal satisfaction to be gained from professional work that serves a valuable public mission. This is no small matter, as the personal and social meaning of one's work has been shown to be critical for professional satisfaction and retention in a field. (See, for example, Colby, Sippola, and Phelps, 2001; Gardner, Csikszentmihalyi, and Damon, 2001.)

Although it was not a focus of our study, we noted other important opportunities to develop the professional spine of a program. Participation in extra-curricular and cocurricular activities (such as Engineers Without Borders, FIRST, Formula SAE, and mini-Baja), undergraduate research, and co-op placements give students exposure to actual practice situations and provide authentic problems to formulate and solve. Co-op experiences, for example, go a long way "to impart first-hand knowledge of . . . the execution in industry/government of engineering designs, business principles, and developments in all career fields" (Atkins, 2005, p. 62). Many programs make participation in such activities available to students, but in general it is up to the students to reflect on the experience. It is important that faculty make purposeful use of these experiences, drawing connections with the skills and knowledge the students are developing in their coursework.

Teach Key Concepts for Use and Connection

Organizing engineering education around a professional spine does not imply the neglect of the traditional core, engineering sciences. It does mean that faculty and other program designers will need to make some hard choices about what kind of theoretical, scientific, and technical knowledge is fundamentally important. Moreover, it requires that engineering educators reach for teaching strategies that encourage students to develop the thinking skills of engineering practice. Fortunately, research on learning points the way.

The danger in separating the learning of concepts from the sites of their application is that the concepts become mere "lists of disconnected facts" (Bransford, Brown, and Cocking, 2000, p. 24). Because, as we have seen, students learn more effectively when they can connect their efforts with the practice for which they are being prepared, there is an important pedagogical reason for providing a professional spine in engineering programs. Students can learn the core knowledge basic to engineering in ways they will remember, truly understand, and be able to use in appropriate ways.

For example, courses that provide basic or core knowledge, including the mathematics and science courses most students take in their first two years, can be enhanced by the use of illustrative cases drawn from actual engineering experience. However, over time, students need to learn not only how to apply key concepts when the problem clearly calls for them, but also to identify for themselves which key concepts are needed in complicated, open-ended problem-solving situations. For this reason, teaching key concepts comes even closer to learning in context when it employs a more inductive approach: presenting students with open-ended problems and asking them to identify the basic underlying concepts that are most applicable to understanding and solving the problem. The use of cases as emphases within engineering science courses exemplifies this potential.

A PLACE TO USE THE TOOLS OF ENGINEERING These developments are receiving theoretical support from the emerging understanding of how engineers use knowledge-based tools. For example, Cardella's 2006 study of the use of mathematics in engineering conceptual design revealed the complex and varied ways in which mathematics supports the work. Although content knowledge and knowledge of how to use tools and mathematical terminology—the so-called mathematical knowledge base—were important in the process, equally important were the ability to tap into appropriate problem-solving strategies, skill in using and monitoring resources, personal beliefs about mathematics, and an understanding of domain-specific mathematical practices.

Gainsburg (2006), looking at the use of mathematics by structural engineers, found that mathematical modeling is central to and ubiquitous in their work, but found that the types of models that engineers actually use are not well reflected in the modeling tasks typically represented in education, certainly at the K–12 level and also, to a significant degree, in undergraduate education. The mathematics courses required for engineering students generally do not present the ways in which engineers use mathematical tools and concepts. Even when they teach math to engineering students, mathematicians are more likely to represent the evolution of mathematical principles and the way these principles are used by mathematicians (Wu, 1996; Redish and Smith, 2008).

The application of mathematics in engineering is not straightforward; it often involves approximation and estimation. This finding, we think, argues for the need to teach the application of mathematics to engineering as integral parts of mathematics courses for engineering students.

EXAMPLES FROM THE FIELD This is an area in which engineering education needs to develop new ways of teaching, and we identified some useful experiments toward this end. For example, at Olin College, faculty in mathematics, the sciences, and engineering collaborate on designing and delivering introductory courses that teach mathematics so that it reflects use in practice and connects with other technical tools (Kerns, Miller, and Kerns, 2005). In 1992, the Drexel University faculty began integrating material, including mathematics, from thirty-seven existing courses in the traditional lower-division curriculum into four interwoven sequences for freshman and sophomore engineering students (Quinn, 1995; Fromm, 2003). Stanford University offers freshman- and sophomore-level mathematics courses taught by engineering faculty in vector calculus, ordinary differential equations, and linear algebra. These courses are taught with an emphasis on engineering applications.

A PLACE TO DEVELOP USABLE KNOWLEDGE We believe that the other bodies of knowledge that are important for engineering—in particular, physics, chemistry, bioengineering, mechanics, and physiology—also need to be taught in ways that are most likely to yield *usable* knowledge. Research similar to that on mathematics in use is emerging; researchers are examining how scientific knowledge is used in practice, what leads to effective learning of science for use in engineering, and how the concepts taught in these subject matters is interrelated. (See McKenna, McMartin and Agogino, 2000; Tuminaro, 2004; *Journal of Chemical Education,* 2000; Mintzes, Wandersee, and Novak, 1998; Penberthy, Priest, Kosciuk, and Millar, 1997; Harris, Bransford, and Brophy, 2002; see also the work of VanNTH ERC at http://www.vanth.org.) These investigations provide insights for rethinking and reformulating curriculum and teaching strategies.

For example, the Integrated Mathematics, Physics, and Engineering Curriculum (IMPEC) at North Carolina State University requires that students take courses in mathematics, science, and engineering concurrently; a multidisciplinary faculty team integrates the ideas and concepts using traditional and alternative instructional methods, including cooperative learning, activity-based class sessions, and extensive computer simulations. Assessment of students participating in the IMPEC demonstrated higher pass rates in core courses than for students in conventional courses, along with marked increases over the term in self-rated confidence in abilities in chemistry, engineering, computing, speaking, and writing, while the confidence levels of a comparison group declined dramatically in chemistry and writing, and slightly in engineering, computing, and speaking (Ohland and others, 2003; Felder and others, 1998). Similar findings have been reported for students participating in Drexel's Enhanced Educational Experience for Engineers (E4) curriculum, noted earlier, which integrates mathematics, physics, chemistry, and biology as foundational elements of engineering. It is particularly noteworthy that the E4 curriculum has also resulted in higher rates of student retention and progress toward a degree, particularly among women and minorities (Quinn, 1995).

This new understanding of how tools such as mathematics and sciences are used in engineering work has the potential to stimulate highly productive (and perhaps highly charged) conversations among faculty, both inside and outside of engineering, who are responsible for educating future engineers. We believe that this body of research provides strong support for the benefits of shifting the basic model of engineering education toward a more networked form. With professional practice providing the spine through and around which the fundamental technical disciplines are woven, there is great potential to provide essential usable knowledge more coherently by emphasizing learning in context, which links engineering thinking more effectively with the mathematical and scientific disciplines.

Integrate Identity, Knowledge, and Skills Through Approximations to Practice

Teaching for professional practice calls for teaching strategies that embody the principles of effective learning that we described in Chapter Twenty: faculty need to make clear what expert practice looks like, modeling or otherwise making visible both thinking and doing. Faculty need to find creative ways to structure and support students' beginning efforts to imitate competent performance and to provide timely and informative feedback on those performances, through both informal means and formative assessments. To these requirements, we add one more: all these efforts should move in a common rhythm, starting from more distant and moving toward closer approximations of the full complexity of practice.

The importance of this principle of progressive approximation to practice is most evident in design and laboratory courses. Many faculty already understand that exercises in laboratory and design experiences are most effective when they are organized to challenge students repeatedly to acknowledge and work with ambiguity and finite resources in order to define a problem and create and execute a plan.

In some of the programs we visited, working on practice-related or integrative exercises starts early and progresses in complexity toward more authentic simulations of practice—or to practice itself, in some cases of capstone design studios. In the best of the examples we observed, the program scaffolds student learning, starting with simple laboratory and design exercises in the freshman-level courses, in which the number of aspects of practice is limited and students receive a high level of faculty input and feedback, and building toward exercises more representative of engineering practice by the senior year. The senior-level exercises often require that students coordinate with others and persist to see the problem through to its resolution, even if the first, second, and third approaches do not work. Some schools involve practicing engineers, who are able to confirm for students that many aspects of the senior-level exercises are representative of engineering practice, including the students' high level of autonomy and the calculated fading of their instructors' intervention.

We emphasize that a focus on professional practice does not mean that students should be immersed in the full complexity of authentic engineering practice from the outset. This is neither a realistic nor even a good idea. The recent work of Stanford education professor Pamela Grossman, looking at how various fields bring practice-oriented experiences into the classroom, questions the assumption—widespread in many fields of professional education—that more authentic educational experiences are necessarily better. She and her colleagues introduce the term *approximations of practice* to capture the idea that course-based experiences do and should vary in the degree to which that they authentically resemble the professional practices in which students will eventually be involved (Grossman and others, 2009).

Any particular approximation of practice is defined by two factors: (1) the nature of participation required of both the novice and the professional educator, and (2) what the novices experience and learn. Both factors relate to authenticity: "the extent to which these classroom-based experiences replicate or distort the conditions of real practice." Grossman describes how approximations can be made to vary from less authentic to more authentic by increasing the number of facets of practice that are highlighted, the students' level of participation, and the extent to which the time frame is close to real time (therefore, the degree to which it is an actual performance versus a rehearsal).

Grossman argues that educational experiences that more authentically replicate practice are not necessarily better at every stage of the learning process. Her case studies of professional preparation of teachers, clergy, and clinical psychologists illustrate instances in which it is more effective to focus intentionally on only some aspects of practice so as to master, through rehearsal, a subset of especially challenging skills. Drawing analogies from the worlds of athletics or music performance, one might compare this to focused practice and training on batting or running in baseball (done in conjunction with learning to perform those skills in the actual context of the game), or focused practice or rehearsal of scales and études (done concurrently with learning to play more complex musical compositions and to perform with an ensemble).

The principle, then, is to design learning experiences that are more systematic and intentional in the degree to which and the ways in which they approximate practice. In our observations, design and laboratory courses currently offer the best examples of this approach. Indeed, we observed that weaving design and laboratory experiences throughout the curriculum helps students make connections among the disparate areas of knowledge and skills, integrating these at various stages of their education as knowledge and skill develop.

However, it is important to reiterate a key point: a more practice-centered education does not mean abandoning the central and critical role that learning and applying technical and contextual knowledge plays in engineering education and practice; rather, it means reframing and teaching this knowledge in ways and in contexts that more directly connect it with engineering thinking and action.

So understood, the professional spine courses can connect with the goals typical of analysis courses by intentionally aiming to develop habits of integrated thinking in which the scientific, technological, and ethical dimensions of engineering become routine aspects of increasingly sophisticated professional thinking. By selecting which aspects of practice to make salient for the learners, educators can ensure that design courses aid in the learning of the network pathways back and forth between high-level concepts and the constraints of particular contexts without overburdening the learners with all the pressures and responsibilities of actual practice.

Place Engineering in the World: Encourage Students to Draw Connections

When, in an introductory design course at Michigan, the instructor asked students to think through the consequences of various design decisions by showing them castoff electronic communications tools such as cell phones, students were challenged to provide alternative designs with fewer negative social and environmental effects. As one student told us pointedly, the class discovered that human values and assumptions were already embedded in what seemed to be purely technical questions about the constraints on designing communication hardware. With equal force, they discovered that engineering inevitably means intervening in the world, so that all engineering projects carry with them responsibility for the effects of those interventions.

We saw that this course brought together the key principles of a networked model focused on professional practice. Students discovered through their own simulations of engineering intervention how important some conceptual tools were to safe and effective device design. They also discovered that being an engineer is a serious as well as a significant business. Like medical students on their first introduction to the clinical care of actual patients, the students discovered they needed to know a lot more than they did, and that they had to be able to understand connections better than they could at present—social and ethical connections as well as electrical and mechanical. Engineering work was suddenly connected to everything else in their college education and, indeed, everything else in their lives. They had discovered that engineering—and engineers—live in and participate in the world, with all its complexities.

Contrast those students' discovery with the way in which undergraduate courses are typically constructed, certainly in engineering and the sciences but in many other disciplines as well. A course is usually framed around a small set of principles and concepts, and students learn to understand those concepts by, at most, applying them to limited range of situations. Presenting concepts of principles from practice, separated from context, is known to weaken the motivation to learn. It also truncates the very idea of a college education and certainly of an adequate preparation of future engineers.

EXAMPLES FROM THE FIELD In our study, we encountered imaginative ways to overcome this problem. For example, in "Engineering Cultures," offered as an elective at Virginia Polytechnic Institute and State University (Virginia Tech), students learn about the professional identity of engineers in various countries and cultures, how their values, methods, ethical frameworks, and beliefs have evolved, and how one learns to work effectively with people who define problems differently from oneself. Cases in which both sides clearly have a defensible perspective, such as a 1920s dispute at General Motors between older manufacturing engineers and new R&D engineers, explore controversies or disagreements among engineers, illustrate engineers' life histories, and call attention to different ways of understanding what it means to be an engineer.

By focusing on the behavior of individual engineers and the consequences of these behaviors, students can connect issues of identity and professionalism as related to cultural traditions. A number of situation-based writing assignments (for example, resolving an issue from the standpoint of an engineer trained in another tradition) can help students understand that what counts as an ethical problem varies significantly from place to place. They learn to recognize that in a given situation of conflict or disagreement, some engineers may be predisposed to see an ethical problem at stake whereas others do not. In the words of Gary Downey, who teaches the course, "Our view in general is that helping students understand such differences is a necessary prerequisite to being a sensitive ethical problem solver in international environments" (Downey, 2006; see also Downey and others, 2006, and Downey, 2008). In addition to providing students with concrete examples of why the ABET standards around teamwork and communication are so important, these courses bring questions of professional identity and purpose into situations that are imaginable futures for the students in the course.

We saw the same approach, putting concepts into relationship with the demands of practice, in effective ethics teaching. Some faculty in both design and analysis courses, for example, ask students to pay attention to the values assumptions underlying trade-offs between design considerations such as product cost and safety.

International service learning projects in engineering illustrate a quite different approach to helping students confront the limits of their understanding of the contexts of their work, while acknowledging their responsibility for possible harm their interventions might do. Co-op and extracurricular programs that include this kind of experience provide a rich opportunity for students to connect conceptual and technical learning with the complexities of practice.

Another promising strategy for motivating and enabling students to widen their understanding of what they are doing and who they could become is the growing number of engineering programs that provide a general, non-field-specific knowledge base in the first one to two years, complemented with some components of engineering specialization. For example, the engineering program at the University of California–Berkeley is moving toward a common freshman curriculum including modules that introduce specific fields or branches of engineering. After this common first year, students select an engineering field or specialty. Howard's "Introduction to Engineering" provides beginning students a common core of understanding of the field, its branches, history, and various career paths. These approaches to specialization encourage students to think through their choice of engineering specialty in a more reflective and informed way than would otherwise be likely.

Significant intellectual resources for exploring identity, purpose, and context in engineering remain severely underutilized. Downey's "Engineering Cultures" and similar engineering ethics courses draw on the interdisciplinary field of science, technology, and society (STS) that we mentioned earlier. Beginning with the nascent environmental and social concerns about the impacts of technology that appeared in the 1970s, STS has developed important concepts and, as we have seen, ways of thinking and teaching about these matters that enable students to make sense of the social, ethical, and environmental contexts and responsibilities of engineering.

For this task, the linear model—with its overloaded, information-focused curriculum—can offer little. In contrast, a networked model with a focus on professional practice can offer much. Courses that reflect on engineering work and its significance, especially when connected to the professional spine, serve to provide a broad picture of the world toward which the student is headed. There may be a bright future for such courses, especially if the motivational value of increased integration is taken seriously.

There is some evidence that well-integrated (well-networked) design-and-knowledge courses taken early in the program may make students more likely to remain in engineering, because these courses provide a firmer view of the nature of engineering work than most of today's students bring with them to college. When faculty at Ohio State University replaced separate first-year engineering courses with an integrated two-course sequence that introduces engineering, graphics, and problem solving, and includes hands-on laboratory experiences and design/build projects, retention rates rose from less than 40 percent to well over 60 percent (Demel, Freuler, and Fentiman, 2004). Similarly, by introducing a first-year engineering design projects course, the University of Colorado has seen a 10-percent increase in student persistence by the seventh semester, from 54 percent to 64 percent, with the changes being especially marked for female students (Knight, Carlson, and Sullivan, 2007).

We believe that taking this principle one further step, to include reflection on the forms, history, and place of engineering in the larger world, is a natural development of these trends. This is not happening to any significant degree outside of STS programs, however. In fact, in our fieldwork we saw few examples of strong connections between engineering learning and the kinds of liberal arts education that could speak directly to these issues of the broader context and meaning of engineering. This observation reveals how poorly connected with the central goal of preparing the new-century engineer the typical liberal arts requirements really are.

Bringing Practice Forward

We believe that networked components centered on preparation for professional practice provide the way forward for engineering education. An important possibility opened by such an approach lies in its potential for incorporating the humanities and social sciences as sources of insight and skill for understanding and navigating social contexts. Perhaps most significant, placing design in interactive contexts as the end in view of engineering education would bring issues of ethical concern from the margins toward the center of attention. If engineers are professionals who draw upon both scientific and humanistic knowledge to formulate ways of intervening technologically to better the world, then it is not hard to introduce the notion of responsibility for the effects of one's interventions.

In a similar way, other aspects of context and identity begin to get more serious attention as well. Operating in such a new model, faculty would explicitly teach the abilities to learn from one's own and others' experience and to participate responsibly in an effective professional community. Engineering education would focus less on teaching technical skills and more on developing professionals who are committed to remaining technically competent, accountable, and socially responsible for their work, because being technically competent today and tomorrow is a natural outcome of the conception of the engineer as professional. Competency, responsibility, and accountability would be held up as core features of professional practice. In this sense, one of our hopes is that integrated, networked components focused on preparation for professional practice would provide an intellectual rationale and incentive for making undergraduate engineering education more whole, precisely in order to make it more motivating and relevant to students as they begin to understand the demands of their professional futures.

22

GETTING FROM HERE TO THERE

ALL EDUCATIONAL INNOVATIONS FACE the crucial question of means. This is not solely, or even primarily, a question of resources, but one of personnel. After laying out the why, what, and how of any new approach, there comes the question, who will teach it? For the engineering education we need, for today and the future, will this be the deal breaker? With all that is at stake for engineering in the United States, a failure to press forward for lack of faculty initiative and imagination would not only be disappointing; it would also be self-defeating.

We do not expect this to happen. On the contrary, from the excitement about reforms we observed on our visits, as well as from the movement generated by the work of the NSF and the NAE, we conclude that engineering education will be able to reshape itself to advance the cause of the profession in this new century. In that process, the engineering faculty will, of necessity, be the key players.

Although faculty are the primary architects of a revitalized approach to preparing the next generations of engineers, of course, they do not have a totally free hand in this. Like practicing engineers facing a design problem, faculty, too, must work interactively with others. The perspectives of professional organizations and societies and current students and alumni, the predilections of their colleagues, and institutional priorities all must be factored in. However, ultimately it is the energy, creativity, and initiative of the faculty that will determine how their programs might be made more integrated and cohesive. In other words, it is up to the faculty to create a program that is better aligned with practice both within individual courses and across the total student experience.

We are under no illusions as to what will be required. Reconceptualizing undergraduate engineering will demand an enormous effort on the part of faculty. It will involve more than learning about, designing, and implementing integrated curricular structures and active pedagogies. It will involve fundamentally rethinking the role and even the makeup of the faculty, for the educational model we are recommending makes quite different demands on the instructor than does the old model. Among other things, the new model gives more importance to teachers and researchers who are sympathetic to professional concerns and have some interest in them.

Engineering faculty are key stewards of the engineering profession. It is their job to fan the creative fire, feed technological curiosity, and foster the social responsibility of the next generation of men and women engineers. We fully recognize that this is no small job, even with sufficient resources, recognition, and rewards, as faculty must balance and integrate teaching and other educational responsibilities with those of research and service.

The Role of Other Leaders and Stakeholders

Imagining strategies for effecting a transformation of engineering education quickly brings the realization that the engineering faculty will not be able to do all this alone. Nor should they, for the effects of their effort have implications throughout the program, institution, higher education, and field of engineering. They may be key leaders, but they cannot be the sole actors. They need engagement and support from many quarters.

Both engineering education and higher education at large offer rich networks of faculty, campus leaders, and national organizations working to align curriculum and teaching strategies with the demands of a new century and the discoveries about learning. However, it is not clear to what extent engineering faculty are taking advantage of the field's increased understanding of engineering work and student learning to inform their teaching practices. Although it is heartening to see that over 3,500 faculty attended the 2007 ASEE Annual Conference and that many take advantage of the continued annual offerings of the National Effective Teaching Institute (www4.ncsu.edu/unity/lockers/users/f/felder/public/NETI.html), we note that this is just a fraction of the U.S. engineering faculty. Campus leaders and administrators have a role to play in supporting their colleagues and in transforming the engineering programs that are so important to their institutions. Engineers, industry leaders, and the leaders of national professional engineering organizations likewise can contribute at many levels, whether in the classroom or through policy and resources.

Administration

The revitalization of engineering education we propose cannot happen without administrative leadership that is highly supportive and engaged in the endeavor. This can take a variety of forms, from providing faculty with release time for course creation, to fund-raising for new teaching laboratories, to developing recognition systems for faculty who are involved with curricular change, to being part of the leadership in all these efforts. This type of support is also critical for sustaining curricular renewal and is essential for building a faculty community that is emboldened to experiment with innovative pedagogies and curricular structures.

Local collaboration is sometimes easy to encourage and support: at Rowan University, for example, engineering faculty turned to their colleagues in the communications department to develop integrated writing assignments in design courses. There is, however, a larger need calling for the attention of program and institution administration: as professional educators, engineering faculty need to develop or deepen their knowledge about important lessons from research on student learning. Faculty members need to be supported in this learning as part of their basic teaching responsibility.

In today's university, this concern for the quality of student learning links the engineering school or program with the arts and sciences departments as well as other professional schools. For example, few faculty-reward models recognize continuous professional development around teaching as important, though the development of new areas such as the scholarship of teaching and learning (see, for example, Boyer, 1990; Huber and Hutchings, 2005) are beginning to change this situation for the better. Prince, Felder, and Brent's 2007 paper on the relationship between faculty research and teaching outlines the actions that the academic community might take to better utilize the growing understanding of how people learn and how to teach more effectively. Engineering could play a useful role by taking leadership in establishing cross-department and cross-field support for faculty study and development in incorporating the results of learning research into their teaching practice.

To develop the new prototypes, faculty will have to imitate the best of contemporary practice by developing new approaches to teaching, employing integrated, collaborative teaching efforts. A number of large and sustainable curricular efforts serve as examples. Cornerstone design courses using project-centered learning can accommodate large numbers of first-year students if multiple faculty members work in coordination. Faculty team efforts provide useful models; these include the freshman-year redesign at Ohio State (Demel, Freuler, and Fentiman, 2004), the Learning Factory at Penn State (Lamancusa, 2006), the Integrated Teaching and Learning Lab at the University of Colorado, the Gateway Curriculum Reform Project led by Drexel (Fromm, 2003), and curricular reform efforts based on the Conceive-Design-Implement-Operate framework developed at Massachusetts Institute of Technology (Crawley, Malmquist, Ostlund, and Brodeur, 2007).

Many engineering schools will face significant obstacles to emulating these achievements. Such a level of collaboration in teaching and curriculum design may be new and daunting to some faculty members. In many instances, faculty reward systems are not equipped to recognize collaborative teaching contributions. Administrative leadership may balk at what looks like an expensive teaching arrangement unless faculty can establish that the investment will yield significant gains in student learning and can demonstrate that program assessment can complement and inform curricular revision.

This is not an easy time to serve as a dean of engineering, but it is probably the most important and exciting time in half a century to do so.

Practitioners and Industry

It is important that engineering educators engage practitioners from business, industry, and government. Practitioners can play several roles to assist in the effort to place professional practice at the center of engineering education. With professional societies, they can, of course, join a national call for change. They can also develop local, regional, and national partnerships with the academy and professional societies. At the local level, they can work along with individual schools to redesign programs.

They can also work with faculty to help bring approximations of professional practice into the classroom. They can work with faculty to develop ways in which students and practitioners can interact with one another as a component of or complement to coursework. From industry fieldtrips to invited lectures and client-sponsored design projects, these engagements can be organized as stand-alone courses or used as enhancements to more technically based engineering science courses.

For example, an interactive class session with a working engineer can combine short lecture segments with small-group learning exercises on the application of a set of technical ideas. Practitioners can guide students in observing and analyzing work practices in the field. Working engineers might facilitate collaboration with a company, over the course term, to solve a particular problem. Of course, the specific activities should be designed according to learning goals for the course and program.

Although faculty whose training and professional experiences are exclusively from the engineering academy are prepared to teach core engineering concepts and skills, they are not necessarily prepared to teach or integrate across the many domains of knowledge and skill (theory, practice, and professionalism) that make up engineering work. Programs will need to include those with engineering work experience and those with complementary disciplinary backgrounds. Practitioners can be engaged as adjunct faculty, for example, working beside regular faculty to bring a more practice-based perspective to a particular body of material. There are already examples in place: Massachusetts Institute of Technology has created the "professor of practice" faculty role, with assessment of performance and rewards in keeping with the job description. Practitioners can also provide useful insights to program-level review committees attempting to assess a program's overall approach and framework. Whatever the capacity they serve in, the successful integration of these faculty into a program requires that their unique contributions be understood and valued by the entire faculty as well as by the administration.

In all these cases, industry can play a valuable role as a partner in discussion with the schools and, where it seems mutually beneficial, as provider of resources for research and experiment.

National Leadership

Finally, national leadership organizations such as the NAE, NSF, and ABET, and the professional societies can play important, catalytic roles. Many of these organizations have already been influential in moving engineering education toward the future. They should continue to play multiple roles in enabling emerging prototype programs to become more integrated and practice-oriented. The national leadership organizations are vital in articulating the importance of educational innovations in their publications, speeches, and funding announcements. They are also central to the task of promoting, recognizing, and rewarding educational programs and faculty that boldly engage in thoughtful questioning of and experimentation with their educational practices.

We call on the national leadership organizations to support engineering programs in this national-level design problem and to provide resources and infrastructure for developing and sharing prototypes. Moreover, we call on national leadership to make this effort a national priority. Like a pressing professional design problem, such as developing alternative energy sources or more efficient transportation, this educational challenge deserves to be addressed in a national conversation, including debates and idea sharing among the broadest possible range of stakeholders.

Bringing Professional Practice Forward

The work ahead is not easy. What we have so easily termed "pockets of innovation" represent enormous amounts of time and creative energy from faculty and many others. The scope and scale of a national effort would be exponentially greater.

However, who better to define the problem and design its solution than engineering educators? We imagine that the process will be as fruitful as the product, for the work calls for the exercise of new professional "muscles," new skills and thinking. It may also yield some surprising new colleagues across campuses and institutions, across the academy and the profession.

The work to be done is not simply worth the effort; it is vitally important. The public, national and global, has a serious stake in the preparation of engineers to design and manage our technological world. We are convinced that an approach that integrates knowledge, skill, and purpose through a consistent focus on preparation for professional practice is better aligned with the demands of more complex, interactive, and environmentally and socially responsible forms of practice. We hope others will join us in this conclusion and in the effort to educate competent, creative, and wise engineers for the years ahead.

How might we start this work? By reflecting, assessing, debating, designing, and prototyping a truly networked undergraduate engineering program, one that engages both teacher and student in learning in the context of professional practice. By engaging as colleagues and making the redesign of engineering education an intensive national undertaking for the next five years. By redesigning engineering education to prepare the new-century engineers that today's problems—and tomorrow's—demand.

APPENDIX
ABOUT THE STUDY

Our study placed special emphasis on the question of how educational practices support the preparation of engineering practitioners. Because we intended our profile of educational practices to be representative and richly descriptive, we employed both quantitative and qualitative research methods.

We began by examining national studies of engineering education and engineering workforce, including the National Science Foundation database, *Journal of Engineering Education*, and Frontiers in Education. From this, we wrote several papers describing national-level practices and selected forty engineering schools (or more than 10 percent of the engineering schools in the United States) for closer examination. This purposeful sampling of schools was based on a combination of several factors, including the Carnegie Classification; evidence of reflective practice among faculty, as demonstrated, for example, through publications in engineering education conferences; the particular programs offered; and recent and successful accreditation with the new ABET criteria (Prados, Peterson, and Lattuca, 2005).

From these forty schools we collected about one hundred ABET self-study reports spanning mechanical, electrical, bioengineering, and environmental engineering undergraduate education programs. We used these reports as a means of getting deeper insight into programmatic practices because they answer a consistent set of questions posed by the profession about programs and are therefore less variable than, for example, a school's presentation of itself on its Web site. A team of researchers read and coded the reports to identify typical or extraordinary practices, themes, and common issues as a means of refining our understanding of practices.

Programs for In-Depth Study

On the basis of our review of ABET self-study documents, and after piloting our methodology, we selected seven engineering schools for in-depth investigation, looking at eleven programs in mechanical and electrical engineering, each with a unique but representative approach. We divided the institutions into two clusters: engineering programs at technology-oriented institutions and programs situated within universities.

The technology-oriented institutions included California Polytechnic State University (Cal Poly), Georgia Institute of Technology (Georgia Tech), and Colorado School of Mines (Mines). Cal Poly, which emphasizes "learning by doing," serves a diverse student population; the engineering program employs project-based learning (PBL) and has strong links with industry. Georgia Tech, a large public university, offers opportunities for students to participate in research and development activities. The engineering school also provides opportunities for students to participate in major competitions or industry projects through a strong cooperative education program. Mines, also a public university, is focused specifically on engineering and applied science. Its engineering division specifically offers an interdisciplinary undergraduate engineering degree that provides students with breadth while offering them an opportunity for disciplinary focus.

The engineering schools within universities that we visited were Carnegie Mellon University (CMU), Howard University (Howard), and the University of Michigan, Ann Arbor (Michigan). A former technical institute, CMU offers a flexible undergraduate engineering educational experience to serve a wide range of students with diverse backgrounds and interests. Students have some freedom in determining their program of study based on their interests or career goals. Howard, a historically African American university, emphasizes design and a culture that fosters leadership and commitment to community. The University of Michigan, Ann Arbor, gives students early exposure to design experiences while also promoting a strong research culture.

Our pilot school, Santa Clara University, not only allowed us to practice our methodology for site visits, but also helped inform our thinking: educating in the Jesuit tradition, the university seeks to impress on its students the importance of professional responsibility as they develop knowledge and skills.

Campus Observations

Our interdisciplinary research team spent two to three days at each campus early in 2002, interviewing over two hundred engineering students, faculty, and administrators, and observing more than thirty classes in mechanical and electrical engineering programs. In one-on-one interviews and focus groups, we explored faculty's and students' conceptions of engineering work; the program's goals, curricular arrangements, and teaching strategies; and future challenges and opportunities engineering education faces. In classroom observations, we gathered data on teaching and learning strategies and attitudes.

All interviews were digitally recorded and transcribed. Interview transcripts and observation field notes were then coded to identify themes and patterns that allow us to elucidate the ways in which today's engineering programs go about preparing students to engage in the complexities of professional practice.

REFERENCES

ABET. Criteria for Accrediting Engineering Programs, Effective for Evaluations During the 2008–2009 Cycle. ABET, Engineering Accreditation Commission, 2007. http://www.abet.org/Linked%20Documents-UPDATE/Criteria%20and%20PP/E001%2008-09%20EAC%20Criteria%2012-04-07.pdf.

Adams, J. "The Project in a World of Lectures." Paper presented at the Annual Winter Meeting of PSW-ASEE, December 1971.

———. *Conceptual Blockbusting: A Guide to Better Ideas*. New York: Basic Books, 2001.

Agogino, A. "Human-Centered Sustainable Product Design." Presentation at Northwestern University, April 22, 2008.

———. "Longitudinal Study of Project-Based Learning Course in New Product Development." Presentation at Technion-Israel Institute of Technology, July 6, 2008.

Agogino, A., and Hsi, S. "The Impact and Instructional Benefit of Using Multimedia Case Studies to Teach Engineering Design." *Journal of Educational Hypermedia and Multimedia*, 1994, *3*(3–4), 351–376.

Altshuller, G. *40 Principles: TRIZ Keys to Technical Innovation*. L. Shulyak (trans.) and S. Rodman (ed.). Worchester, MA: Technical Innovation Center, 2005.

American Council on Education and others. "Addressing the Challenges Facing American Undergraduate Education, A Letter to Our Members: Next Steps." 2006. http://www.acenet.edu/AM/Template.cfm?Section=Home&CONTENTID=18317&TEMPLATE=/CM/ContentDisplay.cfm.

American Society for Engineering Education (ASEE). "Final Report: Goals of Engineering Education." *Journal of Engineering Education*, 1968, *58*(5), 372–446.

American Society of Mechanical Engineers (ASME). Society Policy Ethics, Code of Ethics of Engineers. 2006. http://files.asme.org/ASMEORG/Governance/3675.pdf.

Astin, A. *What Matters in College? Four Critical Years Revisited*. San Francisco: Jossey-Bass, 1993.

Atkins, T. "A Brief Summary of Cooperative Education: History, Philosophy, and Current Status." In *Educating the Engineer of 2020: Adapting Engineering Education to the New Century* (pp. 61–68). Washington, DC: National Academies Press, 2005.

Atman, C., Kilgore, D., and McKenna, A. "Characterizing the Development of Engineering Design Expertise." *Journal of Engineering Education* (special ed.), 2008.

Bella, D., and Jenkins, C. "The Functionary, the Citizen, and the Engineer." *Journal of Engineering Education*, 1993, 82(1), 38–42.

Bordogna, J. "Engineering—The Integrative Profession." *NSF Directions*, 1992, 5(2), 1.

Boyer, E. *Scholarship Reconsidered: Priorities of the Professoriate.* San Francisco: Jossey-Bass, 1990.

Bransford, J., Brown, A., and Cocking, R. (eds.). *How People Learn: Brain, Mind, Experience, and School: Expanded Edition.* Washington, DC: National Research Council of the National Academies Press, 2000.

Brown, A., and Palincsar, A., "Guided, Cooperative Learning and Individual Knowledge Acquisition." In L. Resnick (ed.), *Knowing, Learning, and Instruction: Essays in Honor of Robert Glaser.* Hillsdale, NJ: Erlbaum, 1989.

Brown, J., Collins, A., and Duguid, P. "Situated Cognition and the Culture of Learning." *Educational Researcher*, 1989, 18(1), 32–42.

Bucciarelli, L. *Designing Engineers.* Cambridge, MA: MIT Press, 1996.

———. "Design Delta Design: Seeing/Seeing As." Paper presented at the 5th International Design Thinking Research Symposium on Design Representation, Cambridge, MA, April 1999.

Bucciarelli, L., and Kuhn, S. "Engineering Education and Engineering Practice: Improving the Fit." *Between Craft and Science: Technical Work in U.S. Settings.* Ithaca, NY: Cornell University Press, 1997.

Butler, W. "Simulators for Experimental Learning." Paper presented at the Engineering Foundation Conference on the Undergraduate Engineering Laboratory, Henniker, NH, July 1983.

Cardella, M. "Engineering Mathematics: An Investigation of Students' Mathematical Thinking from a Cognitive Engineering Perspective." Unpublished doctoral dissertation, Department of Industrial Engineering, University of Washington, 2006.

Chandrupatla, T., and others. *Engineering Clinics: Integrating Design Throughout the ME Curriculum.* New York: American Society of Mechanical Engineers, 2001.

Chaplin, C. *The Education and Training of Chartered Engineers for the 21st Century: Creativity in Engineering Design—The Education Function* (No. FE4). London: Fellowship of Engineering, 1989.

Cochran, K. "Pedagogical Content Knowledge: Teachers' Integration of Subject Matter, Pedagogy, Students, and Learning Environments." In R. Sherwood (ed.), *Research Matters ... to the Science Teacher*. Manhattan, KS: NARST, 1997.

Colby, A., Sippola, L., and Phelps, E. "Social Responsibility and Paid Work in Contemporary American Life." In A. Rossi (ed.), *Caring and Doing for Others: Social Responsibility in the Domains of Family, Work, and Community*. Chicago: University of Chicago Press, 2001.

Collins, A., Brown, J., and Newman, S. "Cognitive Apprenticeship: Teaching the Crafts of Reading, Writing, and Mathematics." In L. Resnick (ed.), *Knowing, Learning, and Instruction: Essays in Honor of Robert Glaser*. Hillsdale, NJ: Erlbaum, 1989.

Coxe, E. "Technical Education." The Annual Address to the Montreal Meeting in June 1894 of the American Society of Mechanical Engineers. *Transactions of the American Society of Mechanical Engineers* XV, 1894.

Coyle, E., Jamieson, L., and Oakes, W. "EPICS: Engineering Projects in Community Service." *International Journal of Engineering Education*, 2005, 21(1), 139–150.

Crawley, E., Malmquist, J., Ostlund, S., and Brodeur, D. *Rethinking Engineering Education: The CDIO Approach*. New York, London: Springer, 2007.

Dean, R. "Laboratory Experience for Engineering Students." Paper presented at the Engineering Foundation Conference on the Undergraduate Engineering Laboratory, Henniker, NH, July 1983.

Demel, J., Freuler, R., and Fentiman, A. "Building a Successful Fundamentals of Engineering for Honors Program." Paper presented at the American Society for Engineering Education Annual Conference, Salt Lake City, UT, June 2004.

DeRego, F., Zoltowski, C., Jamieson, L., and Oakes, W. "Teaching Ethics and the Social Impact of Engineering Within a Capstone Course." Paper presented at the Frontiers in Education Conference, Indianapolis, IN, October 2005.

Dominick, P., Reilly, R., and McGourty, J. "The Effects of Peer Feedback on Team Member Behavior." *Group & Organization Management*, 1997, 22, 508–520.

Downey, G. "Are Engineers Losing Control of Technology? From 'Problem Solving' to 'Problem Definition and Solution' in Engineering Education." *Chemical Engineering Research and Design*, 2005, 83(A8), 1–12.

————. Private e-mail message to S. Sheppard, August 25, 2006.

————. "The Engineering Cultures Syllabus as Formation Narrative: Critical Participation in Engineering Education Through Problem Definition." *University of St. Thomas Law Journal*, 2008, *5*(2), 101–130.

Downey, G., and others. "The Globally Competent Engineer: Working Effectively with People Who Define Problems Differently." *Journal of Engineering Education*, 2006, *95*(2), 107–122.

Dreyfus, H., Dreyfus, S., and Athanasiou, T. *Mind Over Machine: The Power of Human Intuition and Expertise in the Era of the Computer.* New York: Free Press, 1986.

Duderstadt, J. *Engineering for a Changing World: A Roadmap to the Future of Engineering Practice, Research, and Education.* Ann Arbor, MI: The Millennium Project, The University of Michigan, 2008.

Dym, C., and Little, P. *Engineering Design: A Project-Based Introduction.* New York: Wiley, 2008.

Dym, C., and others. "Engineering Design: Thinking, Teaching, and Learning." *Journal of Engineering Education*, 2005, *94*(1), 103–120.

Engineers' Council for Professional Development. *Code of Ethics of Engineers: Engineers' Council for Professional Development 46th Annual Report 1977–78* (No. 23). New York: Engineers' Council for Professional Development, 1978.

Erikson, E. *Identity: Youth and Crisis.* New York: Norton, 1968.

Eris, O. *Effective Inquiry for Innovative Engineering Design: From Basic Principles to Applications.* Boston, MA: Kluwer Academic Publishers, 2004.

Evans, D., McNeill, B., and Beakley, G. "Design in Engineering Education: Past Views of Future Directions." *Engineering Education (ASEE)*, 1990, *80*(5), 517–522.

Eyler, J., and Giles, D. *Where's the Learning in Service-Learning?* San Francisco: Jossey-Bass, 1999.

Farah, B., and Samaan, N. "Effective Approaches for Teaching of Fundamental Subjects in Electrical Engineering." Paper presented at the International Conference on Engineering Education, Oslo, Norway, August 2001.

Feisel, L., and Rosa, A. "The Role of the Laboratory in Undergraduate Engineering Education." *Journal of Engineering Education*, 2005, *94*(1), 121–130.

Felder, R., and others. "Update on IMPEC: An Integrated First-year Engineering Curriculum at N.C. State University." Paper presented at the American Society for Engineering Education Conference and Exposition, Seattle, WA, June–July 1998.

Felder, R., Woods, D., Stice, J., and Rugarcia, A. "The Future of Engineering Education II. Teaching Methods That Work." *Chemical Engineering Education*, 2000, *34*(1), 26–39.

Finelli, C., Harding, T., Carpenter, D., and Mayhew, M. "Academic Integrity Among Engineering Undergraduates: Seven Years of Research by the E[3] Team." Paper presented at the American Society for Engineering Education Conference and Exposition, Honolulu, HI, June 2007.

Flexner, A. *Medical Education in the United States and Canada.* Bulletin Number Four. New York: The Carnegie Foundation for the Advancement of Teaching 1910.

Fromm, E. "Innovations That Changed the Engineering Educational Environment." *Global Journal of Engineering Education*, 2003, *7*(2), 173–178.

Gainsburg, J. "The Mathematical Modeling of Structural Engineers." Unpublished doctoral dissertation, Department of Education, University of Washington, Seattle, WA, 2006.

Gardner, H., Csikszentmihalyi, M., and Damon, W. *Good Work: When Excellence and Ethics Meet.* New York: Basic Books, 2001.

Gharabagi, R. "Coverage of Legal and Ethical Aspects in Electrical and Computer Engineering Curriculum." Paper presented at the American Society for Engineering Education Conference and Exposition, Honolulu, HI, June 2007.

Grayson, L. *The Making of an Engineer: An Illustrated History of Engineering Education in the United States and Canada.* New York: Wiley, 1993.

Grinter, L. "Report of the Committee on Evaluation of Engineering Education." *Journal of Engineering Education*, 1994, *83*(1), 74–94. (Originally published 1955.)

Grossman, P., and others. "Teaching Practice: A Cross-Professional Perspective." *Teachers College Record*, 2009, *111*(9). http://www.tcrecord.org/Content.asp?ContentId=15018.

Harding, T., Carpenter, D., Finelli, C., and Passow, H. "Does Academic Dishonesty Relate to Unethical Behavior in Professional Practice? An Exploratory Study." *Science and Engineering Ethics*, 2004, *10*(2), 311–324.

Harris, T., Bransford, J., and Brophy, S. "Roles for Learning Sciences and Learning Technologies in Biomedical Engineering Education: A Review of Recent Advances." *Annual Review of Biomedical Engineering*, 2002, *4*, 29–48.

Hazel, E., and Baillie, C. *Improving Teaching and Learning in Laboratories.* Canberra, Australia, Higher Education Research and Development Society of Australasia, 1998.

Hebert, E. *The Power of Portfolios: What Children Can Teach Us About Learning and Assessment.* San Francisco: Jossey-Bass, 2001.

Herkert, J. "ABET's Engineering 2000 Criteria and Engineering Ethics: Where Do We Go from Here?" 1999. http://www.onlineethics.diamax.com/cms/12053.aspx.

———. "Engineering Ethics Education in the USA: Content, Pedagogy, and Curriculum." *European Journal of Engineering Education,* 2001, *25,* 303–313.

———. "Continuing and Emerging Issues in Engineering Ethics Education." *The Bridge,* 2002, *32*(3), 8–14.

Hoover, T., and Fish, J. *The Engineering Profession.* Stanford, CA: Stanford University Press, 1950.

Howe, S., and others. "Work in Progress: Designing for Economic Empowerment in Nicaragua." Proceedings of the Frontiers in Education Conference, Global Engineering: Knowledge Without Borders, Opportunities Without Passports. 2007. http://fie.engrng.pitt.edu/fie2007/index.html.

Huber, M. T., and Hutchings, P. *The Advancement of Learning: Building the Teaching Commons.* San Francisco: Jossey-Bass, 2005.

Hudson, L. *Contrary Imaginations: A Psychological Study of the English Schoolboy.* London: Methuen, 1966.

Hughes, T. *Human-Built World: How to Think About Technology and Culture.* Chicago: University of Chicago Press, 2004.

IEEE. Code of Ethics. 2006. http://www.ieee.org/web/aboutus/ethics/code.html.

Irby, D. Private e-mail message to S. Sheppard, July 1, 2008.

Journal of Chemical Education. ConcepTests for Use in Chemistry. Madison, WI: Chemistry Department, University of Wisconsin-Madison, 2000. http://jchemed.chem.wisc.edu/JCEDLib/QBank/collection/ConcepTests/index.html.

Kerns, S., Miller, R., and Kerns, D. "Designing from a Blank Slate: The Development of the Initial Olin College Curriculum." In *Educating the Engineer of 2020: Adapting Engineering Education to the New Century.* Washington, DC: National Academies Press, 2005.

King, P., and Kitchener, K. *Developing Reflective Judgment: Understanding and Promoting Intellectual Growth and Critical Thinking in Adolescents and Adults.* San Francisco: Jossey-Bass, 1994.

King, R., and others. "A Multidisciplinary Engineering Laboratory Course." *Journal of Engineering Education,* 1999, *88*(3), 311–316.

Kipnis, K. "Engineers Who Kill: Professional Ethics and the Paramountcy of Public Safety." *Business and Professional Ethics Journal,* 1981, *1*(6), 253–256.

Knight, D., Carlson, L., and Sullivan, J. "Improving Engineering Student Retention Through Hands-On, Team Based, First-Year Design Projects." Paper presented at the International Conference on Research in Engineering Education, Honolulu, HI, June 2007.

Koen, B. *Discussion of the Method: Conducting the Engineering Approach to Problem Solving.* New York: Oxford Press, 2003.

Kohlberg, L. "Continuities in Childhood and Adult Moral Development Revisited." In P. Baltes and K. Schaie (eds.), *Life-span Developmental Psychology: Personality and Socialization.* New York and London: Academic Press, 1973.

Kopplin, J. "A Proposed Vertical Laboratory Program." Paper presented at BUILD Conference on Laboratory in the Electrical Engineering Curriculum, Urbana, IL, April 1965.

Kroes, P. "Technical and Contextual Constraints in Design; An Essay on Determinants of Technological Change." In J. Perrin and D. Vinck (eds.), *The Role of Design in the Shaping of Technology*, COST A4 Social Sciences Vol. 5, Brussels: European Commission Directorate General Science, R&D, 1996, 43–76.

Lamancusa, J. "The Reincarnation of the Engineering Shop." Paper presented at 2006 ASME International Design Engineering Technical Conferences and Computers in Engineering Conference, Philadelphia, PA, September 2006.

Lattuca, L., Terenzini, P., and Volkwein, J. "Engineering Change: A Study of the Impact of EC2000." Baltimore, MD: ABET, 2006.

Layton, E. "Technology as Knowledge." *Technology and Culture*, 1974, *15*(1), 31–41.

Leifer, L. "Remarks on Provisional Notions of Design Education." Remarks made at the International Workshop on Project-Based Learning, Palo Alto, CA, August 1995.

Little, P., Hink, R., and Barney, D. "Living Up to the Code: Engineering as Political Judgment." *International Journal of Engineering Education*, 2008, *24*(2), 314–327.

Mann, C. *A Study of Engineering Education, Prepared for the Joint Committee on Engineering Education of the National Engineering Societies.* No. 11. New York: The Carnegie Foundation for the Advancement of Teaching, 1918.

McCabe, D. "Classroom Cheating Among Natural Science and Engineering Majors." *Science and Engineering Ethics*, 1997, *3*(4), 433–445.

McGinn, R. "Mind the Gaps: An Empirical Approach to Engineering Ethics, 1997–2001." *Science and Engineering Ethics*, 2003, *9*(4), 517–542.

McKenna, A., McMartin, F., and Agogino, A. "What Students Say About Learning Physics, Math, and Engineering." Paper presented at the Frontiers in Education Conference, Kansas City, MO, October 2000.

McMasters, J. "Student Design Projects from Industry." Unpublished manuscript, The Boeing Company Summer Intern Program, September 12, 1997.

McMasters, J., and White, B. *Report on the Second Boeing-University Workshop on an Industry Role in Enhancing Engineering Education.* Seattle, WA: The Boeing Company, 1994.

Merriam, S., and Caffarella, R. (eds.). *Learning in Adulthood: A Comprehensive Guide.* San Francisco: Jossey-Bass, 1999.

Mintzes, J., Wandersee, J., and Novak, J. (eds.). *Teaching Science for Understanding: A Human Constructivist View.* San Diego: Academic Press, 1998.

Montgomery, K. *How Doctors Think: Clinical Judgment and the Practice of Medicine.* New York: Oxford University Press, 2005.

National Academy of Engineering (NAE). *The Engineer of 2020: Visions of Engineering in the New Century.* Washington, DC: National Academies Press, 2004.

National Research Council's Board on Engineering Education. *Engineering Education: Designing an Adaptive System*, National Research Council Report. Washington, DC: National Academies Press, 1995.

Neeley, L. "Adaptive Design: A Theory of Design Thinking and Innovation." Unpublished doctoral dissertation for the Department of Mechanical Engineering, Stanford University, 2007.

Oberst, B., and Jones, R. "Offshore Outsourcing and the Dawn of the Post-Colonial Era of Western Engineering Education." *European Journal of Engineering Education*, 2006, *31*(3), 303–310.

Ohland, M., and others. "Integrated Curricula in the SUCCEED Coalition." *Proceedings, 2003 American Society for Engineering Education Conference and Exposition.* Nashville, TN: ASEE, 2003.

Ohland, M., and others. "Persistence, Engagement, and Migration in Engineering Programs." *Journal of Engineering Education*, 2008.

Pascarella, E., and Terenzini, P. *How College Affects Students: A Third Decade of Research.* San Francisco: Jossey-Bass, 2005.

Penberthy, D., Priest, S., and Kosciuk, S., with Millar, S. *Overview of Attitudinal Outcomes and Learning Process Information About UW-Madison's New Traditions, Topic-Oriented Approach to General Chemistry (104) Course.* Formative feedback report No. 2. Madison, WI: University of Wisconsin-Madison, LEAD Center, 1997.

Perlow, L. *Finding Time: How Corporations, Individuals, and Families Can Benefit from New Work Practices.* Ithaca, NY: ILR Press, 1997.

Perry, W. *Forms of Intellectual and Ethical Development in the College Years.* New York: Holt, Rinehart and Winston, 1968.

Pister, K. "A Context for Change in Engineering Education." *Journal of Engineering Education,* 1993, 82(2), 66–69.

Prados, J., Peterson, G., and Lattuca, L. "Quality Assurance of Engineering Education Through Accreditation: The Impact of Engineering Criteria 2000 and Its Global Influence." *Journal of Engineering Education,* 2005, 94(1), 165–184.

Prince, M., Felder, R., and Brent, R. "Does Faculty Research Improve Undergraduate Teaching? An Analysis of Existing and Potential Synergies. " *Journal of Engineering Education,* 2007, 96(4), 283–294.

Quinn, R. "Implementing Large Scale Curricular Changes—The Drexel Experience." Paper presented at the Frontiers in Education Conference, Atlanta, GA, November 1995.

Redish, E., and Smith, K. "Looking Beyond Content: Skill Development for Engineers." *Journal of Engineering Education,* 2008.

Richkus, R., Agogino, A., Yu, D., and Tang, D. "Virtual Disk Drive Design Game with Links to Math, Physics and Dissection Activities." Proceedings of the Frontiers in Education Conference, Designing the Future of Science and Engineering Education. 1999. http://fie.engrng.pitt.edu/fie99/.

Rosenthal, L. "Guided Discovery Teaching in Engineering Laboratory." *Journal of Engineering Education,* 1967, 58(3), 196–198.

Rubinstein, M. *Patterns of Problem Solving.* Upper Saddle River, NJ: Prentice-Hall, 1975.

Ryle, G. *The Concept of Mind.* Chicago: University of Chicago Press, 2000. (Originally published 1949.)

Saffer, D. "Thinking About Design Thinking." 2005. http://odannyboy.com/blog/new_archives/2005/03/thinking_about.html.

Savery, J., and Duffy, T. "Problem Based Learning: An Instructional Model and Its Constructivist Framework." *Educational Technology,* 1995, 35, 31–38.

Sax, L., and Astin, A. "The Benefits of Service: Evidence from Undergraduates." *Educational Record,* 1997, 78 (Summer–Fall), 25–33.

Scott, T. "Mechanical and Aerospace Engineering Laboratories at the University of Virginia." Paper presented at the Engineering Foundation Conference on the Undergraduate Engineering Laboratory, Henniker, NH, July 1983.

Seymour, E., and Hewitt, N. *Talking About Leaving: Why Undergraduates Leave the Sciences*. Boulder, CO: Westview Press, 1997.

Shavelson, R., and Huang, L. "Responding Responsibly to the Frenzy to Assess Learning in Higher Education." *Change*, 2003, *35*(1), 10–19.

Sheppard, S. "Mechanical Dissection: An Experience in How Things Work." Paper presented at Engineering Education: Curriculum Innovation and Integration, Santa Barbara, CA, January 1992.

Sheppard, S., Chen, H., Schaeffer, E., and Steinbeck, R. *Assessment of Student Collaborative Process in Undergraduate Engineering Education by Stanford Center for Innovations in Learning*. Final report to the National Science Foundation. Palo Alto, CA: Stanford University Press, 2004.

Shimmel, K. "ABET 2000—Can Engineering Faculty Teach Ethics?" Proceedings of the 3rd Christian Engineering Conference, June 23–35, Waxhaw, NC, 1999. http://engr.calvin.edu/ces/ceec/schimmel.htm

Shulman, L. "Those Who Understand: Knowledge Growth in Teaching." *Educational Researcher*, 1986, *15*(2), 4–14.

———. "Theory, Practice, and the Education of Professionals." *The Elementary School Journal*, 1998, *98*(5), 511–526.

Shuman, L., Besterfield-Sacre, M., and McGourty, J. "The ABET Professional Skills: Can They Be Taught? Can They Be Assessed?" *Journal of Engineering Education*, 2005, *94*(1), 41–56.

Smith, K., Sheppard, S., Johnson, D., and Johnson, R. "Pedagogies of Engagement: Classroom-Based Practices." *Journal of Engineering Education*, 2005, *94*(1), 87–101.

Society for the Promotion of Engineering Education. *Report of the Investigation of Engineering Education, 1923–1929*, Vol. 1. Pittsburgh, PA: Office of the Secretary of the Society, F. L. Bishop University of Pittsburgh, 1930.

Steneck, N. "Co-Opting Engineering Models and Methods to Teach Engineering Ethics." Paper presented at the American Society for Engineering Education Annual Conference, Charlotte, NC, June 1999.

Steneck, N. "A Checklist of Ethical Concerns for Use in the Engineering Classroom." Private e-mail message to A. Colby, August 21, 2007.

Streveler, R., Litzinger, T., Miller, R., and Steif, P. "Learning Conceptual Knowledge in the Engineering Sciences: Overview and Future Research Directions." *Journal of Engineering Education*, 2008.

Sullivan, W., and others. *Educating Lawyers: Preparation for the Profession of Law*. San Francisco: Jossey-Bass, 2007.

Tryggvason, G., and others. "The New Mechanical Engineering Curriculum at the University of Michigan." *Journal of Engineering Education*, 2001, *90*(3), 8.

Tsang, E. "Service-Learning as a Pedagogy for Engineering: Concerns and Challenges." In E. Tsang (ed.), *Projects That Matter: Concepts and Models for Service-Learning in Engineering*. Washington, DC: American Association for Higher Education, 2000.

Tuminaro, J. "A Cognitive Framework for Analyzing and Describing Introductory Students' Use and Understanding of Mathematics in Physics." University of Maryland, 2004. http://www.physics.umd.edu/rgroups/ripe/perg/dissertations/Tuminaro/.

U.S. Department of Labor, and Bureau of Labor Statistics. *Occupational Outlook Handbook: Engineers*. Washington, DC: U.S. Department of Labor, 2007.

Vincenti, W. *What Engineers Know and How They Know It: Analytical Studies from Aeronautical History*. Baltimore, MD: The Johns Hopkins University Press, 1990.

Wankat, P., and Oreovicz, F. *Teaching Engineering*. New York, McGraw-Hill, 1993.

Williams, R. *Retooling: A Historian Confronts Technological Change*. Cambridge, MA: MIT Press, 2002.

Wood, D. "An Evidence-Based Strategy for Problem Solving." *Journal of Engineering Education*, 2000, 89(4), 443–459.

Wu, H. "The Mathematician and the Mathematics Education Reform." *Notices of the American Mathematical Society*, 1996, 43(12), 1531–1537.

Wulf, W. "Great Achievements and Grand Challenges." *The Bridge*, 2000, 30(3/4), 5–10.

Yang, M., and Cham, J. "An Analysis of Sketching Skill and Its Role in Early Stage Engineering Design." *Journal of Mechanical Design*, 2007, 129(5), 476–482.

INDEX

MORE TITLES FROM THE CARNEGIE FOUNDATION
FOR THE ADVANCEMENT OF TEACHING:
PREPARING FOR THE PROFESSIONS SERIES

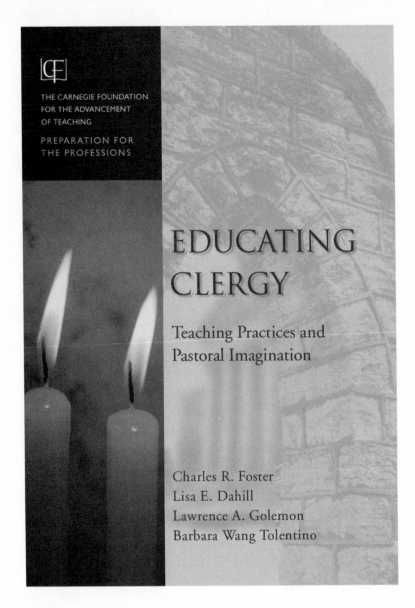

THE CARNEGIE FOUNDATION
FOR THE ADVANCEMENT
OF TEACHING

PREPARATION FOR
THE PROFESSIONS

EDUCATING CLERGY

Teaching Practices and
Pastoral Imagination

Charles R. Foster
Lisa E. Dahill
Lawrence A. Golemon
Barbara Wang Tolentino

Educating Clergy
Teaching Practices and Pastoral Imagination

by Charles R. Foster, Lisa E. Dahill, Lawrence A. Goleman,
and Barbara Wang Tolentino
978-0-7879-7744-3

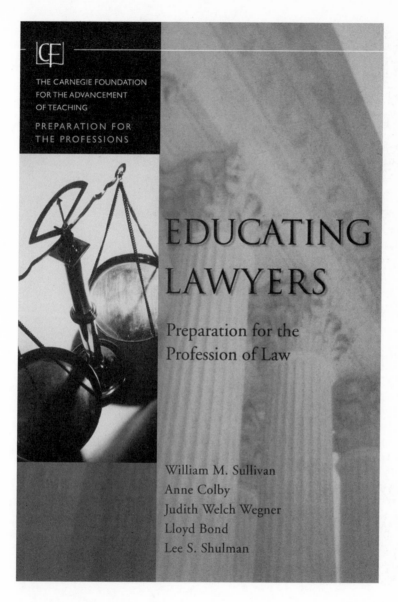

THE CARNEGIE FOUNDATION
FOR THE ADVANCEMENT
OF TEACHING

PREPARATION FOR
THE PROFESSIONS

EDUCATING LAWYERS

Preparation for the
Profession of Law

William M. Sullivan
Anne Colby
Judith Welch Wegner
Lloyd Bond
Lee S. Shulman

Educating Lawyers
Preparation for the Profession of Law

by William M. Sullivan, Anne Colby, Judith Welch Wegner,
Lloyd Bond, and Lee S. Shulman
978-0-7879-8261-4

FORTHCOMING TITLES FROM THE CARNEGIE FOUNDATION FOR THE ADVANCEMENT OF TEACHING: PREPARING FOR THE PROFESSIONS SERIES

Educating Nurses
Teaching and Learning a Complex Caring Practice

by Patricia Benner, Molly Sutphen, Victoria Leonard, and Lisa Day
978-0-470-45796-2

Educating Physicians
Preparing Doctors for a Lifetime of Practice

by Molly Cooke, David Irby, and Bridget O'Brien
978-0-470-45797-9